THE LOW ACHIEVEMENT TRAP

THE LOW ACHIEVEMENT TRAP
COMPARING SCHOOLING IN BOTSWANA AND SOUTH AFRICA

EDITED BY: MARTIN CARNOY | LINDA CHISHOLM | BAGELE CHILISA

The UBotswana-HSRC-Stanford Research Team
Martin Carnoy | Linda Chisholm | Bagele Chilisa
Nii Addy | Fabian Arends | Hlengani Baloyi
Jesse Foster | Margaret Irving | Thenjiwe Major
Lillian Mokgosi | Kolentino Mpeta | Paul Nleya
Erin Raab | Cheryl Reeves | Ingrid Sapire
Alejandra Sorto | Nnunu Tsheko

Published by HSRC Press
Private Bag X9182, Cape Town, 8000, South Africa
www.hsrcpress.ac.za

First published 2012

ISBN (soft cover) 978-0-7969-2368-4
ISBN (pdf) 978-0-7969-2369-1
ISBN (e-pub) 978-0-7969--2370-7

© 2012 Stanford University

Exclusive print rights Southern and East Africa: HSRC Press
© Design and cover, this edition only: HSRC Press

Copyedited by Louis Botes
Typeset by Robin Taylor
Cover design by Georgia Demertzis
Printed by Paarl Media Paarl

Distributed in Southern and East Africa by Blue Weaver
Tel: +27 (0) 21 701 4477; Fax: +27 (0) 21 701 7302
www.oneworldbooks.com

Contents

Figures and tables vi
Preface x
Executive summary xii
Acronyms and abbreviations xx

Introduction 1

1 Background to the study 6

2 Exploring policy differences and similarities 13

3 Conceptual framework and methodology 35

4 The school profile in the Botswana and North West samples 52

5 The school context: Characteristics of principals and instructional leadership 61

6 Learner knowledge of mathematics 73

7 Teacher knowledge of mathematics 89

8 Teacher proficiency to teach mathematics 105

9 Opportunity to learn and teaching and learning mathematics in Grade 6 classes 114

10 Are more knowledgeable teachers better teachers and do they provide more opportunity to learn? 128

11 Testing the overall model of student achievement 136

12 Conclusions 150

References 159
Contributors 167
Index 169

Figures and tables

Figures

Figure 1.1   Sixth Grade mathematics test score by country and SES quintile, 2000   11
Figure 2.1   Botswana: Number of primary and secondary teachers, 1996–2009   24
Figure 2.2a Botswana: Median female monthly earnings, post-secondary degree holders, 2002–03   27
Figure 2.2b Botswana: Median male monthly earnings, post-secondary degree holders, 2002–03   27
Figure 2.3   Trends in graduates from colleges of education and higher education, 1994–2006   31
Figure 3.1   Conceptual framework   36
Figure 4.1   Botswana and South Africa: Gross domestic product per capita, 1995–2009   53
Figure 4.2   Border area: Botswana-South Africa, including boundaries of former Bophuthatswana   57
Figure 4.3   Political map of Botswana showing districts   58
Figure 5.1a North West Province: Length of tenure as principal, 2009   62
Figure 5.1b Botswana: Length of tenure as principal, 2009   62
Figure 5.2a North West Province: Principals' perceived frequency of violence against learners, 2009   65
Figure 5.2b Botswana: Principals' perceived frequency of violence against learners, 2009   65
Figure 5.3   Botswana and North West Province: Distribution of sampled classrooms by level of reported violence index, 2009   66
Figure 5.4   Botswana and North West Province: Reporting of violence in the school by group, 2009   67
Figure 5.5a North West Province: Tasks on which principals report spending most time, 2009   68
Figure 5.5b Botswana: Tasks on which principals report spending most time, 2009   68
Figure 5.6a North West Province: Management issues on which principals report spending least time, 2009   69
Figure 5.6b Botswana: Management issues on which principals report spending least time, 2009   69
Figure 5.7   Botswana and North West Province: Perception of principals on whether teacher absenteeism is a problem, 2009   71
Figure 5.8a North West Province: Principals' perceived reasons for teacher absenteeism, 2009   72
Figure 5.8b Botswana: Principals' perceived reasons for teacher absenteeism, 2009   72
Figure 6.1   North West Province and Botswana: Average of individual learner initial mathematics test score by test item, late March, 2009   74
Figure 6.2a North West Province: Average of individual learner pre-test and post-test mathematics score, by test item, late March and late October, 2009   75
Figure 6.2b Botswana: Average of individual learner pre-test and post-test mathematics score by test item, late March and late October, 2009   75
Figure 6.3a North West Province: Pre- and post-test scores by item and curriculum category of items, 2009   78
Figure 6.3b Botswana: Pre- and post-test scores by item and curriculum category of items, 2009   78

Figure 6.4a	North West Province: Test score gains, by item and curriculum category of items, 2009 79
Figure 6.4b	Botswana: Test score gains by item and curriculum category of items, 2009 79
Figure 6.5a	North West Province: Learner achievement on pre-test and average learner socio-economic background by classroom, 2009 81
Figure 6.5b	Botswana: Learner achievement on pre-test and average learner socio-economic background by classroom, 2009 81
Figure 6.6a	North West Province: Pre- and post-test scores by item and mathematics and language difficulty of item, 2009 83
Figure 6.6b	Botswana: Pre- and post-test scores by item and mathematics and language difficulty of item, 2009 83
Figure 6.7a	North West Province: Test score gains by item and mathematics and language difficulty of item, 2009 84
Figure 6.7b	Botswana: Test score gains by item and mathematics and language difficulty of item, 2009 84
Figure 6.8a	North West Province: Pre- and post-test scores by item and by alternative specification of mathematics and language difficulty of item, 2009 85
Figure 6.8b	Botswana: Pre- and post-test scores by item and by alternative specification of mathematics and language difficulty of item, 2009 85
Figure 6.9a	North West Province: Test score gains by item and by alternative specification of mathematics and language difficulty of item, 2009 86
Figure 6.9b	Botswana: Test score gains by item and by alternative specification of mathematics and language difficulty of item, 2009 86
Figure 7.1	North West Province and Botswana: Sampled teachers by age, 2009 90
Figure 7.2a	North West Province: Percentage of teachers by years of teaching experience, years teaching in current school and years teaching mathematics, 2009 90
Figure 7.2b	Botswana: Percentage of teachers by years of teaching experience, years teaching in current school and years teaching mathematics, 2009 91
Figure 7.3a	North West Province and Botswana: Teacher mathematics test results by test item, 63-item grading, 2009 95
Figure 7.3b	North West Province and Botswana: Teacher mathematics test results by test item, 24-item grading, 2009 95
Figure 7.4a	North West Province: Teacher test score by Grading A, Grading B and level of teacher education, 2009 98
Figure 7.4b	Botswana: Teacher test score by Grading A, Grading B and level of teacher education, 2009 98
Figure 7.5	North West Province: Teacher questionnaire score and average classroom student socio-economic background, 2009 100
Figure 7.6a	North West Province: Initial student achievement score and teacher test score graded giving equal weight to each question (Grading B), 2009 101
Figure 7.6b	Botswana: Initial student achievement score and teacher test score graded giving equal weight to each question (Grading B), 2009 101
Figure 8.1	Flow of the lesson in a typical Grade 6 lesson in both countries 106
Figure 8.2	North West Province and Botswana: Mathematical content of the lessons, 2009 107
Figure 8.3	North West Province and Botswana: Mathematical proficiency strands, 2009 108
Figure 8.4	North West Province and Botswana: Levels of cognitive demand, 2009 109
Figure 8.5	North West Province and Botswana: Teachers' observed knowledge, 2009 111
Figure 8.6	North West Province and Botswana: Overall teacher quality ratings, 2009 113
Figure 9.1	North West Province and Botswana: Number of classrooms by percentage of test topics covered, 2009 115

Figure 9.2   North West Province and Botswana: Percentage of sample classes by overall level of cognitive demand, 2009   119
Figure 9.3   North West Province and Botswana: Frequency of observed mathematics lessons, 2009   121
Figure 10.1a   North West Province: Teacher mathematics teaching overall rating (higher of the two ratings when two videotaped lessons) and teacher mathematics knowledge, 2009   130
Figure 10.1b   Botswana: Teacher mathematics teaching overall rating (average of the two ratings when two videotaped lessons) and teacher mathematics knowledge, 2009   130
Figure 10.2   North West Province and Botswana: Teacher mathematics teaching highest overall rating and teacher mathematics knowledge by level of teacher test score, 2009   131
Figure 12.1   Botswana and North West Province: Production possibilities curves and school achievement   154
Figure 12.2   The combination diamond of learner performance improvement   157

Tables

Table 1.1   SACMEQ: Reading and mathematics scores, Grade 6 by country, 2000 and 2007   10
Table 1.2   SACMEQ: Background variables on students, school resources and access by country, 2007   10
Table 2.1   Botswana: Mean monthly earnings for post-secondary degree holders by gender and occupation, 2002–2003   26
Table 2.2   South Africa: Growth in learner and teacher numbers, 2001–2007   29
Table 3.1   Example of topic complexity in the framework   46
Table 3.2   South Africa and Botswana: OTL dimensions, variables, data sources, time of data collection and data collection instruments   50
Table 4.1   Botswana and South Africa: Income inequality comparisons   53
Table 4.2   Botswana and South Africa: Human Development Index and its components   54
Table 4.3   Botswana and South Africa: Public spending on education as a percentage of total government spending and proportion of government spending on education by level of education, 2003–2009   55
Table 4.4   Botswana and South Africa: Public spending per pupil in primary and secondary education, 2003–2009   56
Table 4.5   Botswana: Distribution of sampled schools, by location and district, 2009   57
Table 4.6   Distribution of schools by geography in the Mahikeng and Ramotshere Moiloa local municipalities, 2009   60
Table 6.1   North West Province: Analysis of average learner test score and common distractors in selected mathematics test items, 2009   77
Table 6.2   North West Province: Learner scores by fees of school and urban/rural, 2009   82
Table 7.1   North West Province and Botswana: College at which teachers in sample trained, 2009   91
Table 7.2a   North West Province: Highest degree of training for teachers in the sample, 2009   93
Table 7.2b   Botswana: Highest degree of training for teachers in the sample, 2009   93
Table 7.3   North West Province: Mean teacher test score and overall and teaching mathematics teacher experience   99
Table 7.4   North West Province and Botswana: Teacher mathematics knowledge and average student socio-economic background, by test grading method, 2009   100
Table 7.5a   North West Province: Initial student achievement score and teacher test score, 2009   102
Table 7.5b   Botswana: Initial student achievement score and teacher test score, 2009   102

Table 9.1	North West Province and Botswana: Number of mathematics topics related to test items covered between the pre- and post-test, 2009 115
Table 9.2	North West Province and Botswana: Number of topics covered in each of the five content areas, 2009 116
Table 9.3a	Coverage of topics in main content areas in North West classrooms, 2009 118
Table 9.3b	Coverage of topics in main content areas in Botswana classrooms, 2009 118
Table 9.4	North West Province and Botswana: Number of lessons that each class spent on topics per content area, 2009 120
Table 9.5	Number of mathematics pieces (recorded lessons) of daily work in Grade 6 workbooks by the end of October/beginning of November 2009 121
Table 9.6	North West Province and Botswana: Correlations of various measures of opportunity to learn with classroom SES, 2009 122
Table 9.7a	North West Province: Estimated gains on test items per classroom related to opportunity to learn and average pre-test score, 2009 124
Table 9.7b	Botswana: Estimated gains on test items per classroom related to opportunity to learn and average pre-test score, 2009 125
Table 10.1	North West Province and Botswana: Teacher mathematics teaching quality as related to teacher mathematics knowledge, by type of teacher test grading, 2009 129
Table 10.2	North West Province and Botswana: Opportunity to learn related to teacher test score, by type of opportunity to learn and teacher test grading, 2009 133
Table 11.1	North West Province and Botswana: Estimates of individual student achievement gains as a function of student characteristics, 2009 138
Table 11.2	North West Province and Botswana: Estimates of learner post-test mathematics achievement as a function of learner initial (pre-test) achievement, classroom 'fixed effects' and learner socio-economic background, 2009 140
Table 11.3	North West Province and Botswana: Cross-section and value-added estimates of teacher and other classroom variables on learner mathematics achievement, 2009 144
Table 11.4a	North West Province: Estimates of teacher quality on average classroom learner achievement gains by curriculum category of items, 2009 147
Table 11.4b	Botswana: Estimates of teacher quality on average classroom learner achievement gains by curriculum category of items, 2009 148

Preface

This project would not have been completed without the support of numerous people at different times and in several universities and institutions who gave willingly of their time.

The project emerged from a long-standing relationship between Stanford and a consortium of South African universities' schools of education and between Stanford and the University of Botswana. The aim of these relationships and the consortium was to develop the research capacity and greater depth of research among students and staff at southern African universities' schools of education. These included the Universities of Cape Town, KwaZulu-Natal (UKZN), Western Cape, Witwatersrand (Wits), and the University of Botswana. A fellowship programme began in 2000 with support from the Spencer Foundation for doctoral fellowships in these schools and faculties of education. A substantial number of students gained their doctorates as a result of the support they received from this programme and have gone on to occupy leadership positions, as intended, in universities, government and other walks of life. In addition, thanks to the support of the United States Department of State, Stanford engaged in an exchange programme with these southern African institutions. Faculty and graduate students traveled from Stanford to Botswana and South Africa, and from various universities in South Africa and Botswana to Stanford.

One of our main aims was to run a large comparative research project involving students in various aspects of researching education. With the participation of the consortium, we reached agreement on the topic with which such a research project should be concerned – the exceptionally low achievement of South African learners in literacy and numeracy – and began efforts to raise funds for the project. Again, a main aim was to build capacity.

Martin Carnoy provided intellectual leadership and travelled extensively between southern Africa and Stanford in the conduct of the research. Linda Chisholm coordinated the project in South Africa, while Bagele Chilisa did so in Botswana. They were also responsible for the overall writing of the study. Cheryl Reeves, Ingrid Sapire and Alejandra Sorto led major sections of the study (opportunity to learn, learner knowledge of mathematics, and teacher proficiency to teach mathematics). Margaret Irving also contributed to the writing. Thenjiwe Major and Nnunu Tsheko led the data collection effort in Botswana, which included the involvement of Paul Nleya, Onalenna Senwedi, Bose Emmanuel Ketlhaotswe and Onyetswe Tshabo. Nii Addy, Fabian Arends, Kolentino Mpeta and Margaret Irving played major roles in organising and analysing the data.

Six PhDs (Nii Addy, Fabian Arends, Hlengani Baloyi, Jesse Foster, Margaret Irving and Erin Raab) were initiated as a result of this project. Three masters degree theses were completed (Victor Bome and Gift Madwala in mathematics education and Tina Sukhjinder Kaur in research and evaluation). Jeffery Marshall (with support from Luis Benveniste) provided crucial early training for local data collectors and the analysis team. Many thanks to them. In addition, the assistance of Ronel Paulsen (UNISA), Judah Makonye (Wits), Bronwen Wilson-Thomson (Wits), Jessica Sherman (Wits) and Corin Mathews (Wits) in data capturing resulted in skills transfer. Interactions with staff and students at UKZN, who conducted the same project with separate funding, also resulted in the sharing of research knowledge and skills.

One of the great advantages of doing this project with a team of researchers who covered both the data gathering and data analysis aspects is that everybody in the team who was analysing and writing up data had an intimate knowledge of the conditions on the ground as well as the data collection process. 'Feeling' the numbers is important in quantitative analysis and in drawing conclusions from that analysis. This became clear when we met in Mafeking in July 2011 with 70 of our 120 teachers in our Botswana and North West province samples who accepted our invitation to discuss the results of the study. We, the researchers, had been with these teachers in their classrooms and were therefore able to have a different kind of conversation with them about our results. As a consequence, they were unusually open with us. We hope that in presenting the results in these pages, we have been able to convey the very processes we are trying to measure.

Thanks especially to the parents, teachers, principals and learners who were willing to be part of this study, also to departmental officials in South Africa and Botswana, and unions in South Africa, for giving us access to the schools.

Ultimately it was again the Spencer Foundation that believed that something of value could come out of this collaboration – and we have no doubt that something has. We are grateful for their support. Finally, we would like to thank the critical readers of this report, Mark Orkin and William Schmidt (Michigan State University), who gave generously of their time and insights to help improve the document. Thanks also to Charles Simkins, who looked at an earlier report on the South African data.

Gaborone, Botswana; Pretoria, South Africa; and Stanford, California
September, 2011

Executive summary

This study compares student learning in primary schools in the border region of two neighbouring countries, South Africa's North West Province and South East Botswana. Like several other studies in recent years, it tries to identify schooling factors that affect student achievement significantly. This research, however, distinguishes itself by addressing physically proximate, culturally and socio-economically similar learners attending the same grade in two different school systems. It focuses on the characteristics of teachers and teaching that may contribute to student learning gains in Grade 6 of a group of lower- and lower middle-income schools shaped in different historical settings. We sampled 60 schools in each of the two countries, 62 Grade 6 mathematics teachers in North West schools and 64 teachers in Botswana, covering a total of 5 500 students in those 126 classrooms. The data were collected in 2009.

Background and contexts

South Africa has a bigger and more diversified economy, and more complex government institutions and civil society than Botswana. It is often viewed as the economic powerhouse of and gateway to Africa. However, Botswana has a higher gross domestic product (GDP) per capita than South Africa and saw a phenomenal 8.2 per cent average economic growth rate over three decades after achieving independence in 1966. Economic development in South Africa slowed significantly from the 1980s, whereas Botswana is widely acknowledged as a 'star performer', a 'miracle' and a 'developmental state' in the African context.

Botswana and South Africa are not poor countries in terms of their per capita incomes. The GDP per capita in South Africa in 2009 was more than $10 000, and in Botswana, more than $13 000. These are levels in the range of Lebanon, Chile or Argentina for Botswana; and Brazil and Costa Rica for South Africa.

Yet, Botswana and South Africa have among the most unequal income distributions in the world (Botswana has a Gini coefficient of 0.61 compared to South Africa's 0.58), suggesting that despite high national average GDP per capita, low-income families in both countries are still very poor. Both economies also share jobless growth and high youth unemployment and are among the countries with the highest incidence of HIV/AIDS in the world.

Despite the similarly large gap between rich and poor, Botswana ranks higher (98th) than South Africa (110th) on the United Nations' Human Development Index (HDI) – Botswana has somewhat more highly developed human capabilities and services than South Africa.

Botswana and South Africa spend similar amounts on education per student as other countries with the same levels of GDP per capita. According to our estimates from World Bank data, Botswana spends about $1 500 per primary school student, and South Africa, about $1 300. Costa Rica and Brazil spend somewhat more per student than South Africa, Chile about the same as Botswana, and Argentina somewhat more than Botswana – but the differences are not large. Furthermore, young people in these two southern African countries almost universally attain Grade 6.

In summary, Botswana has higher income per capita than South Africa, but a more unequal income distribution. It has traditionally put a lower fraction of its resources into primary education, but having more resources, has spent more per pupil in primary schools, and has somewhat better conditions in primary schools in terms of teacher pupil ratios and the proportion of certified teachers. The primary school education spending differences between the two countries seem to have been declining in the past decade. Nonetheless, despite having higher levels of inequality and spending more or less the same as South Africa on primary schools, Botswana enjoys a higher ranking on human development indices and performs better on international and regional tests of literacy and numeracy. Our study investigates why this might be the case by closer examination of what goes on inside classrooms.

Historical and policy contexts are relevant. The different political and education policy trajectories of the two countries have influenced contemporary schooling contexts. Botswana gained independence in 1966; South Africa in 1994. The legacy of British colonialism in Botswana was relatively light by contrast with apartheid's legacy in South Africa. For almost three decades after 1966, while South Africa was subject to authoritarian, racially-based unequal development, Botswana pursued a path of liberal democratic nation building, growth and development based on the discovery of diamonds in 1967. The most significant differences as a result are the relatively more conflictual processes of political and education policy change in South Africa over the past half century when compared with Botswana, and the earlier extension of state control over African education under more favorable conditions, as well as the more incremental process of education policy change in Botswana than in South Africa.

There are also important education policy similarities and differences between the two countries. Whereas both adopted an outcomes-based curriculum in the 1990s, the form and content in each differed substantially. In Botswana, a closely calibrated system of clearly specified curriculum-texts-tests and supervision has come into being. In contrast, South Africa's curriculum, design and assessment requirements have proved challenging for teachers. Testing has not (until very recently) been high on the reform agenda, teacher education has been disrupted, supervision virtually non-existent, and texts variable in availability and quality. There have been difficulties in each country with the expected form of pedagogy. Each country struggles with the transition from mother tongue to English as language of instruction, but curriculum planning and implementation processes in Botswana are generally longer and more sustained than in South Africa.

Botswana does suffer shortages of well-trained mathematics teachers, but far less than South Africa, which has major deficiencies in adequately prepared teachers. Teacher training in South Africa shifted from teacher education colleges to higher education in the late 1990s, disrupting the supply of teachers to schools. Botswana has had no such disruption in its provision of teacher education. South Africa is only now moving in the direction of centralised teacher recruitment and hiring, a longtime feature of Botswana's system. Teachers are relatively well paid in Botswana, while in South Africa, improvements since the mid-1990s and changes initiated in 2008 have resulted in a gradual closing of the wage gap between teachers and other professionals.

South African teachers are highly unionised and over 80 per cent of teachers in public schools belong to unions, with the vast majority of these belonging to the South African Democratic Teachers' Union (SADTU) and smaller numbers to the National Association of Professional Teacher Organisations of South Africa (NAPTOSA) and the Suid-Afrikaanse Onderwysersunie (SAOU). Teacher unionism has been a major feature of the educational landscape in South Africa for three decades. It has become so only very recently in Botswana. A number of analyses suggest that the expression of teacher unionism at the local level constrains the ability of government to pursue its policy objectives of improving literacy and numeracy and broader educational outcomes.

Together, these contextual features help us to understand the process of what happens inside classrooms. But they do not explain everything. For this, we need to probe the classroom context.

The method

The method we use and the data collected make ours a unique study of schooling. The details on learning, teacher skills, the schooling process and the schooling environment give us insights into what and how students in the two countries learn mathematics that go far beyond those in other studies of schooling – even most studies outside southern Africa. Further, the comparison of the schooling processes in a border area of two countries helps us draw broader conclusions about school improvement strategies than are possible in single country studies. And, unlike other studies in the region, the same researchers who designed the instruments and collected the data in the classrooms did the empirical analysis and interpreted the results. Once the study was completed, the researchers also met in a collective meeting with most of the teachers who participated in the study to discuss the results. The discussion in that meeting appears in a separate report of this study.

Unlike previous research, this study does three things that make it innovative and especially relevant to policy-makers:

First, it is a large, comparative study that focuses directly on differences in educational systems. Such differences give us insights into why similar students learn more under certain 'system conditions' than others do, and what those conditions are. One element in our innovative approach is to exploit a 'natural experiment.' The natural experiment results from the similarity of primary school student populations but differing school systems on either side of the border area of two neighbouring southern African countries, Botswana and South Africa, namely, North West Province and South East Botswana. The children attending school in this border region, as in many border regions of the world, are very alike linguistically and culturally, yet they attend schools that have been subject to different political, economic and education policy histories. The school and classroom contexts are therefore likely to be different in a number of aspects, including the way teachers are trained, the social organisation of the schools, including teacher culture, and the way the teachers interact with the curriculum.

Second, the study measures gains in student learning in mathematics in each region over the course of an academic year in Grade 6. Such changes in achievement in Grade 6 can be associated directly with the quality of teachers and other classroom conditions that students experienced in that year.

Third, the study also measures a number of different characteristics for each teacher that may be related to each other and could likely contribute to how much mathematics students learn during their year in Grade 6. These characteristics are as follows:
- The teacher's knowledge of mathematics, as measured by a test of mathematics content and pedagogical content knowledge (how well the teacher understands common mistakes that students make and how to correct them) related to the subject matter in the Grade 6 curriculum.
- The quality of teaching assessed through videotape analysis of mathematics lessons given during the school year.
- The nature of teaching experience and teacher preparation gleaned from teacher questionnaires.
- How much and what mathematics was taught during the school year, based on detailed information taken from student notebooks in each class. We call this last set of information the opportunity to learn (OTL) provided to their students by the teachers in our sample.

The sample

For the North West study, we used a two-level stratified random sampling methodology applied to public schools with Grade 6 learners. We selected 60 schools in the Mahikeng (formerly Mafikeng) and Ramotshere Moiloa local municipalities. These border Botswana and contain two of the major urban centres in the province, Mahikeng and Zeerust. A total of 155 schools with a learner population of 9 157 constituted the sampling frame. We oversampled urban schools to correspond to the sample on the Botswana side of the border. Our surveys in North West Province covered 62 mathematics teachers and 3 800 learners in 58 of the 60 schools sampled.

For South East Botswana, we used a simple stratified random sampling methodology, appropriately weighted, to select primary schools spread across four districts: Gaborone, South East, Southern and Kgatleng districts. The schools are located close to the capital city of Gaborone and the town of Lobatse and are within a radius of about 80 kilometers. Both Gaborone and Lobatse are near the South African border posts of Tlokweng and Mahikeng. A total population of 107 schools with enrolment of 6 835 Grade 6 learners constituted the sampling base. We sampled a total of 60 schools. Of these, 58 agreed to participate in the study. Our Botswana surveys covered 64 mathematics teachers and about 1 700 learners in the 58 schools.

The results

Our results for Botswana and North West Province provide an enormous amount of carefully gathered information on student background, student learning, teacher knowledge and pedagogical skills, school environments, and the amount of mathematics actually taught to students during their Grade 6 year. This is useful in understanding the conditions in a broad range of Botswana and South African primary schools serving students of relatively modest socio-economic background, albeit in only one region in each country. The systematic analysis of this information allows us to draw important conclusions regarding the role of teachers and teaching in Botswana and North West in students' learning. Our results for the students in these classrooms become part of the broader analysis comparing Botswana and South African educational policy and practices.

- The large majority of the 5 500 students in our sample were from lower-income families and attended fee-free schools. Even so, the learners in our study came from considerably varied socio-economic backgrounds. Students in both countries did poorly on the mainly 5th grade level test we gave them (average of 28.6 per cent on the initial test in North West and 33.5 per cent in Botswana) and made relatively small gains in the seven months between the pre- and post-test (3 percentage points in North West and 4 percentage points in Botswana).
- Many learners in both countries had better knowledge of some parts of the mathematics curriculum, such as patterns, but had very poor knowledge of much of the Grade 6 curriculum, especially measurement and data handling. Learners in both countries tended to do poorly or well on the same test items. The learner test results were marked by rather high variation, and the learner gains by even greater variation compared to the mean gain. The bottom line is that students in Botswana scored significantly higher on the initial test and made higher gains over the academic year.
- As was to be expected, there were differences in achievement level between teachers and learners in schools in higher and low-income neighbourhoods. Urban learners scored significantly higher than rural learners did on both tests, although their achievement gain was smaller than for the lower scoring rural students.
- The language of instruction was English (or Afrikaans in South Africa, as chosen by the school governing body). Although we observed that the majority of students spoke English with difficulty, students in Botswana seemed to have greater English facility. When we assessed how well learners

did in both countries on test items that were rated according to how difficult the mathematics and language was we found that mathematics difficulty is more important than language difficulty in how well learners scored on a particular item. On a classification of test items according to the numeric, symbolic and language complexity of items, there was very little difference in achievement, suggesting that language itself does not necessarily make things harder for learners. However, this finding is in the context of quite low average scores on the test as a whole.

- Teachers' mathematics knowledge (as measured by a test given to teachers), the quality of their teaching (as measured by assessing videotapes of lessons) and the amount of mathematics teaching they actually did during the year (as measured by an assessment of student notebooks) were all statistically related to each other. Teachers who did better on our mathematics test also, on average, taught mathematics more effectively and taught more lessons on the topics covered by our student test. This relationship was more evident in North West Province than in South East Botswana.

- Teachers in Botswana and North West Province are, on average, quite senior, and almost all are trained in teacher secondary school level training colleges. However, teachers in Botswana scored significantly higher on our teacher mathematics test and taught significantly more total mathematics lessons during the academic year. The analysis of 100 videotapes of Grade 6 mathematics lessons taught by the teachers in North West (1.6 per teacher) and the 83 videotapes in Botswana (1.3 per teacher), showed that the level of mathematics content knowledge displayed by the teachers in the observed lesson averaged significantly higher in Botswana. Many of the teachers taught moderately well pedagogically in their classrooms, but especially in North West, they tended to cover subject matter that should be taught in the 4th and 5th grades. Relatively few teachers in either country (somewhat more in Botswana) were rated as 'best quality,' due mainly to their low level of mathematics pedagogical content knowledge.

- The results of our assessment of student notebooks showed that the amount of time during the year that teachers actually teach learners mathematics is disturbingly low in both countries, but especially low in North West Province. Descriptive data reveal that the average number of mathematics lessons given by most teachers is considerably less than the number of lessons officially intended, indicating that 'time on task' is a problem in many of the sample schools and classrooms. Rather than teaching the 130 lessons or more that were programmed in the period for which we were able to observe recorded lessons in their notebooks (beginning of the academic year up to the beginning of November), we counted an average of 50 daily lessons during that period in North West and 78 in Botswana. Teachers did not teach 60 per cent of the lessons they were scheduled to teach in North West and almost 40 per cent of the lessons scheduled in Botswana. There was considerable variation in the number of lessons taught from classroom to classroom, but this very low average figure in North West Province implies that students were not getting much exposure to mathematics during their Grade 6 year. They were getting more in Botswana, but much less than they were due.

- Teachers and principals we interviewed did not consider teacher absenteeism a major issue, and principals reported that the biggest reason for absenteeism was ill health followed by domestic responsibilities. However, even teachers who are actually present in school on a particular day may not teach their scheduled mathematics lessons for a host of other reasons. One of these, brought up by many North West teachers, is the 'lack of confidence' teachers feel in teaching the required elements of the Grade 6 mathematics curriculum. In discussions, teachers attributed this lack of confidence to lacking the knowledge needed to teach the subject.

- There is considerable evidence from the notebooks in both countries of a slow pace of work within lessons, as reflected in the number and type of written mathematical tasks that learners completed daily. This slow micro-pacing suggests that teachers may be having difficulty in determining the amount of time students should have for completing exercises, or that students are taking a long time to complete exercises, or that teachers wait until the last pupil has finished, leaving faster pupils unoccupied and bored. Descriptive data on OTL also confirm that the sample of Grade 6 teachers most commonly focus on topics related to the content area 'numbers, operations and relationships', and mainly engage students in routine mathematics procedures, and not with underlying knowledge principles. We cannot ascertain from our data whether this situation prevails because teachers find they need to address gaps in students' knowledge, or because teachers themselves are less confident about, or are not competent enough to teach certain content areas or topics at higher levels. Later discussions with teachers suggest that both factors are important in explaining the reasons for the slow pace of lessons.

- However, we learnt through our teacher questionnaires and our interviews that teachers in North West are often also pulled away from school by teacher in-service training and union meetings, and in Botswana by departmental meetings. Even if learners were involved in mathematics activities during the year that were not recorded in their notebooks, the outcomes-based education (OBE) system that formed the basis for accountability in Botswana and South African schools makes it doubtful that there would be many such unrecorded class activities. The low exposure to the curriculum is therefore an obvious problem that needs to be corrected if learners are expected to improve their knowledge of mathematics. That this is not widely recognised as a major issue by teachers and principals makes the problem more difficult to solve.
- Our study also found that teacher test scores in both countries are positively and significantly related to the average classroom student pre-test score. This suggests that better teachers tend to be attracted to schools with better performing learners; although the mobility profile of teachers indicates that the majority tend to teach close to where they trained and trained close to where they grew up. Few teachers were from outside the region; those who were tended to locate in high socio-economic status schools.
- The differences in achievement gains by students in the two regions are explained by the aggregation of relatively small differences in teaching skills and the process of delivering education in the two countries. The results suggest that Botswana is able to produce higher achievement gains because it has somewhat better teacher resources (teachers with greater mathematics knowledge and teaching skills) and delivers education a little more effectively than South Africa does. Effective delivery here means that teachers teach more mathematics lessons during the year and stick more closely to the curriculum.
- Although Botswana is able to produce greater Grade 6 learning gains than South Africa, our estimates suggest that there is little room for gains in Botswana from improving teacher skills or opportunity to learn in the range of inputs now available in low/middle social class Botswana classrooms. In South African schools, however, it appears that much larger gains can be made from improving teacher skills and the opportunity to learn in the range observable in these schools. For Botswana to make larger gains would require significantly increased teacher mathematics knowledge and mathematics teaching skills.
- Another way to interpret this is that even though teachers in Botswana schools are quite diverse in their mathematics knowledge, teaching skills and the number of lessons they devote during the year to various items on our learner test, there is something more regularised about the process of teaching in Botswana schools. This reduces the effect of that variation on learner academic performance. In South Africa's North West Province, however, the variation in observed and unobserved classroom conditions appears to have a large impact on learner gains, probably because classroom processes are more heterogeneous in South Africa.

Policy implications

The detailed picture provided by our analysis of schools in North West Province and Botswana may be rather dismal, but the relationships we measure do point to specific ways to make that picture better.

Should policy-makers take our results seriously, we believe that student performance in mathematics would improve.

Previously estimated differences in learner achievement between Grade 6 learners in Botswana and South African classrooms are significant but not terribly large. Our study not only confirmed this, but also showed that the reasons for those differences are rooted in a combination of differences in the quality of teacher inputs – teachers' mathematical knowledge and the quality of classroom teaching – and the amount of coverage of the required curriculum, which is certainly greater in Botswana than in North West Province classrooms. These 'little things' apparently add up to produce the greater achievement gains in Botswana classrooms. Over the years, greater achievement gains apparently accumulate, so that by the end of Grade 6, the very culturally and socio-economically similar students in North West Province schools find themselves one-half a standard deviation in achievement score behind Botswana students.

We would speculate that the education systems of both countries are marked by relatively low subject matter and subject teaching skills for teachers and consequently low academic expectations for teachers and students. This begins with teacher training in the knowledge and skills considered necessary to teach subjects such as mathematics, and continues on to the expectations concerning teacher responsibility for student learning, and the expectations of how thoroughly teachers are expected to know and cover all elements of the national curriculum. More emphasis in teacher training on mathematics content knowledge and pedagogical mathematics content knowledge, as well as how to teach the required national curriculum, could produce more academic achievement in both countries without significantly increasing the current resource expenditure per student.

Unfortunately, improving the overall quality of teachers already in the system has proven to be extremely challenging. South Africa and Botswana have many teachers already in service who are inadequately trained and who are likely to remain in the system for many years. Despite numerous attempts to improve existing teacher quality through upgrading programmes for un- and under-qualified teachers, most programmes appear to have had almost no effect on the quality of learning outcomes in schools. Clearly, new approaches to in-service training are needed. To improve, teachers may be required to spend large parts of their vacation periods learning how to teach mathematics and language more effectively by focusing on improved content knowledge and increasing the content demand in their teaching. It might well be more effective in the short term to focus on ensuring that already employed teachers and those about to enter teaching teach subjects they are qualified to teach. But even in the short term, making a concerted effort to increase the mathematics content and pedagogical content knowledge of current teachers should have multiple effects, including increasing the number of lessons they teach and improving learners' mathematics skills.

Findings from our study also suggest that emphasising opportunity to learn through time spent overall on mathematics work, content coverage, spread of topics across each grade year and cognitive and curricular pacing within and across grades, could be an effective strategy to increase learning, especially in poorly performing schools, such as most of those in our sample. To accomplish this, teachers need to acquire more content knowledge and should be held accountable for teaching their classes. Were such a strategy added to the current effort to provide and use efficiently a well-structured and carefully designed textbook and workbook series, as well as other material, it could greatly improve student learning with almost no increase in per student spending (especially in North West Province). This is provided that teachers actually use the books purposefully.

In both countries, but especially on the South African side of the border, more knowledgeable teachers teaching more effectively in classrooms and covering more material, result, not surprisingly, in students learning more. If the North West provincial authorities were to assess and take steps to correct the nature of teacher shortages in subjects such as mathematics, implement a serious in-service teacher training programme and ensure that teachers taught mathematics lessons every day as scheduled, there is no doubt that mathematics learning in North West Province schools would improve and probably reach current levels of achievement gains in South East Botswana. Of course, Botswana should be taking exactly the same steps to improve their students' achievement. But, as we argue, there is less room in Botswana to make as large gains with existing resources.

The name of the education game in southern Africa, as we show rather exhaustively in this study, is to get out of the low achievement trap. Botswana has a more effective education system than South Africa and has somewhat better resources going into education, but, given how much it has to spend, is nonetheless producing rather low levels of learner knowledge. Policy-makers in Botswana need to reassess their benchmarks for educational quality and raise expectations across the board if they hope to reach levels of student achievement commensurate with their GDP per capita.

In some sense, South African policy-makers have an easier task in that South African education is so inefficient and under resourced in terms of teacher quality that the steps needed to reach Botswana levels of student achievement gains are more apparent. We have shown what those steps are and the high payoff that taking them would have for the vast majority of South African students. However, as we have also analysed, the steps may be evident, but taking them in the South African political and social context may be exceedingly difficult. This will require changing a now deeply ingrained culture of inefficiency in producing learner achievement. Most schools in the South African educational system have, plainly and simply, organised themselves to produce something that is not student achievement. That suggests that our recommendations, evident as they may be to most, represent more than just showing teachers and principals how to improve their effectiveness. It may require changing the underlying school culture from one that places first priority on teacher autonomy to one that focuses much more clearly on making students academically competent.

This does not mean that South African education has to give up on its other goals, such as infusing learners with a sense of their new destiny as equals in building a new society with justice for all, and being politically aware and politically active. Nevertheless, unless all learners have the opportunity to be academically adept in the knowledge society, they will automatically be at a disadvantage and unlikely to gain crucial elements of the equality that they deserve. The school system will effectively have prevented them from realising their full potential.

Acronyms and abbreviations

ANC	African National Congress
BODMAS	Brackets of division, multiplication addition and subtraction
COSATU	Congress of South African Trade Unions
CK	Content knowledge
DBE	Department of Basic Education
DoE	Department of Education
GDP	Gross domestic product
GNP	Gross national product
HLM	Hierarchical linear model
HSRC	Human Sciences Research Council
IEA	International Association for the Evaluation of Educational Achievement
IPET	Initial professional education of teachers
IQMS	Integrated quality management system
KZN	KwaZulu-Natal
MKT	Mathematical knowledge for teaching
NAEP	National Assessment of Educational Progress
NEEDU	National Education and Evaluation Unit
NCS	(South African) National Curriculum Statement
OBE	Outcomes-based education
OECD	Organisation for Economic Co-operation and Development
OLS	Ordinary Least Squares
OTL	Opportunity to learn
PCK	Pedagogical content knowledge
PISA	Programme for International Student Assessment
PPP	Purchasing power parity
PTRs	Pupil:teacher ratios
SACMEQ	Southern African Consortium for Monitoring Education Quality
SADTU	South African Democratic Teacher's Union
SERCE	Segundo Estudio Regional Comparativo y Explicativo
SES	Socio-economic status
TIMSS	Third International Mathematics and Science Survey
UB	University of Botswana
UNDP	United Nations Development Programme

Introduction

Thanks to the spread of international tests, such as the Trends in International Mathematics and Science Study (TIMSS) and the Programme for International Student Assessment (PISA), pundits have become obsessed with the reasons for high student performance in countries such as Finland, Korea, Taiwan and Singapore. Students in those countries score at the top of the league tables on international tests. We can probably learn many things from observing their education systems, but in practice, the economic, social, and educational conditions there have little relevance for most lower-income developing countries. It is much more interesting for Latin American countries, for example, to understand why Cuban and Costa Rican students do so much better than students in the rest of the region when neither Cuba or Costa Rica is especially well off economically (Carnoy et al. 2007; Segundo Estudio Regional Comparativo y Explicativo, SERCE 2008). Similarly, it is much more relevant for African countries to understand why students in some countries do better academically than those in other countries with similar resources (see Southern African Consortium for Monitoring Education Quality, SACMEQ 2010).

Aim of the study

With this in mind, we set out to understand why students in primary schools in one African country seem to perform at a higher level than do students in another. Our innovative approach is to exploit a 'natural experiment'. This natural experiment is based on the similarity of primary school student populations, but differing school systems, on either side of the border in two southern African neighbours, Botswana and South Africa. The children attending school in this border region, as in many border regions of the world, are very alike linguistically and culturally,[1] yet they attend schools that have been subject to different political and policy histories. Botswana has been an independent country since 1966, developing its social and educational institutions under a democratic non-racial government. South Africa pursued a policy of separate development, enforced with great violence, in which most black Africans were required to live in 'homelands', segregated from white South African territory. One of these, Bophutatswana, was located along the Botswana border, had its 'own' Bantu education, and was ultimately swept up by the conflict with the 'Apartheid South African State'. These different histories caused school and classroom contexts to differ in the way teachers are trained (even today), the social organisation of the schools (including teacher culture) and the way teachers interact with the curriculum. We were further motivated to undertake the study because the results of international student performance studies in the early 2000s showed that pupils in Botswana achieve at significantly higher levels those in South Africa. In both the TIMSS and SACMEQ II studies, which tested 8th and 6th graders respectively, the bottom 80 per cent of Botswana students by social class

---

1 It is important to note that whereas all the students in our sample of schools in both countries are by definition 'Africans,' apartheid in South Africa left a legacy of racial classification that divided people into categories of African, coloured, Indian and white. Apartheid further classified black Africans into ethnic groups that constituted the basis for the homeland policy. The black consciousness movement of the 1970s popularised the view that all people designated as Africans, Indians and coloureds suffered racial discrimination and oppression and should collectively be termed 'black'. To track whether racial redress has occurred, the South African census still collects data differentiating between white, Indian, coloured and African, but education statistics are not collected using these categories. These nomenclatures remain in use (and we refer to them where necessary in this study while recognising their socially-constructed character), although in theory there are no longer any differential privileges associated with them.

background scored significantly higher than students in South Africa. SACMEQ III, conducted in 2007, shows similar results. Even so, Botswana students scored considerably lower on the SACMEQ than students tested in many other African countries. The test results from a decade ago and from the most recent SACMEQ III show little change in either Botswana or South Africa's scores. Thus, although most students in both countries are learning at rather low levels, schools in Botswana seem to be preparing them better than do schools in South Africa.

Botswana and South Africa are not poor countries in terms of their per capita incomes. According to World Bank data, measured in purchasing power parity (PPP) dollars (dollars adjusted for the prices of a typical consumer basket of good in different countries compared to the United States), the GDP per capita in South Africa in 2009 was more than $10 000, and in Botswana, more than $13 000. These are levels of GDP per capita in the range of Lebanon, Chile or Argentina for Botswana; and Brazil and Costa Rica for South Africa. Botswana and South Africa also spend similar amounts per student on education compared with other countries at the same levels of GDP per capita. Based again on estimates we made from World Bank data, in PPP dollars, Botswana spent about $1 600 per primary school student, and South Africa, about $1 300. Costa Rica and Brazil spent somewhat more per student than South Africa, Chile about the same as Botswana, and Argentina somewhat more than Botswana. But the differences are not large. Furthermore, young people in these two southern African countries almost universally attain Grade 6.

We reasoned that this set of circumstances, where two different state-administered and financed school systems provide similar funding to supply education to similar students but produce different academic outcomes, could help us understand how possibly different levels of 'teacher skills' and different 'schooling environments', including educational policies, result in learning differences. Simply put, our study asks the following questions:
- Do children in Botswana learn more during Grade 6 than similar children in South Africa?[2]
- Do children in Botswana learn more because Botswana schools have 'better' resources (teachers, smaller class sizes), or because the resources are 'better organised' – that is, used more efficiently – than in South Africa?
- What does our analysis suggest for policy-makers to improve student learning in the two countries?

Method

The most common empirical method used to analyse the relation of school inputs, such as teacher characteristics to student learning, is the production function (see Hanushek 1986). Production functions estimate the relation between inputs and outputs of a given product, and when comparing two producers, also suggest whether one is more efficient than the other in using similar resources to produce the same output. There have been two major criticisms of the production function approach applied to the education industry:
- First, it is not based on any underlying learning theory and therefore does not model the learning process adequately (Levin 1980).
- Second, its estimates of the contribution of school inputs to student outcomes are biased because students may select themselves to be with certain teachers, and schools and teachers may select themselves to work in certain schools or with certain groups of students in schools (Ladd 2008; Schneider et al. 2007).

---

2 We selected schools along a strip on either side of the border. Throughout the study, we refer interchangeably to the North West Province/North West/South Africa and to South East Botswana/Botswana. Size, representativeness and comparability of the sampling frame allow for generalisation from the part to the whole.

In recent years, researchers have made progress in addressing both these issues. They have dealt with causality in the teacher characteristics-student outcomes relation by using longitudinal studies that measure a student's achievement across grades and various teachers (Clotfelter et al. 2005; Hill et al. 2005; Lankford et al. 2002). They are also beginning to delve into the learning process rather than just using teacher characteristics as proxies for the process (Carnoy et al 2007; Marshall & Sorto 2012). Our approach goes far beyond previous studies in capturing the teaching-learning process. We use a production function methodology that has little resemblance to the traditional input-output models of the past. This methodology also addresses many of the criticisms regarding selection bias and empirically capturing the schooling process. We apply an underlying theory in which student learning is a function of:

- the human and cultural capital the students bring to the school, the teacher's capacity to teach the subject matter (teacher content knowledge and pedagogical content knowledge),
- the cognitive demands teachers make of students in the classroom,
- the amount of time spent on the subject matter that is supposed to be taught (curriculum),
- the quality of the teacher's pedagogy in the classroom, and
- classroom peer conditions, such as average socio-economic background and number of students in the class.

We measure these variables and show how each of them is related to students' learning during their 6th grade year in school. Our theory of change is based on the view that any efforts to improve student learning would necessarily have to address the combination of issues but also focus on those specific features that appear to influence student learning the most.

Classrooms are also part of schools and are embedded in educational systems, larger societies and political cultures. Besides deepening the traditional production function analysis by measuring classroom processes, our study has the advantage that we observe classrooms and schools that are part of two different systems of education with very different histories. We gather data from principals on their schools, such as absenteeism and school violence, that we cross-check with similar questions on the student and teacher questionnaires. We have also been able to analyse, through interviews and secondary data, important differences in the 'culture of schooling' in the two countries that might explain some of our results. One clear difference is that the roles of teachers' unions in Botswana and South Africa are very different. These differences have potentially important impacts on teachers' perceptions of their classroom and school roles. Teacher training has been shaped by significantly different policies in the past 15 years in Botswana and South Africa, and this has influenced the availability of primary school teachers and who the current teachers are in the schools we sampled. Ultimately, African students in South Africa may not perform as well in school subjects as African students in other countries, even when they face teachers with similar subject knowledge and pedagogical skills. This is because of a 'South African effect' – that is, the years of apartheid may still weigh on teachers' and students' perceptions of how successful both can be academically. We shall use our data to explore the possibility of such an effect.

Results

Our study provides carefully gathered information on student background, student learning, teacher knowledge and pedagogical skills, school environments, and the amount of mathematics actually taught to students during their Grade 6 year in the Botswana-South Africa border region. This information is useful in understanding the conditions in a broad range of South African and Botswana primary schools serving students of relatively modest socio-economic background, albeit confined to specific regions of the two countries. The systematic analysis of this information allows us to draw important conclusions regarding the role of teachers and teaching in students' learning. The method we use and the data collected make this a unique study of schooling. The details on learning, teacher skills, the schooling process and the schooling environment give us insights into what and how students in the two countries learn mathematics that go far beyond those in other studies of schooling, even most studies outside southern Africa. In addition, the comparison of the schooling processes in a border area of two countries helps us draw much broader conclusions about school improvement strategies than are possible in single country studies.

Our analysis produced four major findings:
1. Grade 6 learners in Botswana have higher mathematics achievement gains than a very similar set of Grade 6 learners in South Africa, but students in both countries learn mathematics at relatively low levels and make relatively small gains during the Grade 6 year.
2. The pattern of learning mathematics is very similar in the two countries. Students in both countries mainly learn how to do operations rather than being taught the underlying mathematics or how to reason mathematically. They also learn the same elements of the mathematics curriculum.
3. The differences in achievement gains are explained by the aggregation of relatively small differences in teaching skills and the process of delivering education in the two countries. The results suggest that Botswana is able to produce higher achievement gains than is the case in South Africa because it has somewhat better teacher resources (teachers with somewhat greater mathematics knowledge and somewhat better teaching skills). Botswana also delivers education somewhat more effectively than in South Africa (teachers teach more mathematics lessons during the year and stick more closely to the curriculum).
4. Although Botswana is able to produce greater Grade 6 learning gains than South Africa, the production function estimates suggest that there is little room for gains in Botswana from improving teacher skills or opportunity to learn in the range of inputs now available in low/moderate social class Botswana classrooms. In South African schools, however, it appears that much larger gains can made from improving teacher skills and the opportunity to learn in the range observable in these schools. Another way to interpret this is that even though teachers in Botswana schools are quite diverse in their mathematics knowledge, teaching skills, and the number of lessons they devote during the year to various items on our learner test, there is something more regularised about the process of teaching in Botswana schools. This reduces the effect of that variation on learner academic performance. In South Africa's North West Province, however, the variation in observed and unobserved classroom conditions appears to have a large impact on learner gains, probably because classroom processes are more heterogeneous in South Africa.

Presentation of the study

We present our analysis in twelve parts:
- Chapter 1 provides the background to the study – previous research on the classroom and school factors that contribute to student learning, especially the impact of teacher quality on achievement.
- Chapter 2 compares the educational policy history and teacher preparation policies relevant to our research in Botswana and South Africa's North West Province.
- Chapter 3 presents the conceptual framework, methodology, and a description of the data collection process, including the instruments used and an analysis of the data collection problems faced. The chapter is long, but the conceptual framework and methodology are a major contribution of the study, and the instruments and data collection itself are important details supporting the validity of the empirical results. This chapter is also important for researchers in replicating the study in other regions and countries.

- Chapter 4 describes the characteristics of the schools sampled in North West Province and Botswana in terms of the schools' location.
- Chapter 5 describes the context of the schools in our sample and some of the features of the schools' leadership through the lens of the principals' questionnaire.
- Chapter 6 analyses the results of the learner pre- and post-tests in mathematics, with a detailed item analysis of the results of the two tests and of the item gains.
- Chapter 7 describes the characteristics of the teachers in our sample, including their mathematics skills as measured by a Grade 6 level mathematics and mathematics pedagogy test.
- Chapter 8 analyses the 180 videotapes of classroom mathematics lessons we filmed of the teachers in our two samples to compare what teachers are teaching in the classrooms in the two countries and at what level they are teaching mathematics to 6th graders.
- Chapter 9 does an extensive analysis of the opportunity to learn provided to students as measured from student mathematics notebooks, which provide an archaeology of the academic year in these sampled classrooms.
- Chapter 10 compares our analysis relating teacher mathematics knowledge to teacher teaching quality, analysed from the lesson videotapes, to the opportunity to learn provided by teachers to their students in schools on either side of the border.
- Chapter 11 estimates the relationship between learners' achievement gains, student socio-economic background, language, and social capital, our various measures of teacher quality, and our measures of school context in the two countries, and presents an overall analysis that estimates possible learner gains in North West Province from implementing teacher improvement policies.
- Chapter 12 develops some brief conclusions of the study.

CHAPTER 1

Background to the study

The past two decades have witnessed a worldwide shift in the education policy discussion toward improving 'educational quality' – that is, toward increasing student learning at each level of schooling in addition to increasing the number of years students complete (Hanushek & Woessman 2008; UNESCO 2005). An accelerated pace of international and national testing around the world has contributed to this shift. The new emphasis on student achievement has reached developing countries, including those in Africa. The educational quality issue in Africa differs in degree and historical context from that in high-income societies and in Latin American and Asia, but it shares a common conundrum. Despite widespread acceptance of the notion that improving student performance may have a high economic and social payoff, policy analysts in all countries have surprisingly little hard data on which to base educational strategies for raising achievement. In South Africa, this question is all the more pressing in a context where government's own evaluations of progress since the transition to democracy can show little improvement in educational outcomes despite significant policy changes (Department of Education, DoE 2006a).

A major difficulty in gleaning significant policy conclusions from analyses within one country or one region within a country is that many key macro-educational policy variables, such as teacher recruitment, teacher training and school supervision, are fairly uniform within a nation, and certainly within a region. In addition, it is difficult to identify the effects of school resources on student achievement. For one, much of the variation in student achievement across schools can be explained by the socio-economic background differences of students (Rothstein 2005). Further, the distribution of school resources is highly correlated with the family resources students bring to those schools (Barbarin & Richter 2001). One way to overcome the limits of single country educational policy research is to undertake comparative studies of neighbouring countries (or regions) with similar socio-economic conditions, but significant differences in student performance and, possibly, educational policies (for example, the United States and Canada, Finland and Norway, Costa Rica and Panama – for the latter, see Carnoy et al. 2007). Some have called a situation where national social conditions are similar but policies and outcomes differ, a 'natural experiment' (Knight & Sabot 1990).

In southern Africa, we have such a ready-made comparative case: South Africa and Botswana. The peoples inhabiting the region near the border are of the same language and culture, but students' school performance and, for historical reasons, the educational conditions and policies in the two countries differ substantially. With this 'natural experiment' in mind, we investigate (a) the impact that school inputs make on gains in student learning; (b) differences in educational policies in these two neighbouring countries; and (c) the role of such policies in shaping the quality of school inputs.

This is a complex task, since it requires estimating relationships between school inputs and student outcomes that approach 'causality' (Schneider et al. 2007), as well as identifying educational policies that could improve those school inputs. We believe that we can make these connections for the teaching competence input by relating student mathematics learning to teacher knowledge/teaching quality, and, in turn, relating teacher knowledge/teaching quality to policies relating to teacher recruitment, pre-service education and teacher assignment.

Thanks to a Spencer Foundation planning grant, researchers from the Human Sciences Research Council (HSRC), several South African universities, and Stanford were able to test the feasibility of our approach in a South African setting. We conducted a pilot study in the 6th grade classrooms of 40 schools in Gauteng, South Africa, in July–October, 2007. We developed and piloted a student 5th/6th grade mathematics test, a student questionnaire, a teacher questionnaire and mathematics test of teachers' content and pedagogical content knowledge, a principal questionnaire, mathematics lesson videotaping of 40 teachers, and two rubrics to analyse the videotapes for teacher time use and teaching quality. The pilot study provided a great deal of original data that the research team analysed. The data suggested that the approach we used could produce important insights into the contribution of teacher skills and other school inputs to student learning, and that the relationships we estimated could be linked to teacher education and teacher assignment policies.

Building on what we learnt from the pilot study, we tested our model in a sample of primary schools along the South Africa/Botswana border. In South Africa, we included schools from North West Province. The North West Province/South East Botswana comparison allows us to estimate the relationship of student performance to teacher and school inputs within each country and to estimate the sample differences across countries in teacher quality and school context variables. We suspected that we would find large differences in teacher mathematics skills between the two countries, especially at lower student socio-economic status (SES) levels, as well as rather high variation of teacher skills within North West Province/South Africa.

The research focuses on mathematics learning. We chose mathematics performance because comparisons across countries of mathematics knowledge and teaching would be more straightforward than comparisons of teachers' language skills and language pedagogy across language groups. Nevertheless, a similar study could be made of student reading performance.

Empirical questions used in the comparison study

These are the empirical questions used in the comparison study:
1. Do students in South East Botswana learn more mathematics in the 6th grade than do students in North West Province?
2. Do teachers in Botswana have more knowledge of mathematics than do teachers on the other side of the border?
3. Are teachers with more mathematics knowledge on either side of the border more likely to be 'better' classroom teachers of mathematics and more likely to teach more mathematics lessons to their students?
4. Are teachers in North West Province with more mathematics knowledge and teaching skills more or less likely than teachers in South East Botswana to be teaching in schools with higher socio-economic background students?
5. Do teachers' mathematics knowledge and teaching skills significantly influence student mathematics achievement gains, particularly among lower socio-economic urban and rural students in North West Province and South East Botswana classrooms?

6. Do other factors – notably the curriculum-teacher skills interaction, the degree of curriculum coverage (opportunity to learn/teacher accountability), language of instruction, and class size – play an important role in explaining student learning gains?

Research background

Estimating the relation of school inputs to student outcomes

Most national and international studies that analyse the role of teacher characteristics and other school variables in student achievement are cross-sectional – they estimate these relationships based on the level of student performance at a single point in time. Such surveys are useful for benchmarking achievement, but are less useful in explaining why students in some classrooms achieve more than in others. Student and teacher data are usually not linked, and endogeneity issues inherently plague the estimates – that is, it is difficult to determine, whether students are achieving at higher levels because they have better teachers or because better teachers end up teaching in classrooms with higher scoring students. Many of the studies recognise these limitations, although there is little that can be done about them. These studies almost universally show little impact of teacher characteristics on student achievement.[1]

Recent longitudinal studies

Recent longitudinal studies of student performance gains, however, show that some teachers achieve consistently higher gains in their students across student cohorts, and some, consistently lower gains (Boyd et al. 2009; Clotfelter et al. 2007; Rivkin et al. 2005; Sanders 1998). Many of these studies had difficulty identifying what it is about teachers that makes them good at producing high student learning gains. Those that are able to make this identification show that teacher experience and teacher preparation linked to practice seem to be related to greater student learning. Other studies that measure teacher knowledge show that it is significantly related to student gains (for example, Hill et al. 2005). Two studies in Mexico suggest that students in schools where primary and secondary teachers scored higher on a general ability test were likely to have larger gains (Luschei 2006; Santibanez 2002). Another study in Germany, following up on students who took the 2003 PISA test, shows that mathematics teachers' subject knowledge had a significant positive effect on high school students' learning gains in mathematics (Baumert 2006).

The consensus among researchers, based on these studies and others, is that student performance in school is the result of a confluence of factors, including:
- the quality and quantity of educational inputs that families invest in their children,
- the physical resources schools have available,
- the degree of teacher presence or 'effort' (the number of days that teachers show up to teach and their curriculum coverage (Kremer et al. 2004),
- the opportunity to learn that teachers provide students and that students expose themselves to by coming regularly to school (Reeves 2005),

---

1 Some of the international research focuses on the impact of differences in mathematics curriculum on student mathematics achievement, mainly in developed countries (Carnoy et al. 2004; Schmidt et al. 2001). Others focus on the role of state driven social capital on achievement (Carnoy & Marshall 2005); and yet others on the relative role of student socioeconomic background and school inputs (Hanushek & Kimko 2000; Organisation for Economic Co-operation and Development, OECD 2003; Willms & Somers 2001).

- teachers' content knowledge and pedagogical content knowledge, including the language and pedagogical use of language knowledge they have (Shulman 1986),
- childrens' access to schoolbooks,
- schools' 'efficiency' in using available resources (the organisation and the instructional accountability system of the schools), and
- the school's social context, such as the absence of violence in schools, the general importance accorded education in a particular society for both boys and girls, community services provided to low-income students and the absence of child labour outside the home.

Because most research in Africa on student achievement also generally uses cross-section data, it has not been able to say much about the impact of teaching or other school factors on student outcomes. South Africa participated in the 1995, 1999 and 2003 TIMSS tests, and South African students scored the lowest among all countries in all three years. The analysis of the 1995 TIMSS data suggests that South African 7th and 8th grade students were older than those taking TIMSS in other countries and performed poorly, even on questions that were supposed to be covered in the South African curriculum. They came from much poorer home environments than students elsewhere, they had much less homework than students in other countries, and only 21 per cent of them wrote the TIMSS test in their home language, even though all of them wrote the test in the school's language of instruction (Howie 1997). Results in 2003 showed very little change between 1995 and 2003 (Reddy 2006).

However, two studies in southern Africa stand out because they are based on academic year student achievement *gains*. In 1990, Fuller et al. (1994) carried out a pre- and post-test in English and mathematics in 53 junior secondary schools (8th and 9th grades). They applied teacher, student and school questionnaires, and observed teachers' time use in mathematics and English lessons. Their results suggest that teaching capacity is distributed more equally across classrooms in Botswana than in South Africa. Unfortunately, since students face a number of different teachers in junior secondary school, it was impossible to identify a teacher directly with a student. Rather, they averaged teacher characteristics in each grade in each school. The study estimated that an additional year in school seemed to increase learning more than was the case in developed countries, but they had difficulty finding significant relations between student learning gains and teacher characteristics (Fuller et al.1994). Our Gauteng pilot study in 2007 suggests that this may have been the case because Fuller et al. have no measure of teachers' subject matter knowledge (Carnoy et al. 2008). They also seem to have faced an issue of relatively low variation in teaching skills among classrooms, perhaps caused by considerable uniformity in teacher pre-service education in Botswana and rather equitable teacher assignment policies.

An excellent recent study by Cheryl Reeves has the advantage of measuring student mathematics learning in the 6th grade over an entire academic year. This study was able to identify students with their mathematics teachers and estimate how much teachers covered the curriculum. She conducted the study in 24 schools in the Western Cape and showed that OTL is significantly related to students' mathematics gains, but that teachers' teaching methods are not (Reeves 2005; 2006).

Comparative studies of student achievement also exist in Africa, although these too use only cross section data. A UNESCO-organised consortium of African education ministries, SACMEQ, has conducted three rounds of testing (1997, 2000 and 2007) in eastern and southern Africa. A number of comparative studies based on these data have focused on the relationship between socio-economic background and student achievement (Filmer & Pritchett 1999), participation levels and student achievement (Crouch & Fasih 2004; Fleisch & Perry 2006) and school resources/SES and achievement (Van der Berg 2005; Van der Berg & Louw 2006).

TABLE 1.1 SACMEQ: Reading and mathematics scores, Grade 6 by country, 2000 and 2007

Country	Average reading score		Average mathematics score	
	2000	2007	2000	2007
Mauritius	536	574	585	623
Swaziland	530	549	517	541
Botswana	521	535	513	520
Mozambique	517	476	530	484
South Africa	492	495	486	495
Namibia	449	497	431	471
Malawi	429	434	431	447

Source: Unesco, International Institute of Educational Planning, IIEP 2010: 4.

Table 1.1 shows the SACMEQ 2000 and 2007 results. The table shows that reading and mathematics scores went up in six of seven southern African countries. The scores in Mozambique went down, but Mozambique greatly increased the number of students reaching the 6th grade between 2000 and 2007, which probably explains the decline in scores. Students in Botswana scored among the highest of the southern African countries, third behind Mauritius and Swaziland, whereas students in South Africa scored about 0.25 standard deviations lower in mathematics than students in Botswana in both years.

TABLE 1.2 SACMEQ: Background variables on students, school resources and access by country, 2007

Country	2007 GDP/capita (2005 PPP $)	SES*	Per student spending on primary school, 2007	P:T ratio, 2007	Students with mathematics textbooks, 2001* (%)	GER, 2007	NER, 2007	Primary school completion rate, 2007 (%)	Cohort reaching final grade primary school, 2007 (%)
Namibia	5 848	475	994	29.9	52	113	90	81	76
Malawi	697	435	70	72.2ª	59	113	85	54	36
South Africa	9 366	550	1 356	31.0	43	105	87	86	86
Botswana	12 600	540	1 590	25.4	80	110	87	99	87
Swaziland	4 507	520	734	32.4	77	108	83	72	74
Mozambique	741	440	108	64.1	58	110	75	46	44
Mauritius	10 987	625	1 154	21.5	96	98	92	91	98

Source: Variables marked with an asterisk are derived from the SACMEQ II (2000) database. All other variables are compiled from the World Bank, World Development Indicators database.[2]

Abbreviations: GER, gross enrolment rate (all students including repeaters as a per cent of the age group); NER, net enrolment rate (students net of repeaters as a per cent of the age group).

ª Datum for 2000.

2 The World Development Indicators database is available at http://data.worldbank.org/data-catalog/world-development-indicators

FIGURE 1.1 *Sixth Grade mathematics test score by country and SES quintile, 2000*

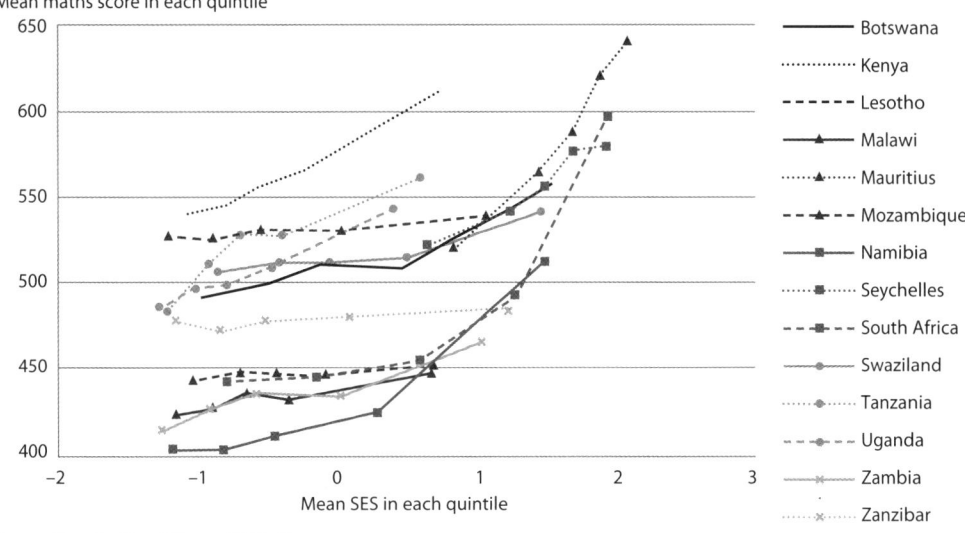

Source: Van der Berg & Louw 2008: 60.

In Table 1.2, we compare socio-economic and school variables for the same set of countries. Of the seven countries, two – Malawi and Mozambique – have much lower per capita incomes and lower primary completion rates (the latter could bias the test scores in 6th grade upward). Mauritius has the highest test scores, especially in mathematics, but also (by far) the highest student SES levels, although not the highest GDP per capita, which belongs to Botswana. South Africa has a lower GDP per capita in purchasing power equivalents than does Botswana, but it is still quite high, and SES as measured from the SACMEQ student questionnaire is somewhat higher than in Botswana. Botswana and South Africa also spend about the same per student in primary school. Despite similar spending on schools and higher SES, students in South African schools do not do nearly as well as Botswana students on the SACMEQ tests.

The SACMEQ data suggest that there exists considerable variation in average student performance among these countries even when controlling for student socio-economic background. As Figure 1.1 (using 2000 data) suggests, South African and Namibian 6th graders not only have considerably lower achievement levels than pupils in neighbouring countries, such as Botswana and Swaziland,[3] but these differences appear to be largest among low and middle SES students.

The data for 2007 show a similar pattern. In the bottom 25th percentile of SES, Botswana students scored 479 on the mathematics test, whereas South African students scored 446. In the top SES quartile, Botswana students scored 553 and South African students, 579. Rural Botswana scored 501 in mathematics versus 457 in South Africa, whereas urban Botswana scored 539 versus 533 in urban South Africa. Thus, there exist much larger differences between urban and rural students in South Africa than in Botswana and even larger differences between student performance in the highest and lowest quartile of SES in South Africa.

---

3   It should be remembered, however, that a smaller percentage of students reached 6th grade in Swaziland than in South Africa or Botswana, which should drive observed test scores up, assuming that the lower scoring students drop out.

It is also important to note, in comparing South Africa and Botswana, that Botswana's economic growth since 1995 has been much more rapid than South Africa's (see Chapter 2). Until very recently, high growth has allowed Botswana to increase spending per pupil in primary school more rapidly than is the case in South Africa. Whether this has had any impact on the kinds of individuals entering teaching or the availability of textbooks is an important question that we cannot answer, but it does give more flexibility to the government to pay teachers more, to improve teacher education, and so forth.

The data in Table 1.2 on SACMEQ countries provide a few other clues as to why some schools within these countries do better than others and why lower-income students in Botswana score so much higher than lower-income students in South Africa. The data indicate that class sizes are smaller in Botswana and that students in Botswana are more likely to have had a mathematics textbook in 2001, suggesting some major policy differences between the two countries. Further, we can speculate that the 'can do' test-driven curriculum in Botswana that was introduced in the 1990s may have contributed to higher levels of basic mathematics skills.

CHAPTER 2

Exploring policy differences and similarities

Our study provides results that reflect back on the comparative history, socio-economic contexts, contemporary curriculum, and the language and teacher policies that provide a major part of the broader context for the work that is done in schools. Here we examine how differences and similarities in the political histories of the region may have helped to shape some of the differences and similarities we observe in the curriculum, language and teacher policies of the two countries. In Chapter 4 we undertake a comparative perspective on the socio-economic and more immediate context of Botswana and South African schools to fill in this context.

In this chapter we highlight two dimensions of the comparative history of education in Botswana and South Africa that help us gain insight into the more 'regular' classroom environments that our study suggest are more prevalent in Botswana than in South Africa. First, we consider the earlier extension of state control over schooling in Botswana, and second, the conditions under which state schooling was extended to education for Africans in Botswana and South Africa. The former gave Botswana a head start of two to three decades of educational development over South Africa, and the second resulted in similar policies but very different models of implementation in each country.

The political histories of Botswana and South Africa are critical to understanding these differences. From 1885 until 1966 (the year of Botswana independence), the British administered Botswana as the Bechuanaland Protectorate. In 1895, British Bechuanaland became part of the Cape Colony and was administered from Mafikeng. According to Robinson et al. (2003: 12), the Bechuanaland Protectorate was in fact administered by the British from South Africa until 1961 when South Africa broke ties with the Commonwealth. If 1885 and 1966 are the key turning points in Botswana's history, then 1910, 1948, and 1994 are the turning points in the history of South Africa. In 1910 South Africa unified under white rule, which took a particularly harsh form from 1948 when formal apartheid, Bantu Education and the Bantustans were introduced. In 1994, almost three decades after Botswana celebrated independence, South Africa gained its freedom. This history marked education policy change in each country in distinctive ways.

Education policy change in Botswana, we argue, has been gradual and incremental, consolidating what exists and working through reform of teacher education in order to reach teachers first. Education policy change in South Africa, by contrast, has been more or less continuously disruptive, attended by massive repression for three decades after the 1950s. This pattern of disruptive change continued after 1994, albeit under different social and political conditions. Although conflict has been and is increasingly part of the educational process in Botswana, and harmonious forms of interaction and development are not foreign to South Africa, the broad patterns are very different and shape how education policy unfolds.

In this chapter we examine four key moments in educational change, showing and comparing how the nature of education policy change has shaped the nature of curriculum and teacher policy and labour markets in Botswana and South Africa since 1994. These four key moments can be defined as:
- 1850–1928,
- 1928–1977,
- 1977–1990, and
- 1990–2004.

The first considers the early beginnings of formal schooling under missionaries in the colonial state, the second looks at differences in how state control was extended over African education in Botswana and South Africa, and the third contrasts the apartheid educational history of 1977–1994 in South Africa with the route taken by an independent Botswana. This history concludes with a note on the legacy of the last years of apartheid and transition to democracy in South Africa.

After considering the history, we move on to compare curriculum and assessment, language and teacher policy in each country. We show that whereas processes of change are marked by the respective histories of gradual and disruptive change, curriculum, assessment and language policies show convergence, while teacher policies differ markedly. The result appears to be that while South Africa has suffered severe teacher shortages and has no teacher supervision system to speak of, Botswana reports limited shortages and has a working system of teacher supervision. In Chapter 4 we also show that spending has differed, with Botswana spending more overall on education than South Africa, but South Africa spending more on primary education

A short history of education in North West Province and Botswana in the twentieth century

Early beginnings (1850–1928)

The history of education in both North West Province and Botswana has its roots in nineteenth century missionary endeavor. Missionaries of different denominations, such as those from the London Missionary Society, German Lutherans, Roman Catholics, Dutch Reformed, and Wesleyans, built schools to attract converts. Church and mission boundaries included communities scattered between Mafiking and Gaborone. Variations in the curriculum depended on ownership of the schools. From the late nineteenth century and accelerating in the early twentieth, increased state aid to mission schools was accompanied by an approach that emphasised a practical and rurally oriented education. This approach was based on the view that Africans were mainly a rural and agricultural people and therefore needed an education system closely aligned to that type of lifestyle (Hunt Davis Jr. 1984a).

Increasing state aid and control of mission education was accompanied in the latter part of the nineteenth and early part of the twentieth century by convergence in the goals of the colonial state. From 1885, Botswana was governed as a British Protectorate. It watched on as the mining revolution in South Africa disrupted far-flung communities on its border in search for labour, and as the South African War (1899–1902) convulsed the region. The Siege of Mafiking was a turning point in the war. The ending of the war, victory for the British and establishment of Union in South Africa in 1910, resulted in the forging of closer ties among colonial Botswana and local white South African authorities and extension of control over African education.

As the grip of the colonial state on the region grew, tensions between missionaries, the colonial state, and the mission-educated elite intensified. The purpose of schooling differed for each (Comaroff & Comaroff 1991). In North West Province, considerable variation in mission schooling continued throughout the early twentieth century, and an academic curriculum, sometimes also aimed at teacher training, continued to feature alongside the vocational curriculum in some mission schools. Tiger Kloof, near Vryburg in North West Province, was one such mission school that attracted not only the sons of South African chiefs, but also those from Botswana. Its curriculum was broad and included agricultural, industrial and academic dimensions.

A common colonial framework and mission networks facilitated educational links between the two countries. In Botswana, the vocational curriculum of an earlier period began to be enforced by an examination set in South Africa or in the Protectorate and administered by the missionaries. The examinations, known as the School Leaving Examination (SLE), included practical agriculture, craftwork and written tests of hygiene and biblical knowledge. Biblical knowledge was an important element of academic achievement as it served the missionaries' role of converting Africans to Christianity. Those who completed the SLE could go on for further training in South Africa.

Resistance to colonial education began to take shape through embryonic nationalist movements. In South Africa, the South African Native National Congress (SANNC), founded in 1912, sought through representations to the colonial state to articulate a different vision of inclusion. In Botswana, resistance to the colonial government and missionary disposition towards vocational education was rebuffed by the chiefs who demanded an academic curriculum that would produce clerks and state secretaries essential for a budding literate bureaucracy in the colonial government of indirect rule. By 1910, most chiefs had erected their own schools, which were run by tribal committees. To meet school costs, some chiefs imposed a voluntary education levy on their own schools, which were run by tribal committees (Botswana National Archives, Dutton Inspector's Reports for 1910, 1911 and 1927).

State control over African education in Botswana and South Africa (1928–1977)

State control of African education came much earlier in Botswana than in South Africa. In 1928, when South Africans were tightening controls over the movement and labour of Africans, and instituted the Carnegie Commission of Inquiry into 'poor whites', the British in Botswana appointed a director of education. His task was to regulate the establishment and control of schools in Botswana. He immediately prescribed the South African Cape Colony Primary School Syllabus, pending the drawing up of a code for the Protectorate. He also institutionalised externally conducted examinations at the end of the primary course. In conjunction with this examination, he introduced a scholarship scheme to assist deserving pupils who had passed with the highest marks. The scholarship scheme sent a message that conforming to the colonial policy would grant opportunities for further education. Schooling for Africans in Botswana was thus placed on a par with schooling for whites in the Cape Colony.

This marked the decisive break with the hitherto relatively common mission-controlled educational history in the region. Ten years later, by the Bechuanaland Proclamation of 1938, the Botswana colonial government instituted control of the curriculum and methods of teaching through the standard examination (Thema 1947). In line with changes occurring for whites in the Union of South Africa, the system was revamped to bring a tight alignment between curriculum, teacher training and accountability: the textbooks to be used in the schools, the equipment necessary, the school hours and days, and the code of work were all to be decided upon by the resident commissioner (see Malherbe 1922; also Tyack 1993). Every school was to be subject to inspection by the director of education or the inspector of schools. Either one of the two would examine the school buildings, ascertain the progress of the pupils, the nature of instruction given, the standing and qualification of the teachers and any other matter relevant to the conduct and discipline of the school. By comparison, African education in South Africa was left to the mercy of missionaries and interested government officials (Hunt Davis Jr. 1984b).

Botswana's head start of more than two decades was also accomplished under conditions markedly different from the conditions in South Africa in the 1950s, when the apartheid state extended control over mission schools through the Bantu Education Act of 1955 (Hyslop 1988a, 1989, 1993). British control over African education in Botswana before its independence in 1966 saw its steady consolidation and extension. This same period in South Africa saw a struggle over the direction of African education. The struggle ended in violent and significant disruption to the patterns that had been emerging over the previous decades. An Afrikaner Nationalist Party victory in 1948 led to the closure of many mission schools. The Bantu Education Act (1955) brought African mission education under state control, introducing a form of mass schooling that was not only extremely poorly resourced but also limited the curriculum for Africans (Hyslop 1988a, 1991a, 1993). The fate of Tiger Kloof school, founded by the London Missionary Society in 1904, points to the fate of the vast majority of mission schools in the country and the area during this period (Irvine 1966). Tiger Kloof was essentially closed and sold off to an Afrikaans-speaking farmer who built a distillery on the premises. Other mission schools were brought under state control and new schools were built.

Botswana and black South Africans were both subject to an overarching colonial ideology of white supremacy. However, this was made more extreme in South Africa by the repressive authoritarianism of Afrikaner nationalist control over education and the Bantustan policy, which relocated much educational development, and especially teacher training, to the Bantustans. South Africa's Bantustan policy drew on the discourses of African independence then sweeping the continent but was essentially a pseudo form of independence granted to areas formerly designated as reserves for Africans under the 1913 and 1936 Land Acts. The policy was central to apartheid's conception of separation of races and ethnic groups, and was distinctive in trying to create ethnic enclaves for African political expression within the overall borders of a South Africa dominated by whites. Bantustans created 'all the trappings of states: development boards were established, capitals built, parliaments established, presidents inaugurated, flags designed, national anthems composed and, above all, mechanisms of control and compulsion devised' (Magubane n.d: 754). The mass removals of populations ensured that Bantustans became consolidated as poverty-stricken reservoirs of labour migration to the cities. As mission schools were closed or brought under state control, state schools and teacher training colleges were built in rural areas of the Bantustans, and the University of Bophuthatswana was brought into being in the late 1970s as a symbol of independence.

By contrast with Botswana's relatively peaceful transition to independence in the 1960s, violence, repression, social dislocation and disruption attended implementation of South Africa's policy of separate development. In June 1964, Britain accepted proposals for democratic self-government in Botswana. The 1965 Constitution led to the first general elections and to independence on 30 September 1966. Seretse Khama, who married a British woman, and was a leader in the independence movement, was elected as the first president. Two years after Botswana gained independence, the apartheid state granted Bophuthatswana its own spurious 'independence' under Chief Lucas Mangope. Bophuthatswana formed a central pillar of South Africa's Bantustan policy (Lawrence & Manson 1994).

Separate development in South Africa, as exemplified by the introduction of Bantu Education and the pursuit of the apartheid ethnic homeland dream, was a policy enforced with great violence. The contrast with Botswana could not be clearer. At the same time as Botswana was anticipating renewal of its social and educational institutions, the apartheid state was crushing resistance, driving it underground and into exile. Botswana did not take kindly to South Africa's new rulers. It began to police the previously open and fluid border between Moiloa's reserve in South Africa and Botswana more strictly, even as Botswana became a refuge for South African exiles fleeing repression at home (see Drummond & Manson 1993).

Bantustan and post-independence educational policy: Education for Popagano and education for Kagisano (1977–1990)

Unlike South Africa's apartheid government during this period, Botswana under Seretse Khama consolidated a democratic, peaceful, non-racial state. Botswana became fully integrated into the development reforms, plans and projects as they swept the developing world in the 1970s and 1980s. South Africa was isolated from these trends, but experimented with them through its Bantustan policy (see Chisholm 2012).

Both Botswana and Bophuthatswana produced education development plans in the late 1970s. Eleven years after independence, in 1977, Botswana set up its first National Commission on Education (NCE) to review the education system. The NCE outlined an educational system built on the four national principles of democracy, development, self-reliance, and Kagisano (social harmony). One aspect of Kagisano is the idea of social justice, which was interpreted as fairness and equity. Government was to promote fair and equitable distribution of resources by providing equal education opportunities for all. There was to be no discrimination on the grounds of sex, ethnic group, religion or sex.

Education policy in the pseudo-independent Bophuthatswana mimicked that in Botswana. If Kagisano was the education plan for Botswana, for Bophuthatswana it was the Popagano Report and the Commission of Inquiry into Education (Republic of Bophuthatswana 1978). These reports encompassed the entire spectrum of education, from early childhood to higher and adult education. Botswana's liberal-democratic, nation-building Kagisano ideals were reflected in the adoption of a learner-centred pedagogy and found expression in the 1980s in Botswana's Primary Education Improvement Project (PEIP) and its Junior Secondary Education Improvement Project (JSEIP) (Tabulawa 2009: 93). Bophuthatswana's Popagano was similarly committed to nation building, but within the context of Bantustan policy, it promoted a narrower ethnic nationalism. Like Botswana's PEIP, Bophuthatswana's Primary Education Upgrade Programme (PEUP) was introduced in 1979 after the Popagano Commission of Inquiry into Education (1978) recommended the overhaul of the education system in the then-Bophuthatswana. Participating in the development discourse was part of Bophuthatswana's effort to normalise and legitimise its existence. The Popagano Report, for example, proposed to imbue primary education 'with what might be called the development spirit' (Republic of Bophuthatswana 1978: 36).

International participation in the policy and local programmes was present from the outset in both Botswana and South Africa. Botswana's PEIP and JSEIP programmes were the concrete expression of an agreement between the United States Agency for International Development (USAID) and the Government of Botswana (Yoder & Mautle 1991: 30). This project was primarily focused on teacher education and linking Botswana with American counterparts, principally from Ohio University. Placing the child and the individual at the centre of the educational enterprise was at the core of this programme (Horgan et al. 1991: 77–103). Considerable synergies developed between this carefully planned and executed ten-year programme and a number of other initiatives supported by the United Kingdom and Scandinavian countries to improve primary education. Bophutatswana programmes were supported among others by the Israelis and British and included a significant curricular innovation, the British Council's Breakthrough to Setswana Literacy Programme (MacDonald 1990).

In both countries, the primary education initiative was driven by states seeking to promote national or ethnic unity. The learner-centred approach was in keeping in Botswana with a liberal-democratic, nation-building project. In Bophuthatswana, it was a contradiction within an overall educational edifice in practice based on authoritarian repression but seeking legitimacy for an ethnic enclave within a wider state through the trappings of liberal democracy. After a few years in the field, the primary education project was brought to a sudden end after an attempted coup against Mangope.

Resistance to the apartheid state swept through almost every school in South Africa between 1976 and 1990. Schools became sites of resistance as student, youth, teacher, and community organisations mobilised around and inside schools to bring apartheid to an end (Hyslop 1988b, 1990a, 1991b). A major dimension of this resistance was resistance to the apartheid State's school curriculum and language policies. In Moila's Reserve, then Bophutatswana, Paterson shows how a 'clash of values' developed as the authorities attempted to impose practical agricultural work on communities: 'teachers frequently opted out of attempting any agricultural or gardening work with learners, or consigned their charges to desultory labour tasks'. (Paterson 2004: 88).

Transition to democracy in South Africa, 1990–1994

Between 1990 and 1994, South Africa negotiated a new Constitution and began the movement away from segregated and unequal schooling. At the same time as South Africans began to articulate education policy for a democratic South Africa, Botswana undertook its second National Commission of Education. Conducted entirely independently of one another, these discussions shared important similarities. But the underlying conditions, especially in schools, were vastly different.

At the very moment that political organisations were unbanned and negotiations for a democratic South Africa began, there was a change in the form of struggles taking place in schools as political structures shifted attention elsewhere. This period left a lasting legacy captured in the concerns for 'the lost generation' and loss of a 'culture of learning and teaching' reverberating throughout the 1990s. Another legacy of this period was a teachers' defiance campaign that resulted in the physical ejection of inspectors, principals and other figures of authority from schools. (Chisholm 1999; Hyslop 1990a; Jansen 2004).

Then and now, the area renamed North West Province under a new dispensation, has been integral to these developments and South Africa's development trajectory. Once again, Tiger Kloof illustrates this. Following democratic elections in 1994, the church bought the land back and re-opened the school. It is now a public school on private land, once again drawing pupils from far and wide. In its new vision, it is attempting to restore the old mission heritage and is committed to a broad liberal education. Tiger Kloof is, however, an anomaly in the broader context of schooling, drawing on a history that touched a minority in the apartheid period. The schools that formed the basis of our study were those poor schools constructed largely by the state or by communities, primarily at the height of apartheid. They were poorly resourced, and their teachers were trained in colleges where they received little if any preparation in mathematics. How has policy since 1994 attempted to overcome the apartheid legacy?

Curriculum policy in Botswana and South Africa (1994–2010)

This section explores the curriculum policy in Botswana and South Africa between 1994 and 2010. We consider the curriculum, the language policy and mathematics education in Botswana, and the processes of teacher supervision and evaluation in the two countries.

Curriculum

Both South Africa and Botswana adopted outcomes-based curricula, although there are significant differences between when they did so, how they did so, the content of the change, and the results of the change. Botswana's curriculum reform process started two decades earlier than in South Africa with the National Commissions on Education of 1977 and 1993 (Nitko 1990; Republic of Botswana 1977, 1993, and subsequent consultancy reports). In South Africa, it began with the introduction of OBE in 1997. In Botswana, it was coupled with massive educational expansion, public pressure for a relevant education system and international trends in curriculum and assessment (Chilisa 1998, 1999). In South Africa, it was linked to the post-apartheid overhaul of Bantu Education, widely seen as the symbol of and underpinning the inequalities between black and white in economic and political spheres.

In Botswana, the process of reform was gradual. In South Africa, it constituted a dramatic rupture and break with the past. In Botswana, reform processes started with teachers and the introduction of new qualifications to upgrade their knowledge. In South Africa, it began with changing the curriculum documents and prescripts with which teachers had to work. Teacher knowledge was delegitimised, as they were asked to abandon all they knew and begin afresh (Jansen & Christie 1999).

The form and content of OBE in Botswana and South Africa also differ. Although the mathematical content contained in each is similar, there have until recently been major differences in the form of presentation of this content to teachers. Curriculum documents in South Africa, especially in the first few years after 1997, were characterised by an impenetrable language and presentation of what was to be taught and learnt. In Botswana, presentation of what was expected of teachers was much clearer, and was expressed in more familiar terms. In Botswana, the curriculum was introduced through new qualifications and formal preparation of teachers; in South Africa, through short workshops.

From the 1990s, the curriculum in Botswana has been tightly linked to testing of students. Botswana opted for criterion-referenced assessment. What is referred to as the Curriculum-Driven-Test-Development Model (CDTDM) (Nitko 1989, 1990) was adopted and implemented in primary schools in 1992 and in the junior secondary schools in 1996. The thrust of the CDTDM is that students' scores are referenced to a well-defined curriculum domain. The curriculum domain makes explicit the cognitive theories of learning and instruction, the instructional materials, classroom activities, content syllabus and curriculum objectives and goals. Since the adoption of the model, Botswana has designed syllabi that outline the content to be taught by topic and further break the topics into general objectives and specific objectives to be achieved. School-based formative and summative assessment is an important component in the new examination model. The intention is to make continuous assessment marks part of the national examination score.

By contrast with this tightly aligned curriculum and testing model, the implementation of South Africa's 1998 Assessment Policy Act saw a heavy emphasis on various forms of continuous assessment to support an under-specified curriculum. It was not aligned to the curriculum until the curriculum was specified more clearly in 2002. Continuous and formative assessment requirements in the curriculum have resulted in major dissatisfaction among teachers about increased workload (Chisholm et al. 2005). In South Africa, the curriculum design and continuous assessment requirements of OBE have proven challenging for teachers. Curriculum reviews of 2000 and 2009 in South Africa (Chisholm et al. 2000; DoE 2009) recommended clearer curriculum content and specification than OBE provided for and the Revised National Curriculum Statement (DoE 2002) and subsequent Curriculum and Assessment Policy Statements (Department of Basic Education, DBE 2011) have given effect to these recommendations.

Without abandoning continuous assessment, government has since 2008 begun national testing of students in literacy and numeracy. The system is now beginning to look more like that of Botswana, which had begun the same process more than a decade earlier. The change in South Africa has once again been introduced rapidly and without much preparation of the schools for the reform (Addy 2012).

In South Africa, the introduction of OBE was sudden, disruptive, contested and controversial. Although teachers supported the principle of change, the nature of the change sorely taxed their sense of what they could and should be doing in the classroom. Teachers found the language and expectations of the curriculum obscure and jargon-filled, the assessment expectations burdensome and the pedagogical prescriptions difficult to implement (Taylor & Vinjevold 1999). In Botswana, the approach has attracted criticism, but not to the point of its abandonment, as has been the case in South Africa. In Botswana, a closely calibrated system of curriculum-texts-tests and supervision has come into being; in contrast with South Africa where testing has not to date been high on the reform agenda, supervision has been non-existent, and texts variable in availability and quality. There have been difficulties in each country with the expected form of pedagogy (Harley & Wedekind 2004; Hoadley 2007, 2008; Hoadley & Muller 2009; Tabulawa 2003).

Language policy and mathematics education in Botswana

In North West Province, as in Botswana, the dominant language is Setswana. Minority languages include Afrikaans, isiXhosa and Sesotho. English, as in Botswana, is mainly spoken as a second language. In both countries, the transition from mother tongue to English is key. While English has long been recognised as important in children's schooling in Botswana, South Africa's official additive bilingual approach has accorded it less significance in schooling until recently.

There are similarities in the approach to language teaching, but also significant differences. In Botswana, the planning period has been longer, and based on improving teachers' knowledge through post-secondary education. In 1994, Botswana's Revised National Policy on Education (RNPE) recommended that English be used as the medium of instruction from Standard 1 (Grade 4 in South Africa) by the year 2000. It was suggested that to establish appropriate conditions for introducing English as the medium of instruction at the primary school level, the envisaged training programme to improve the qualifications and competencies of teachers and to strengthen the role of the head teacher as an instructional leader should also place emphasis on the use of English. In South Africa, there has been no explicit emphasis on the teaching of English and improving teachers' knowledge in this area at teacher training level.

In Botswana, the change from Setswana to English as medium of instruction was planned to take place in Standard 4 (Grade 7) from 1995. An accelerated in-service training of teachers was planned to improve the teaching competencies of teachers in the teaching of English as a subject from Standard 1, with emphasis on oral communication. Teachers were also required to increase the use of English from Standard 1 (Grade 4) onwards in teaching mathematics and science. However, Setswana language was to be taught as a compulsory subject for citizens of Botswana throughout the primary school system. Where parents requested other local languages to be taught to their children, schools could arrange to teach them as a co-curricular activity (RNPE 1994).[1]

There is considerable debate in South Africa about whether poor learning outcomes are attributable to language use or not (for an excellent review of the literature see Fleisch 2008: 98–120). There are three main schools of thought: one considers the use of the mother tongue or home language as key, the second, English proficiency, and the third, the role and importance of code-switching (Alexander 2005; Heugh 2007; Setati 2005; Simkins & Paterson 2005). The National Planning Commission has

---

1   In Chapter 5, we show that when we compare the use of English in teaching mathematics in Botswana and South Africa, approximately 40 per cent of teachers in Botswana never use Setswana or any other African language when teaching the subject compared to approximately 20 per cent in South Africa.

drawn attention to the complex relationships between language, socio-economic status and school functionality in South Africa (NPC 2011) arguing that although students who learn in their second language have a lower socio-economic status than first English and Afrikaans-language speakers, it is not clear why they perform worse (NPC 2011: 27–28).

In South Africa, policy has promoted mother-tongue instruction in the early years and the gradual addition of further languages as learners progress up the grades. Currently some 80 per cent of children in the first three grades learn in their mother tongue (DBE 2011). In terms of the South African Schools Act, school governing bodies make decisions about the language of learning and teaching to be used in schools. In North West Province, as in other provinces, the switch to English as the language of learning and teaching in the majority of schools where Setswana is the home language has occurred in Grade 4 (Standard 1). Since 2010, there has been a shift to emphasise the acquisition of English as a first additional language from Grade 1 alongside the home language. In this study, we examine the relationship between language and mathematics as reported in questionnaires, as taught in the classroom, and through an item analysis of test results.

Teacher supervision and evaluation

In line with an outcomes-based curriculum, Botswana has long emphasised teacher accountability. In a not-altogether conflict-free process, the main consequence of efforts to enforce accountability in schools over the last thirty years has been the introduction of teacher appraisal and competency assessments. These were linked to the introduction of outcomes-based and learner-centred pedagogies.

The first National Commission on Education recommended the strengthening of supervisory roles through effecting a close link between teachers and the Ministry of Education (Republic of Botswana 1977: 9). To strengthen supervision, the Unified Teaching Service (UTS) conducted an annual inspection of schools and produced annual inspection reports. The annual inspection reports are documents based on school visits by a team of education officers from the Ministry of Education. The team usually consists of four to six members and the duration of each visit ranges from one to four days. There are many teams and a given team does not necessarily visit the same school every year. Among the reasons for the school visits, as specified in the reports, are to:
- identify problems and also good practice in the school,
- sample the quality of the teaching process and tone of the school atmosphere,
- understand the operations and functions of the school,
- develop an informed opinion about the quality of learning and teaching that take place in the school,
- appreciate the development and progress in the school, and
- sample the quality of educational provision in secondary schools.

A series of teacher accountability measures were introduced alongside school inspections. To augment the inspection reports, in 1983 the UTS introduced annual confidential reports for teachers (Motswakae 1990: 4; Republic of Botswana 1977: 9). Regulations demanded that the director of the UTS be furnished with a confidential report on each teacher, and that this had to be prepared by the head teacher, supervisory officer, or any other authorised person (Republic of Botswana 1977: 9). These reports were viewed as a strategy to make schools more accountable. To further strengthen supervisory roles and performance, the Government White Paper on Job Evaluation for Teachers was implemented in 1988 (Republic of Botswana 1991: 47). It emphasised the need for continuous assessment of teachers. Job evaluation linked performance appraisal to pay and promotion. Teachers spoke strongly against the implementation of these policies (Republic of Botswana 1994). In 1991, in response to the job evaluation exercise, the current system of teacher appraisal was born (Bartlett 2000: 30; Habagaan 1998: 9; Republic of Botswana 1994: 47). It recommended more regular assistance to and professional development of classroom teachers (Republic of Botswana 1994: 47).

As a result, a Teacher Performance Appraisal instrument was developed, but, again, it was adapted. The instrument used by the new appraisal system is called Teaching Service Management (TMS) (Monyatsi 2003: 147). It seeks to create a non-threatening, valid and comprehensive system, intended to offer teachers the opportunity to learn constructively from their own assessment (Monyatsi 2003: 10). Its primary purpose is to assess objectively the performance of the teacher (Republic of Botswana 1991: 1).

Coupled with innovations on teacher evaluations and appraisals was the introduction of the Botswana Competency Teaching Instrument (BTCI), a mode of instructional supervision that was to promote learner-centred teaching methodologies. BTCI is based on the Teacher Performance Assessment Instrument (TPAI) developed by the University of Georgia, Department of Education. The instrument identifies characteristics of good teaching, and focuses in general on what can be broadly termed child-centred teaching methodologies (Yoder & Mautle 1991). Supervisors were instructed in using BTCI through a national series of intensive workshops conducted over a period of some months in 1984–1985. A videotape and an accompanying manual were subsequently developed to assist in training supervisors and teachers to use the model, and many of the principles developed there continue to be the subject of in-service workshops today. The process involves school heads observing teachers teach and vice versa, education officers observing teachers and vice versa, and teachers observing one another (Tabulawa 2003: 21).

Processes of teacher supervision and evaluation, as described, have not operated in the majority of South Africa's schools for close to twenty years. This was not for want of trying. For more than two decades, the DoE and unions have been locked in battle over the appropriate form of teacher appraisal, and the relationship of evaluation to performance appraisal and development. A key sticking point has been whether departmental officials may enter teachers' classrooms or not.

Difficulties in establishing an effective system of supervision and evaluation date back to the 1980s. Under apartheid, a differentiated system of inspection, control and appraisal existed in which inspection in black schools was characterised by bureaucratic control, and in white schools by a light advisory function (Chetty et al 1993). The reaction to these negative forms of evaluation was overwhelming. Towards the end of the 1980s, in the context of widespread resistance against apartheid authorities in schools, inspectors and subject advisors were routinely and often violently cast out of African schools when they attempted to set foot there, and teachers refused any form of evaluation of their own work and that of their schools. In the process, the entire inspectorate and function of inspection in black South African schools became dysfunctional (Jansen 2004).

A fully functioning and legitimate system is still not in place. Although the education department began to implement an Integrated Quality Management System (IQMS) in 2004, it was bureaucratically difficult to administer and still faces considerable teacher resistance. A Ministerial Project Committee was established in 2009 to recommend a way forward (Jansen et al. 2009). As a consequence of its recommendations, as well as a joint departmental-union National Teacher Development Plan (DBE/DHET 2011), the DBE established the National Education and Evaluation Unit (NEEDU). Its role as an inspectorate is limited to assessment of school functionality; the question of individual teacher appraisal is still in the process of negotiation.

Teacher supervision and evaluation in South Africa is still patchy and uneven, particularly in African schools. Recent government initiatives to intervene in school and learner performance based on test results still raise the question of how to analyse and assess teacher quality in the classroom. Our present study is in part a demonstration of the value of classroom-based assessment of teacher quality for the purposes of remediation.

Differences in teacher education and teacher labour markets in Botswana and South Africa

As we show in this discussion, there are striking differences in teacher education and teacher labour markets between Botswana and South Africa. Whereas Botswana has steadily built up teacher education colleges and higher teacher education sites over the last two decades, South Africa's policy trajectory has involved the closure of its colleges, and their relocation to higher education. This highly traumatic process in South Africa followed immediately after another highly conflictual one of teacher retrenchment and redeployment that saw large numbers of qualified teachers accepting a severance package and leaving the profession. Whereas teacher education curricula are closely linked to school curricula in Botswana, in South Africa the decentralised system of curriculum development in higher education means they are extremely uneven. There are no teacher shortages in Botswana and no shortages of mathematics and science teachers. Salaries are also considered to be better than in South Africa. In South Africa there is a significant shortage in both the quantity and quality of teachers, including Foundation Phase (Grades 1–3) mother tongue and mathematics and science teachers. The introduction of bursaries for teachers in 2005 has started to make a dent in the provision of appropriately qualified teachers, but the recruitment, appointments and allocation processes to schools often results in a mismatch between who is teaching what in many schools.

Teacher education and teacher labour markets in Botswana

In 2009, Botswana had 13 000 primary school teachers for about 331 000 primary school students, or a pupil-teacher ratio of 26:1 (Figure 2.1). This ratio has dropped steadily since the early part of the decade, when it was 29. The number of primary students has remained almost unchanged since 1998, and the number of primary teachers has increased by about 13 per cent. However, the main change since 2003 has been the reduction in the number of untrained teachers. In the late 1990s and early 2000s, the proportion of untrained teachers fluctuated, yet hovered around 10–12 per cent. By 2009, the majority of teachers teaching in the primary grades were trained. Primary teaching is largely a female profession, with around 76 per cent of these teachers being female teachers. Close to 95 per cent of the teachers are Botswana, but the percentage of non-Botswana has risen, from 4 per cent in 1995 to 6 per cent in 2004.

The number of secondary school teachers almost doubled from the mid-1990s to 2006 (Figure 2.1). The number of secondary school students increased by 70 per cent in the same period – from 103 000 to 164 000 in 2006 and almost 171 000 in 2009. Thus, the pupil-teacher ratio has declined substantially in secondary education, from 17:1 to 14:1. Another major change has occurred in the decade from 1995 to 2004. In 1995, more than 30 per cent of secondary school teachers were non-Botswana; in 2006, the proportion had dropped to 8 per cent. This suggests that the main expansion of secondary education was in government and government-aided schools where the teaching force is primarily Botswana. Most of the expansion also took place in grant-aided schools rather than schools run directly by the government. Untrained teachers declined as a percentage of all secondary school teachers, from 15 per cent in 1995 to less than 2 per cent in 2006.

FIGURE 2.1 *Botswana: Number of primary and secondary teachers, 1996–2009*

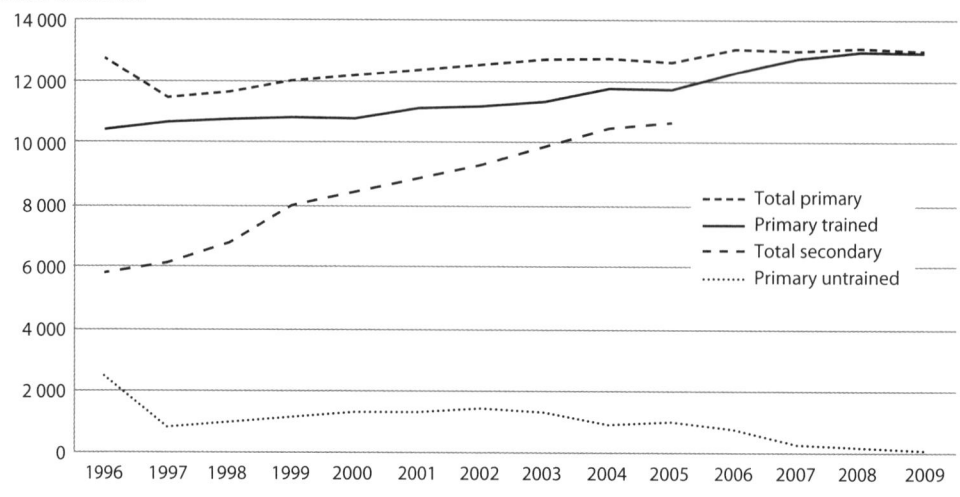

Source: Authors' compilations from Botswana Central Statistics Bureau.

Teacher training in Botswana

Before 1940, persons in Botswana wishing to pursue training as teachers frequently trained in neighbouring South Africa, notably at Fort Hare College near East London, and later the Tiger Kloof College in Vryburg. In 1946, Botswana's first college for training primary teachers was established in Kanye, located in the south-eastern part of the country (Southern District) and later relocated to a location 50 kilometers away from Lobatse. The college offered a programme leading to one of two types of certificates: a two-year programme for junior secondary certificate holders, leading to a Primary Higher (PH) qualification, and a three-year programme for primary certificate holders, leading to Primary Lower (PL) certification.[2]

Nearly 20 years later, in 1963, a second primary teacher training college was established at Serowe village (Central District), and in 1969, a third college in Francistown, originally established to train secondary school teachers, began training primary school teachers. A fourth college was opened in 1985 in Tlokweng village (South East District) just outside the capital city of Gaborone (Max & Yoder 1991). These colleges remain under direct control of the government.

The minimum entry requirements for teacher training undertaken after independence in 1966 was a primary school leaving examination for candidates to be trained to teach lower primary classes, while junior secondary certificate holders were trained to teach upper primary classes. All teachers at the primary level are now required to have a Diploma in Primary Education (DIP). The DIP is a three-year programme. In order to be eligible for the programme, and thereby eligible for primary teacher training, all applicants are required to have completed the Cambridge Overseas School Certificate

---

[2] Botswana operates a 2-7-3-2 structured pre-tertiary education system, with two years of pre-primary (ages 4 to 5 years), seven years of primary (ages 6 to 12 years), three years of junior secondary (ages 13 to 15 years) and two years of senior secondary education (ages 16 to 17 years). Students take their O and A level exams at the end of the junior and senior secondary stages respectively.

(COSC) Ordinary Level or the Botswana General Certificate of Secondary Education (BGCSE). The four primary teacher training colleges enroll about 1 400–1 500 students and graduate about 400 teachers annually; more than 60 per cent of graduates are women.

Those training for the DIP are required to take all the subjects in the Primary School Curriculum. They are also required to select an area of specialisation from one of the following combinations: mathematics and science; English and Setswana; social studies and religious education; or practical subjects (any two from agriculture, arts and crafts, home economics, music and physical education).

A high percentage of teachers in Botswana's primary schools, as reflected in our sample results, were trained before the system required a teacher to have the DIP, and only required a Primary Teacher Certificate (PTC), earlier issued by the same teacher training colleges, but then serving as a post junior secondary rather than a post senior secondary level of education. The PTC qualification is no longer offered.

Those who do not have the DIP (including those holding a PTC) are required to undergo an upgrading course to acquire it. This course is offered by the Centre for Continuing Education at the University of Botswana (UB) in the form of a distance-learning programme. In 2009, 36 per cent of the primary teaching force (almost all women) had the PTC, 50 per cent had the DIP, and 10 per cent had attended university and received a bachelor's degree in education (BEd). The remaining teachers were either untrained, serving in a temporary capacity, or held other forms of certification. The level of education of primary teachers has risen rapidly as DIP holders replace PTC holders. In addition, enrolment in teacher training colleges rose rapidly from 1 056 in 1998 to 1 390 in 2007, increasing sharply for young women and decreasing for young men.

All teachers at the secondary school level are required to have at least a Diploma in Secondary Education (DSE), if they were educated in Botswana, and a bachelor's degree in education, if they were educated outside the country. Unlike at the primary level, where teachers are required to teach all subjects, at this level they are required to teach the subjects they train in. The DSE is also a three-year programme. The qualifications for entry into junior secondary teacher training are the COSC or the BGCSE with specified credits. The DSE is currently offered by two colleges of education, namely Tonota and Molepolole, which currently graduate about 400 teachers annually. Most of these teachers are assigned to junior secondary positions.

In addition to the DIP and DSE offered in teacher training colleges, UB produces teachers in a BEd programme with a specialisation in either primary or secondary teaching. It also offers a one-year post graduate diploma in education for graduates in general degree programmes (BSc and BA) who qualify to teach in secondary schools. Secondary school teachers who have at least six years of teaching experience are eligible to be recruited by the colleges of education for their staff development programmes. In 2006, 32 per cent of secondary teachers held a BEd and another 15 per cent had post-graduate degrees.

Teacher recruitment and hiring in Botswana

Teacher recruitment and hiring is highly centralised in Botswana, with the Department of Teaching Service Management (TSM) in the Ministry of Education responsible for teacher employment in Botswana. TSM manages the recruitment of teachers for all government and government-supported schools in Botswana. The department is also responsible for determining teacher posting, primarily with an aim to ensure that teacher distribution remains equitable in relation to experience and training across schools.

Botswana does not appear to suffer a general shortage of teachers, given that less than 6 per cent of primary and 8 per cent of secondary teachers are expatriates. Expatriate teachers are predominantly male and are concentrated in Gaborone and in private schools. There is no special effort in place to recruit teachers into areas such as mathematics and science. In fact, teacher unions have been actively demanding that differences in salary by level of schooling (primary versus secondary) and type of qualification (diploma versus degree) be removed. They argue that this constitutes discrimination as defined by various International Labour Organization documents.

Teacher salaries in Botswana

As Tables 2.1 and Figures 2.2a and 2.2b show, teachers in Botswana are relatively well paid, particularly in the case of women. As estimated from the 2002/03 household survey, female teachers (combined primary and secondary) earn more than female scientists (scientists includes a broad array of professions that are self-defined as associated with doing science) and non-scientists, even though the scientists tend to have higher level degrees than many of the teachers in the sample. For males, scientists earn considerably more than teachers, providing some evidence for the prevalence of females in the teaching profession, especially at the primary level where salaries are lower. Although these salary comparisons are based on small numbers of observations, they suggest that teacher recruitment among high ability females should not be an issue. This suggests that improving teacher training in the colleges is a feasible strategy to develop higher quality teachers in Botswana primary schools.

Teacher unionism in Botswana

Teacher unionism is a recent phenomenon in Botswana, and teacher unions have not played a strong role in the development of schooling and education policy. Strikes by civil servants in May 2011 represented the first instance of widespread industrial action in the country's recent history.

Teacher education and teacher labour markets in South Africa

The supply and demand of teachers is a matter of both quantity and quality (Chisholm 2009). Where and how teacher education is provided has been regulated by South African teacher labour market dynamics and by political imperatives. Both require some discussion. In South Africa, colleges were the most important providers of teacher education until 2000. According to the National Teacher Education Audit of 1995, the majority of those training to become primary school teachers were enrolled in 104 state-funded colleges of education, with 93 of these providing pre-service teacher education in contact mode, and 14 also offering diploma-awarding in-service education and training

TABLE 2.1 *Botswana: Mean monthly earnings for post-secondary degree holders by gender and occupation, 2002–2003*

Age	Teachers	Scientist (male)	Non-scientist	Teachers	Scientists (female)	Non-scientist
20–24		879	555		223	221
25–29	892	545	722	884	649	605
30–34	1 336	2 733	773	1 044	1 450	693
35–44	1 930	2 046	1 141	782	993	795
45–54	1 366	1 217	1 008	1 673	724	1 246
55–64	2 608	1 683	1 095	634		848

Source: Botswana Household Survey, 2004.

FIGURE 2.2a *Botswana: Median female monthly earnings, post-secondary degree holders, 2002–03*

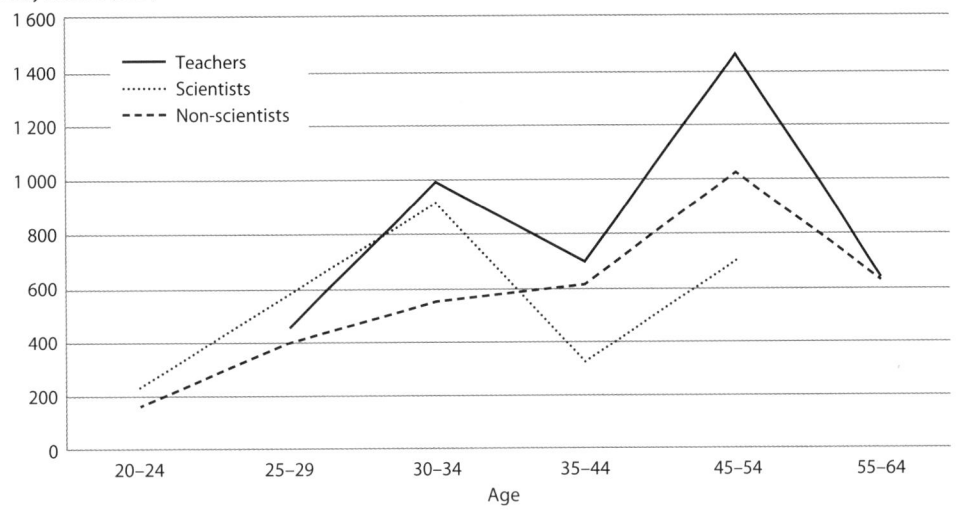

Monthly income (USD)

— Teachers
⋯⋯ Scientists
- - - Non-scientists

Age

Source: Authors' estimates from Botswana Household Survey, 2004.

FIGURE 2.2b *Botswana: Median male monthly earnings, post-secondary degree holders, 2002–03*

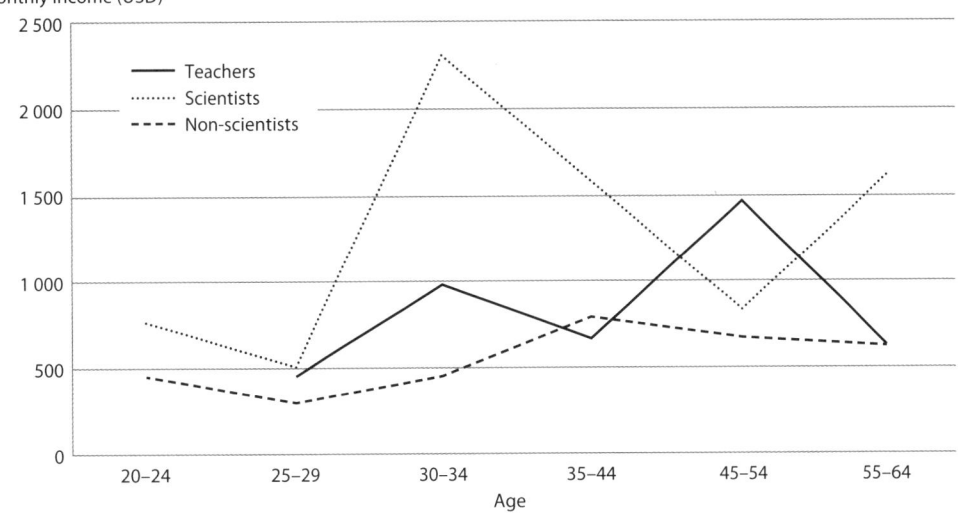

Monthly income (USD)

— Teachers
⋯⋯ Scientists
- - - Non-scientists

Age

Source: Authors' estimates from Botswana Household Survey, 2004.

programmes. The large majority (85 out of 93) catered to black students, and two-thirds were in rural areas (66 out of the 93 colleges) (Jaff et al. 1995). Today, there are only 23 university and technikon-based teacher training facilities, the largest located in urban areas.

At the end of the 1990s, alongside the introduction of a new curriculum, colleges were closed as centres for teacher training or absorbed into existing institutions of higher education. This involved a painful exercise of institutional merger and rationalisation (Kruss 2008, 2009). In North West Province, the Universities of Potchefstroom and Bophuthatswana were merged to become the University of North West, absorbing two colleges: the formerly white Potchefstroom Teacher Education College and the formerly African Mankwe Teacher Education College, which had also been a centre focused on mathematics and science.

Currently, North West Province has eight former teacher education colleges within its borders. Hebron College is now a theological college, Lehurutshe, Taung and Tlhabane have been recapitalised as skills development colleges, and Moretele and North West In-Service Centres serve as departmental offices and training centres. Teacher education is principally provided through the merged University of North West on the Mahikeng and Potchefstroom campuses. But this is by all accounts far from adequate. The consequences are explored below.

An important influence on the shape of teacher education over the last decade was the Norms and Standards for Educators (NSE 2000) which attempted to bring qualifications in line with the curriculum and National Education Qualifications Framework. It identified seven roles for teachers as key criteria for the development of programmes and qualifications in teacher education. These have been variously interpreted by higher education institutions for the purposes of teacher education curriculum development.

A recent Higher Education Quality Council (HEQC) review of teacher education qualifications has identified a number of key characteristics of teacher education in South Africa (HEQC 2009). These are summarised in a draft gazette as reasons for reform of the system (Department of Higher Education and Training, DHET 2010). Few programmes meet minimum standards, the quality of staff, especially in BEd programmes, is 'less than optimum,' many students are not given the opportunity of practice learning and 'more than half of all programme designs focus so strongly on preparing students for the curriculum that students' preparation for a career in teaching, and adapting to future curriculum change, is severely compromised' (DHET 2010: 6). The Draft Policy on Minimum Requirements for Teacher Education also highlights inadequate screening of applicants by institutions, formulaic institutional compliance and inadequate knowledge of the wider challenges facing South African education (DHET 2010). In response to these and other challenges, the DHET has recommended three pathways and five types of disciplinary knowledge that should frame the acquisition and application of knowledge for teaching purposes: disciplinary, pedagogical, practical, fundamental and situational learning (DHET 2010: 7). On this basis it attempts to guide future teacher education qualifications development. However, institutional provision remains the key stumbling block.

One of the single most significant policy interventions of the post-apartheid government to address teacher shortages was undoubtedly the re-introduction in 2005 of full-cost bursaries for teachers in the form of the Funza Lushaka bursaries. These specifically target mathematics, science, and language teachers, especially in the early years of schooling. According to the DBE, the scheme has grown by over 200 per cent in levels of funding and over 150 per cent in number of students funded since 2007. Between 2007 and 2010 some 16 065 students benefited and 5 534 graduated. Of the 812 graduates who qualified at the end of 2007, 99 per cent were in teaching posts by the end of 2008.[3] The majority of bursars were placed in low-income schools.

But there are challenges. There is evidence that provincial departments of education are unable to identify suitable posts in good time to enable effective placement. Provinces employ unqualified

---

3   These figures are from internal unpublished DBE sources.

rather than qualified Funza Lushaka bursars. Schools that need qualified mathematics and science teachers are resistant to employing them. And graduates prefer not to take up positions in rural areas where they are needed and pursue further study or travel rather than teach. Very few take up bursaries in African languages at the Foundation Phase. The capacity of the system to produce teachers also appears to be inadequate to match the need. This points to a complexity that requires greater understanding of teacher labour market dynamics.

Teacher shortages in South Africa

The shortage of appropriately qualified teachers has proved a persistent obstacle to post-apartheid efforts to reform the education system in South Africa. In particular, since the country's first democratic elections in 1994, supply has failed to keep pace with the rapid growth in demand for mathematics, science and Foundation Phase teachers. The Department of Education points to 'a dire shortage of qualified Mathematics and Science teachers' (DoE 2009: 11), and notes in a 2006 report that shortages are similarly serious in the Foundation Phase where students require teachers with mother-tongue competence. Of projected new teacher graduates in 2006, fewer than one in twelve were equipped to teach in African languages in the Foundation Phase (DoE 2006b: 12).

The numbers of learners and teachers recorded by the Department of Education are reproduced in Table 2.2. While the data is problematic, given the discontinuity in reporting between 2004 and 2005, these crude figures nonetheless support the claim that pupil/teacher ratios (PTRs) are gradually rising – an increase mediated only by the capacity of high-income public schools to fund the hiring of additional teachers through fees paid by parents.

It is also likely that South Africa may be subject to hidden shortages. The absolute numbers of teachers may be adequate to meet class size requirements, but a more granular lens reveals a surplus of teacher labour in some geographic regions and disciplinary fields, and a deficit in others. The limited data that are available, while of poor quality, show high vacancy rates in schools across all nine provinces (DoE 2008a).

TABLE 2.2 *South Africa: Growth in learner and teacher numbers, 2001–2007*

	Learners	Reported educators[a]	Estimated educators[b]	L:E ratio[c]
2001	11 738 126	354 201	354 201	33.1
2002	11 917 017	360 155	360 155	33.1
2003	12 038 922	362 598	362 598	33.2
2004	12 176 391	362 042	362 042	33.6
2005	12 217 765	382 133	364 029	33.6
2006	12 293 785	385 860	366 027	33.6
2007	12 401 217	394 175	368 036	33.7
CAGR[d]	0.92%	1.80%	0.64%	

Source: Annual eduation statistics released by the DoE, 2001–2007.

Note: All calculations author's own. Figures are for private and public schools.

[a] Reported educators includes teachers hired by school governing bodies from 2005–2008, but not prior.
[b] Estimated educators reflects an attempt to project growth of the teacher base inferring growth from previous years.
[c] The L:E ratio is the ratio of learners to educators.
[d] CAGR (compound annual growth rate) represents average year-on-year growth between 2001 and 2007).

Unsurprisingly, in light of existing data deficiencies in tracking employed teachers, the DoE has not until recently maintained a database on unemployed, qualified educators and their field of specialisation. It has therefore not been possible to accurately assess whether there is a genuine shortage of educators in certain subject fields (Peltzer et al. 2005).[4] Nonetheless, even if generalised shortages are not a reality in South African schools, reports from school principals, teachers, department officials and union leaders all suggest untenably high PTRs and a lack of qualified teachers in certain subject areas (Mda & Erasmus 2008).

First, there exists a shortage of teachers qualified in technical subjects. This is likely a simple issue of opportunity cost: individuals who are competent in mathematics and science are unlikely to choose teaching as a career when considerably higher returns to these skills may be earned elsewhere in the labour market. In an analysis of teacher wages using South African labour force data, Irving (2010) finds that teachers face a substantial disadvantage relative to individuals with similar levels of education and experience, and are subject to wage structures that allow for less mobility than is typical across the rest of the labour market. This differential is especially striking when compared to professions requiring mathematics and science skills.

While returns to years of education are broadly highly significant and increasing over time for those in technical occupations, teachers have experienced stagnant and uniformly lower returns across years. In mathematics and science professions, each year of education adds on average almost 19 per cent to wages, as against the 6 per cent for teachers. Results for tenure and experience paint a similar picture. Furthermore, salary trajectories within technical professions appear to be significantly steeper than for the labour market as a whole, as indicated by the shorter time (measured by experience) required for movement between salary grades. This further increases the high opportunity cost faced by potential mathematics and science teachers.

Second, shortages exist for properly trained mother-tongue Foundation Phase teachers, particularly in rural areas. Since it is not clear that a high level of technical competence is required for teachers who choose this area of specialisation (DoE 2008b), understanding the mechanisms by which this shortage arises is somewhat less straightforward. Since anecdotal evidence suggests that low-income, rural women traditionally formed the backbone of this segment of the teacher labour market (Paterson & Arends 2009), one explanation might be that this group is now subject to some barrier to entry that limits access to teacher training institutions.

A primary candidate for a barriers to entry explanation would be the migration of the expansive network of apartheid-era teacher education colleges into university and technikon-based schools of education, as described previously. Teacher training arguably became considerably less financially and geographically accessible for many rural communities in the catchment areas of the former colleges as teacher education opportunities migrated to urban areas. Paterson and Arends (2008) suggest that given the mostly urban location of current teacher education facilities, young rural people, especially black females, were cut out of the graduate production process. Also implicit in these changing credential dynamics is the requirement that average remuneration for teachers should rise in response to the higher level of skill required for entry into the profession.

In the absence of information that directly addresses the evolution of teacher shortages, one alternative is to examine enrolment data for Initial Professional Education of Teachers (IPET) programmes over

---

4   A recent DoE report claims that efforts are underway to establish an unemployed educator database (DoE 2008c). As of May 2008 the department reported having captured 724 CVs of teachers trained in mathematics and science.

FIGURE 2.3 *Trends in graduates from colleges of education and higher education, 1994–2006*

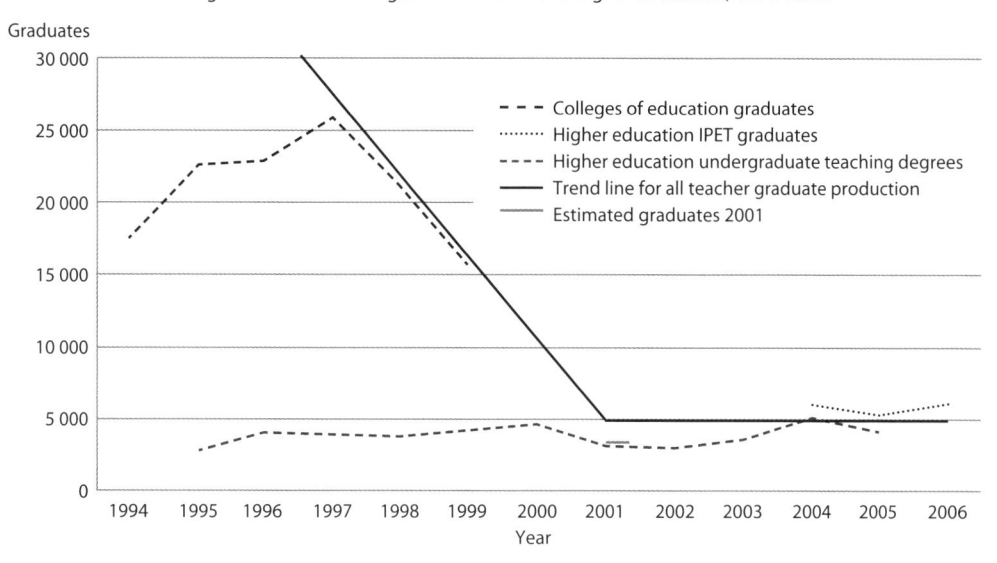

Graduates

- - - Colleges of education graduates
.... Higher education IPET graduates
- - - - Higher education undergraduate teaching degrees
——— Trend line for all teacher graduate production
——— Estimated graduates 2001

Source: Paterson & Arends 2009: 91 (based on the data from Tables 4.82 and Figure 4.22).

Note: Paterson and Arends created the tables and graphs from Higher Education Management Information Systems databases.

time. It is important to recognise that enrolment in teacher education programmes serves as an upper limit on the number of new teachers supplied to the system, since not all those who complete an IPET degree will choose a career as a school teacher. The most complete survey of teacher education patterns to date was conducted by Paterson and Arends (2009). Even here, the authors are unable to accurately report apartheid-era enrolment trends, but synthesise existing sources to describe the changing demography of education students at tertiary institutions in South Africa between 1994 and 2006.

The data show a clear downward trend in IPET graduates, as illustrated in Figure 2.3. However, as the authors observe in an earlier analysis (Paterson & Arends 2008), the issue is not exclusively one of numbers; it is also important to consider the demographic characteristics of students pursuing teacher training. Currently, black women form the largest proportion of educators in South Africa: in 2005, 79 per cent of all teachers employed in public schools were black and 66 per cent female (Arends 2007).

Enrolment data tell their own story. In 1994, the best available information suggests that 78 per cent of students in the colleges of education were 29 years of age or younger. The majority (89.1 per cent) were black, and 65–80 per cent were female. In pre-primary and junior-primary courses, 98 per cent were female (Paterson & Arends 2009). Contrast this with the finding laid out in their 2008 study: while absolute numbers of black women entering IPET programmes appear to be increasing, the proportion of black females 25-and-under stood at 27.6 per cent of all students in 2000 (already a sharp decline from 1994 numbers), but had dropped to 17.4 per cent by 2004. These data, while imperfect, reinforce the need to explore the source of teacher shortages, with the particular phenomenon of declining enrolment among black women potentially explained by either of the shortage narratives outlined previously.

Teacher recruitment and hiring in South Africa

There is simultaneously puzzling evidence to suggest that many new teachers find it difficult to obtain permanent jobs in the public school system, while inappropriately (and under-) qualified teachers continue to be employed by provincial departments of education (DoE 2008a). In a 2004 study of 776 final-year student teachers from 11 higher education institutions, only one-third of the respondents who indicated that they intended to teach in South Africa in 2005 had secured a post by October 2004 for the school year starting in February 2005 (Bertram et al. 2006). Furthermore, almost three-quarters of those respondents who had secured a post indicated that they would be paid by school governing bodies rather than by the provincial government. The authors point to the complexity of teacher shortages: that vacant posts are not being filled by newly qualified teachers suggests that the experience of shortage varies enormously across different locations and in different kinds of schools.

Teacher salaries in South Africa

South African teachers' salaries have been changing steadily over the last decade. According to Gustafsson and Patel (2008) teachers received substantial pay increases in 2006, moderate increases in real terms thereafter, and a falling ratio of teachers' pay to GDP per capita. Their analysis of labour force survey data for 2007 shows that teachers were earning less than other professionals, but that their age-earnings profile was comparatively very different. In their analysis, changes introduced in the 2008 salary negotiations produced real increases, resulting in a gradual closing of the gap between teachers and other professionals, and conversion of the unfavourable age pay-slope into a more favourable one.

Teacher unionisation in South Africa

No discussion of the teacher labour market in South Africa would be complete without mentioning the role of trade unions in shaping the dynamics of teacher behavior. Trade unions are politically powerful in the South African context: the explicit tripartite alliance between the ruling African National Congress (ANC) government, the Congress of South African Trade Unions (COSATU) and the Communist Party, represents an important legacy of the anti-apartheid struggle, but also a powerful constraint on current government action. Within COSATU, the South African Democratic Teacher's Union (SADTU) represents the second largest constituency, with arguably the most educated and relatively affluent members. Estimates vary, but South African teachers are highly unionised, with over 80 per cent of South African public schools teachers belonging to a union. About two-thirds of these teachers are represented by SADTU, the remainder by NAPTOSA and SAOU. Whilst SADTU actively supports the ANC in elections, this is explicitly linked to reciprocal ANC support for pro-SADTU policies.

The union acts as intermediary between government and teachers integral to both the process of policy formation and the shaping of teacher identity. Under apartheid, black schools were frequently hubs of political activity, with this superseding their function as institutions of learning. It appears that this political association continues to play an important role in teachers' sense of purpose, with direct impact on their professional accountability (see Govender 2004 for a history of SADTU). The loyalty granted to the ANC by SADTU under the anti-apartheid struggle generates a complex web of obligations that impacts education policy today. The question is thus to what extent SADTU serves to perpetuate a highly politicised schooling environment, in which teachers perceive their sense of political unity as equal to their sense of duty as educators, and where government education policy is constrained by the pursuit of SADTU objectives, which may not always directly align with the interests of students.

While SADTU plays an important role nationally in ensuring teacher development, a number of observations suggest that the role played by SADTU at the local level may generate negative consequences for learners. Union meetings are generally scheduled during school hours and attendance is considered a legitimate reason for teacher absence. Teacher accountability is also compromised, given SADTU's fierce resistance to inspection in schools: DoE inspectors have largely been prohibited from entering schools since a 'No to Inspectors' campaign instituted as an anti-apartheid measure in the early 1990s (Seekings 2004). There is evidence of the legacy of this mentality today: one reporter records an official as having told members at a union meeting that they, 'should refuse to sign early departure and late arrivals registers because they are linked to apartheid' (Mohlala 2009). This reluctance to allow teachers to be evaluated (and hence provide an avenue for constructive feedback on pedagogical technique) is further evidenced by the unwillingness of South African unions to allow teachers to participate in the teacher test component of the SACMEQ study until 2007.

In the next chapter we outline the conceptual framework we use to probe teacher quality and learning outcomes in these classrooms. Thereafter we provide a profile of the schools that examines their socio-economic, financing and management context. This provides the basis from which we explore results in relation to learner mathematical knowledge and teacher mathematical knowledge and proficiency. From here we build up to and test our overall model of student achievement, which provides us with our overall conclusions.

Conclusion

For Botswana the transition from British colonialism to an independent liberal democratic state was almost as seamless as its transition from a mainly subsistence economy to one based on high value mineral exports. One year after independence in 1966, the fortuitous discovery of diamonds in Botswana resulted in rapid and sustained economic growth over four decades. The combination of sustained economic growth and non-conflictual relationships with its former colonial authority, as well as with its fractious neighbour, resulted in orderly and gradual progress over many years. This was based on the adoption of development plans and programmes that also saw the introduction of the educational conditions to support such growth and national development. Educational strategies, policies and plans for curriculum and language have all taken their cue from international developments considered good for Botswana and have also been implemented with due consideration of the implications for teachers and teaching. How teacher development needs to support wider educational change has been central to how curriculum and language policy has become embedded in regularised routines in practice in classrooms. Of considerable significance is the fact that until recently Botswana has not had a unionised teacher workforce. Although relatively well paid, Botswana's teachers through this long post-independence period have been compliant partners in educational development rather than active adversaries of attempted reforms (as in South Africa).

South Africa's complex and conflict-ridden history has by contrast given rise to a set of pressures on education that have invariably resulted in equally conflictual change processes. Even though there are continuities in its policy trajectory (see Kallaway 2002), discontinuity and rupture have characterised its reform processes since at least the 1950s. The introduction of Bantu Education in the 1950s and the Bantustan system in the 1960s and 1970s were accompanied by physical and symbolic violence: the violence of repression of opposition and the violence of the subordination of aspiration and possibilities through the limited (and limiting) education made available. The student and youth explosion of 1976 did not begin and end in that year, but continued for an entire decade, touching virtually every African school in the country. Rhythms and routines of schooling became destabilised.

The transition years of 1990–1994 saw an escalation rather than diminution of conflict within school walls. Over time, many teachers left the profession. The establishment of a democratic order has brought with it an emphasis on stability and order within schools, and on teaching and learning. Yet, the policy processes set in motion to reverse the effects of apartheid were radical in their impact. While the physical violence and repression of the apartheid years was lifted, the symbolic violence continued through curriculum and teacher policies. The curriculum delegitimised teacher knowledge and practice and demanded that teachers begin as if from a new slate. Teacher policy devalued teachers when it offered severance packages. And teacher education policy closed institutions that had formed networks of knowledge and communities of practice. More recent government initiatives have recognised the importance of institutional provision closer to home and reinvigorated ideas about the centrality of specialised subject knowledge and practice in teacher education and development. In the light of this history and ongoing poor performance in international as well as Annual National Assessments, teacher supply, utilisation and development have become critical priorities.

CHAPTER 3

Conceptual framework and methodology

The core of our broader study is the contribution of teaching (classroom resources/teaching practices) to student performance in the classroom social context of schools in North West Province and Botswana. The purpose of the study is to test whether and how classroom and school factors contribute to student mathematics learning gains. From a classroom perspective, our particular emphasis is on teacher mathematics knowledge, classroom pedagogy and opportunity to learn (including language issues) in a sample of Grade 6 classrooms in North West Province and South East Botswana. From a school standpoint, we focus on school conditions – namely, an indicator of school violence – that contribute to greater or less student learning. We also review the role of principals in our sample of schools.

Our methodology is designed to explore possible variations in teaching and other factors across classrooms and schools (and countries) and to help understand their relation to the variation in student learning gains, if any. We hypothesise that two important constructs of teachers' mathematical knowledge, namely their content knowledge, which is their knowledge of mathematics itself (how well they are able to do mathematics), and their pedagogical content knowledge, which is their understanding of how to teach various mathematical concepts and operations, are related to the breadth and depth of their teaching in classrooms and the effectiveness of their teaching. The study explores this relationship by measuring teacher content and pedagogical content knowledge and by using videotapes to assess the depth of these same teachers' classroom teaching. We were also able to measure the number of lessons teachers taught on test topics during the school year, surveyed school principals and used observations in schools to understand whether differences in school conditions (reported violence and teacher absence) can provide insights into the level and variation of teaching factors in different schools. Overall, the methodology takes us beyond the scope of other studies (which gather data on teachers and teaching through questionnaires) to gain a better understanding of the influences of teaching quality and other factors on differences in student performance.

Among the main distinctions between this study and others, such as SACMEQ, is our focus on learning gains of students rather than just learning levels, on observing how teachers teach classroom lessons in addition to measuring teacher knowledge, and on detailed analyses of student notebooks to measure the degree to which teachers implement the planned curriculum and covered content related to the items in our student pre- and post-tests.

General conceptual framework

At the centre of our analysis is how teacher knowledge, skills and effort may influence the depth of teaching and, in turn, student learning. Figure 3.1 provides a simple conceptual overview of different forms of teacher knowledge and other components of a model of how schools produce student learning. This framework builds on previous work in Latin America (Carnoy, Gove & Marshall 2007; Marshall & Sorto 2012). The focus here is on mathematics, although the framework is general enough to be applicable to all subjects.

The five main components of the model are as follows:
1. The teacher's capacity to teach the material (content knowledge and pedagogical content knowledge).
2. The teacher's pedagogical skills.
3. Two types of opportunity to learn, which may influence student learning gains directly and indirectly, through their interaction with the quality of teaching.
4. The students' socio-economic background, which may influence student learning gains directly and indirectly, through its potential impact on teacher/school expectations of student and the process of teaching itself.
5. The outcome of the process – student learning gains.

We use a structural model to estimate the relationships depicted in Figure 3.1 between student characteristics, teacher capacity (mathematics knowledge), test item coverage (OTL), teacher pedagogical practice, school organisational environment, and student outcomes.

FIGURE 3.1 *Conceptual framework*

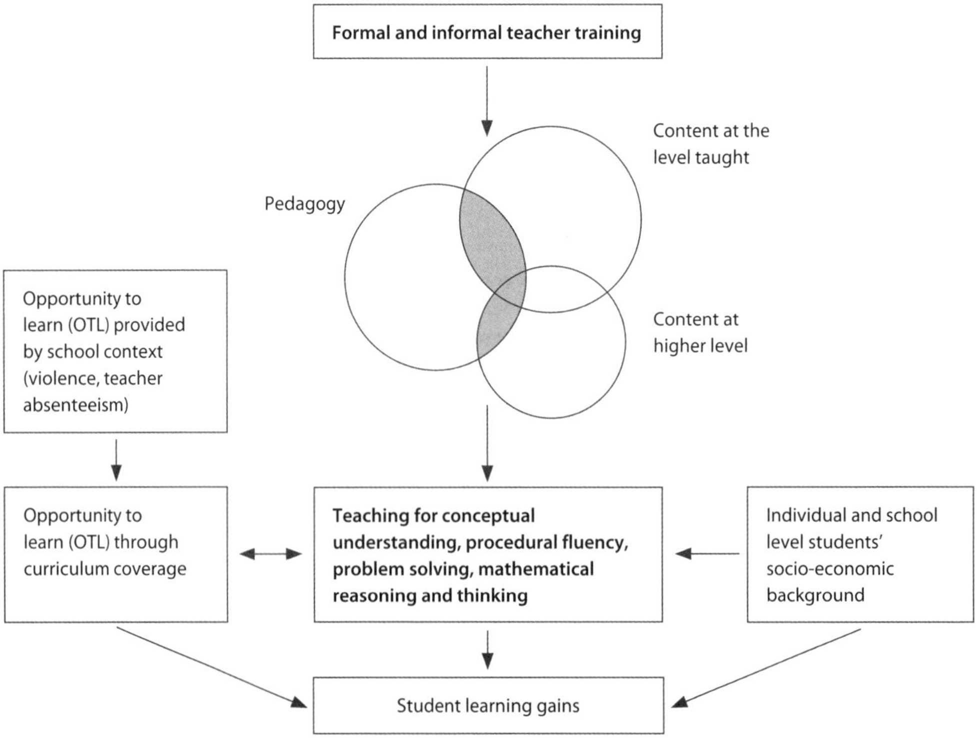

Source: Authors' rendition with special thanks to JH Marshall and MA Sorto

The model hypothesises that:
- teacher pedagogical practice (TQ) and teacher-provided OTL are related to teacher mathematics knowledge and teacher experience (we use a quadratic function of teacher experience), and
- student achievement is cumulative and is a function of previous achievement, SES, teacher mathematics knowledge, teaching quality, OTL, class size, and school context, which includes a reported violence index and the average school/classroom student SES.

For the second function, we estimate two versions of student learning gains: achievement measured at the end of the year as the dependent variable (controlling for student initial achievement as an independent variable), and student achievement gains over the course of the year as the dependent variable.

Equation (2a) that follows assumes that knowledge decays over the course of the year at a constant rate, so that the teacher/school contribution during the year is the sum of new knowledge learned during the year plus the percentage of knowledge decay. This is a typical value-added model, but it presents a problem in that the student's initial achievement may be correlated with the error term (Ladd 2008). This problem is avoided in equation (2b), known as the 'absolute gains model,' but equation (2b) assumes no decay in what the student knew at the beginning of the year, so this means that the teacher/school effect on gains may be biased downward. However, even this formulation does not account for the possibility of non-random assignment of teacher skills to classrooms, or students to teachers on the basis of value added. Students' families may choose teachers whom the families perceive to be better at teaching students more during a given academic year, or a principal may assign teachers to students on the basis of the principal's perception of the teacher's capacity to produce achievement gains. Thus, even the teacher skill coefficients in equation (2b) may be overestimates of the 'true' contribution of these skills to student achievement gains.

We estimate equations (1a), (1b), (2a), and (2b):

$$TQ_j = C + \gamma_{j\,1} TMK_j + \gamma_2 TExp_j + \gamma_3 (TExp_j)^2 + \gamma_4 X_{jk} + e_j \tag{1a}$$

$$OTL_j = C + \beta_1 TMK_j + \beta_2 TExp_j + \gamma_3 (TExpj)^2 + \gamma_4 X_{jk} + e_j \tag{1b}$$

$$A_{ijpost} = C + a_1 A_{ijpre} + \Sigma b_k X_{ijk} + c_1 TMK_j + c_2 TQ_j + c_3 TExp_j + c_4 (TExpj)^2 + \Sigma d_k S_{jk} + f_1 OTL_j + e_{ij} \tag{2a}$$

$$A_{ijpost} - A_{ijpre} = C + \Sigma b_k X_{ijk} + c_1 TMK_j + c_2 TQ_j + c_3 TExp_j + c_4 (TExpj)^2 + \Sigma d_k S_{jk} + f_1 OTL_j + e_{ij} \tag{2b}$$

where
TQ_j = teacher j's observed teaching quality;
OTL_j = opportunity to learn in classroom j;
TMK_j = teacher j's mathematical knowledge (a combination of content and pedagogical content knowledge);
$TExp_j$ = teacher j's years of teaching experience (either total years or years teaching mathematics);
X_{jk} = a vector of average family characteristics k of students in classroom j;
A_{ijpost} = student i in classroom j post-test (November 2009) achievement score;
A_{ijpre} = student i in classroom j pre-test (March 2009) achievement score;
X_{ijk} = a vector of family characteristics k of student i in classroom j;
S_{jk} = a vector of school/classroom conditions k of schools/classrooms j, including X_{jk}; and
e_{ij} = error term.

Fuller et al. (1994) in Botswana and Reeves (2006) in the Western Cape estimate the test score gains functions using a hierarchical linear model (HLM). Wildeman (2010) also uses HLM to estimate the relationship of school resources to test score outcomes (at one point in time) for Grade 6 learners in South Africa. HLM estimates provide some interesting insights into the 'levels' at which variables are correlated. These estimates are also able to deal with fixed and random effects, and provide unbiased estimates of the error terms for the coefficients. However, we will use ordinary least squares (OLS) structural equation modelling, correcting the error terms for clustering, which achieves the same unbiased estimates of error terms as HLM. The results of the structural models are more easily interpreted for policy purposes. Furthermore, HLM models do not correct for selection bias, and it is much easier to adjust OLS models for such bias.

As we discussed earlier, the main difficulty in trying to measure the effect of various school inputs on student achievement is making unbiased estimates of the relations between our independent teaching and social context variables and student performance outcomes. Teacher (and other) resources may be endogenous to student capacity to learn ('better' teachers end up in schools with higher achieving students and students who tend to make greater learning gains may not be randomly assigned to teachers in a school, so it is not possibly to tell which way the causal relationship functions – hence the term 'endogenous'). The Van der Berg and Louw analysis of South African data (2008), work by Motala (2006), our Gauteng pilot study (Carnoy et al. 2008), and recent work by Van der Berg et al. (2011) all strongly suggest that teachers with greater mathematics knowledge teach in schools with higher social class students who do better on mathematics tests. Pedagogical methods may also be endogenous to teacher and student capacity. Teacher resources may be estimated to produce higher achievement gains, but teachers with higher capacity may choose to teach higher gaining students. Whereas a pedagogical method may be estimated to be more effective in producing student achievement gains, mainly teachers with higher content knowledge and students with higher ability may be exposed to that method. In such situations, the estimated effect of pedagogical method on achievement gains would be biased. Since we test students at the beginning and end of the year, we eliminate some of the problem, but students with higher or lower expected gain scores may be non-randomly assigned to schools and classrooms with better trained teachers. This is probably not the case, but it is important to consider the possibility of biases in the estimated coefficients.

Another problem is student 'loss' during the year between the time that we apply the pre-test at the beginning of the school year and the post-test at the end of the school year (Fuller et al. 1994 encountered this problem). The standard way of correcting our estimated relationships for the problem is to estimate the probability of taking both tests based on the family and individual background information gathered on all students who took the initial test and to use that estimation to 'correct' the estimated relationships between our teacher variables and student outcomes (see Heckman 1979). It turned out that we did not encounter this problem, as 90 per cent of the students in our sampled classrooms who took the pre-test also took the post-test.

Measuring teacher mathematical knowledge

There are four distinct knowledge areas depicted in Figure 3.1: lower and higher content knowledge, pedagogical knowledge, and pedagogical content knowledge. At the intersection of pedagogical and content knowledge lies a specialised form of knowledge especially prized by education researchers. This domain is commonly referred to as pedagogical content knowledge (PCK) (Shulman 1986), and its evolution in mathematics reflects a growing emphasis on practice-based metrics for analysing teaching effectiveness in the classroom. Examples include the powerful explanations that teachers use to develop deep understanding of concepts that are part of the curriculum, the ways in which they draw linkages with other elements of mathematics, and the questions they pose to students.

These kinds of skills, it is argued, can only be accumulated through practice or very specialised training activities, although they are still highly related to teachers' knowledge of subject content (Ball et al. 2005; Hill et al. 2005).[1]

The instrument used to measure teacher mathematics knowledge

Following Hill et al. (2005), we combined our instrument's measures of teachers' pedagogical content knowledge and content knowledge into a single measure of 'teacher mathematics knowledge'. The instrument we used was a 24-item, multi-part questionnaire/test that asked teachers to solve two kinds of problems: those related to identifying issues that Grade 6 students commonly face in addressing mathematics problems (mathematics pedagogical problems), and actual mathematics problems (mathematics content) common to the Grade 6 curriculum, or somewhat more difficult. In a few cases, we asked teachers to solve the same problem that appeared on the student test. We will present some of the questions on the teacher questionnaire when we analyse the results.

We graded the teacher test in two ways. In the first, we gave each possible answer equal weight. Of the 24 questions, 11 had multiple parts, so that there were 63 possible answers. Grading A gave each teacher a percentage score based on equal weight for the 63 possible answers. In the second grading scheme, we gave each of the questions equal weight, so that there were 24 possible answers, with partial credit for correct answers to some parts of the 11 multiple part questions. Grading B gave each teacher a percentage score based on the average score of each of the 24 questions.

Measuring teaching quality

We videotaped teachers in our sample of classrooms teaching mathematics lessons on at least one occasion, and usually two. To estimate the level of content taught in mathematics lessons and to categorise the teaching methods used in the classroom from these videotapes, we used a protocol of tasks categorising the level of demand put on students by the teacher and the content complexity of the teaching.

Many educational researchers have observed school classrooms and measured their characteristics for different purposes (Shavelson et al. 1986). The number of classroom observational instruments reviewed by Rosenshine and Furst (1973) and later Brophy and Good (1986) is almost as large as the number of studies reviewed – over 150. These particular instruments measured only behaviours related to teaching in general, such as, pacing of instruction, classroom management, clarity and questioning the learners. More recently, in Latin American countries researchers have measured the time learners spend doing seatwork, recitation activities, group work and 'dead time' to try to explain the differences in learners' outcomes across countries (Carnoy et al. 2007). These aspects of teaching, although important, do not measure if the teacher is using the instructional techniques or behaviours in a way that is effective or consistent with the lesson's content goal.

Perhaps, in response to the need to explain better the mathematical aspects as well as the mathematical pedagogy harnessed during lessons, mathematics educators have turned their attention to the

---

1   For example, Ball et al. (2005) argue that a 'mathematically literate' person would struggle to answer questions these researchers created that measure specialised knowledge.

development of more specific observational protocols and instruments. What follows is a summary of the existing instruments and what constitutes the basis of our coding scheme in the context of North West Province and Botswana schools.

Studying mathematics tasks and learner cognition during instruction

In our review of the literature, we found a set of instruments that focus on mathematical tasks and their implementation. One of them is the instrument used in the TIMSS video study (National Centre for Education Statistics, NCES 2003) to describe instructional practices in seven countries. Some of the aspects considered were 'Making connections', 'Stating concepts', 'Using procedures' and 'Giving results only', as intended by the mathematical content and as a result of the implementation of the lesson. Their major finding was that in Australia and United States the lessons retained the 'Making connections' focus less often than the lessons in the other countries. A related instrument is presented in Henningsen and Stein (1997) where they investigate the factors associated with high-level mathematical tasks presented by the teacher and retained at high level in the implementation by learners in the classroom. The high level refers to one of the levels of cognitive demands defined by the authors as 'the kind of thinking processes entailed in solving the task as announced by the teacher (during the set-up phase) and the thinking processes in which learners engage (during the implementation phase)' (Henningsen & Stein 1997: 529). The thinking processes they considered could range from memorisation to complex thinking and reasoning. They found that the major factor that helps retain a high level of cognitive demand is the effectiveness of the teacher in maintaining learners' engagement by scaffolding and consistently pressing them to provide meaningful explanations or make meaningful connections.

At more specific levels with respect to content, Gearhart et al. (1999) developed an instrument to code videotapes and field notes from 21 primary classrooms. Their purpose was to measure the effect of curriculum and professional development (OTL construct), in the context of teaching fractions, on learner achievement. Their instrument included aspects such as 'the degree to which practices elicit and build upon student thinking, the extent to which conceptual issues are addressed in treatments of problem solving, and the extent of opportunity to utilise and interpret representations in ways that help students build understandings of underlying mathematical concepts' (Gearhart et al. 1999: 292). The last two aspects were shown to significantly affect learners' performance.

Collectively, these studies suggest that when studying the quality of mathematics instruction, it is important to include aspects that describe the mathematics learners are intended to learn by the curriculum or other instructional materials, as well as the way in which the mathematics is presented and assimilated by the learners. In other words, we need to focus on the mathematics that is available to the learner (National Research Council 2001), independent of the way the teacher is teaching it and the learners are learning it, and we need to focus on what learners get out of a mathematics lesson as measured by the level of cognitive demand (see the levels of cognitive demand defined by Henningsen & Stein 1997; Stein et al. 2000).

In the international comparison literature, Carnoy et al. (2007) investigate these two domains in lessons across three Latin America countries (Cuba, Chile, and Brazil) to explain the differences in learner outcomes in those countries. They found that learners in Cuba, which had the best learner outcomes in relation to the other countries, engaged in higher levels of cognitive demand and their curriculum also gave more opportunities for mathematical proficiency (i.e. more representation of all five strands). What this study and the ones mentioned do not take into account is the third key player during instruction – the teacher. Fortunately, there is another body of research that has focused on teachers' knowledge and skills during instruction. We summarise this in the next section.

Studying teachers' knowledge during instruction

Measuring the way teachers apply what they know (mathematically and pedagogically) to teach effectively has been studied more recently. Hill et al. (2008) give an extensive review of literature in this area and provide an instrument that captures aspects focusing on the mathematical quality of instruction (MQI instrument) and its relation to their measures for mathematical knowledge for teaching (MKT). The aspects that this instrument measures are mainly based on the theoretical and empirical work defining the MKT construct (Ball & Bass 2000; Ball et al. 2005; Hill et al. 2004). The MQI instrument measures aspects that focus on the teachers' skills and knowledge during instruction, such as mathematical errors, responding to learners inappropriately or appropriately in terms of the mathematics, connecting practices to mathematics, richness of the mathematics, and mathematical language. In this exploratory study, the authors found a significant association between levels of MKT and the mathematical quality of instruction. Previously, Hill et al. (2005) found a positive association between MKT and learner achievement gains, which supports the contention that the teachers' mathematical knowledge during instruction is ultimately related to learner achievement. In South Africa, Adler and Pillay (2007) and Kazima et al. (2008) have used case studies that build on the work of Deborah Ball and Heather Hill to provide more detailed insights. For example, they argue that the mathematical work that teachers do needs 'to be understood…in relation to particular topics in mathematics, and to particular approaches to teaching' (Kazima et al. 2008: 296). Therefore, when measuring teachers' mathematical work during instruction, we also need to take into consideration the topic or main goal of the lesson and the particular teaching approach, which is related to pedagogical perspectives.

Taking all these aspects into consideration, we designed a new instrument that not only helps describe the teaching quality of the mathematics but, in our larger analysis, can be used to link teacher and learner outcomes. The next section describes the framework used to develop the final instrument.

Framework and instrument development

The framework used to characterise the teaching quality of the lessons for this study is a product of several sources: our experience as mathematics teachers and mathematics teacher educators; our experience studying teaching in developing countries in Latin America; and the existing literature that investigates mathematics instruction. The development of the codes started with observational classroom codes used in rural Guatemala (Marshall 2003; Marshall & Sorto 2011). Even though the addition of new codes helped sharpen the focus on the intended and implemented mathematical tasks, the framework was missing what other authors (Adler et al. 2007, Hill et al. 2008) argue is needed when analysing the quality of mathematical instruction. In response to these concerns, we included one more aspect, the level of the observed teachers' knowledge while teaching. These new codes were tested for the first time in the Panama and Costa Rica study with 50 videotaped lessons (Sorto et al. 2009) and in a large pilot study in the province of Gauteng, South Africa with 42 videotaped lessons.

The four major components of the framework used in the North West Province and Botswana schools are:
- the mathematical content of the lesson,
- the mathematical proficiency learners have the opportunity to acquire,
- the level of cognitive demand the learners are engaged in during the lesson, and
- the observed teacher's knowledge while teaching.

Mathematical content

Mathematical content is measured by the main goal of the lesson using the five learning outcomes from the South Africa National Curriculum Statement (NCS) for mathematics (Grades R–9) and the six modules[2] in the national Botswana Curriculum Guide (or syllabus).
- Numbers and operations: The learner is able to recognise, describe and represent numbers and their relationships, and counts, estimates, calculates and checks with competence and confidence in solving problems.
- Algebra: The learner is able to recognise, describe and represent patterns and relationships, as well as solve problems using algebraic language and skills.
- Geometry: The learner is able to describe and represent characteristics and relationships between 2-D shapes and 3-D objects in a variety of orientations and positions.
- Measurement: The learner is able to use appropriate measuring units, instruments and formulae in a variety of contexts.
- Statistics and probability: The learner is able to collect, summarise, display and critically analyse data in order to draw conclusions and make predictions, and to interpret and determine chance variation.

Mathematical proficiency

Mathematical proficiency is measured by the presence of any of the five strands that form the mathematical proficiency variable, which according to *Adding It Up* (National Research Council 2001: 116) are necessary to learn mathematics successfully. The five strands are:
- Conceptual understanding: Comprehension of mathematical concepts, operations and relations.
- Procedural fluency: Skill in carrying out procedures flexibly, accurately, efficiently, and appropriately.
- Strategic competence: Ability to formulate, represent, and solve mathematical problems.
- Adaptive reasoning: Capacity for logical thought, reflection, explanation and justification.
- Productive disposition: Habitual inclination to see mathematics as sensible, useful, and worthwhile, coupled with a belief in diligence and one's own efficacy.

These strands are not taken as individual goals but rather as an interdependent and interwoven definition of proficiency. If any one of the five elements is missing, the learning process is not considered complete. Nevertheless, in the context of evaluating a (short) lesson it may be unrealistic to expect all five elements to be present, even in a very good class. This argues for some flexibility in how we assess the mathematical proficiency of the lesson. The focus in this component is the mathematics available to the learner.

Cognitive demand

The level(s) of cognitive demand learners engage in during the lesson are derived from a rubric in Stein et al.'s (2000) classification of higher and lower cognitive demand. These include:
- Memorisation: Recollection of facts, formulae, or definitions.
- Procedures without connections: Performing algorithmic type of problems and have no connection to the underlying concept or meaning.
- Procedures with connections: Use of procedures with the purpose of developing deeper levels of understanding concepts or ideas.

---

2   The Botswana Curriculum Guide includes an extra module called Problem Solving. This module was treated as a process module and not as a content module. This process was expected to be observed not as separate content but rather in combination with the content modules.

- Doing mathematics: Complex and non-algorithmic thinking; learners explore and investigate the nature of the concepts and relationships.

The focus in this component is the thinking processes in which learners engage.

Observed teachers' knowledge

We characterise the observed teachers' knowledge in a lesson by focusing on three aspects. The work of Shulman (1986) forms the basis of these categories. These include:
- Grade level mathematics knowledge: The presence of computational, linguistic, and representational accuracy for the mathematics at the grade level being taught. We take into account any mathematical errors during instruction.
- General pedagogical knowledge: The use of general instructional techniques beyond the lecture mode. Elements include how well the teacher has the learners engaged, his/her use of proper classroom management techniques, and the quality of instructional materials.
- Mathematical knowledge in teaching: The degree to which the teacher can appropriately integrate the use of the instructional techniques with the mathematical concept being taught, and its effectiveness in student learning. This includes the use of correct language to clearly convey mathematical ideas.

Together, these four analytical elements make it possible to go beyond a simple reconstruction of each lesson and consider the deeper mathematical meaning of what is being taught. These elements also allow us to assess what the teachers know and how they apply this knowledge in the classroom, which in turn makes for some useful linkages between the lesson analysis and teacher questionnaires. Of course, what is observed in one or two lessons does not measure the entire body of knowledge a teacher has in mathematics, or any of the other kinds of knowledge. But the purpose of looking at the teacher's knowledge for these lessons is not to characterise the entire knowledge of a teacher (for this we would need a case study where we observe a teacher for a long period of time). The purpose is to measure how well the teacher uses these specific knowledge forms in a particular lesson.

Coding and inter-rater reliability

To capture the presence of the 13 different components (one for content, five for mathematical proficiency, four for cognitive demand, and three for observed teacher's knowledge) a coding system was used for each lesson. After observing a particular lesson the researcher adjudicated a code of 'present' (P) or 'not present' (NP) for each component that defines the three elements of teaching mentioned previously. A conservative judgment was used for the 'present' code, that is, if the component was observed at least once during the lesson, a code of P was adjudicated. Other video studies have broken the lessons into small segments of 5 or 10 minutes or episodes to account for the complexity of instruction (e.g. Andrews 2009; Hill et al. 2008). However, when this method was applied to our lessons, we did not find significant differences between the codes considering the lesson as a whole and lessons broken into smaller segments. An overall evaluation of the teaching quality observed in the lesson was assigned using the scale 1 (low), 2 (medium), or 3 (high). These ratings were a holistic composite of the 13 components described.

For the first observation lessons, trained coders worked independently to code each lesson, and for the second observation lessons one expert coder coded all the lessons. A subset of lessons for each set was submitted for inter-rater reliability test. Inter-rater reliability between coders ranged between 65 per cent to 95 per cent for individual codes.

Measuring opportunity to learn

Our second focus in understanding how the learning process works is on opportunity to learn. OTL was first introduced as part of the International Association for the Evaluation of Educational Achievement (IEA)'s cross-country comparative studies when the mathematics and science curriculum was conceptualised as functioning at the three levels of the intended, implemented and attained or achieved curriculum. OTL, defined as the curriculum content made available to students, the cognitive levels at which various topics of sub-topics are covered, and the amount of contact time devoted to teaching the subject area, has since been used in different ways to explore links between whether tested content has been taught, cognitive demand, and the amount of time students had to learn the content and student achievement (McDonnell 1995).

OTL as a measure to deal with the problem of curricular diversity

When researchers use tests as measures of student achievement, they usually try to select or construct test items that represent content areas that should be (or are) common across official curricula of countries (the intended curriculum), or use standard content that subject experts believe students in a particular grade ought to know. This selection is important for the credibility of the test results.

However, a fundamental problem with the use of tests as measures of student achievement, particularly in cross-country comparative research, but even within countries where there is strong central control over the school curriculum, is diversity in the implemented curriculum (the curriculum put into practice). This is because test content does not always match the content actually covered by teachers in schools. Different teachers in different classes, even in the same schools, do not necessarily cover the same topics and sub-topics (McLean 1985). In addition, students in different classes and schools are not necessarily exposed to the same curriculum content, nor do they spend the same amount of time on the various content requirements. It follows that all students do not have the same opportunity to learn.

A construct of OTL that focuses on what takes place in class provides a useful means for measuring differences in the implemented curriculum, as well as for looking at links between the curriculum made available to students in the classroom, test content areas, and student achievement.

OTL as a policy relevant curriculum variable

The results of large-scale international comparative mathematics and science studies together with national studies, especially in the United States, document the empirical relationship between student achievement and the content/conceptual level at which the content is covered. These studies have suggested that curriculum coverage and exposure 'could be an effective lever in efforts to improve student achievement and to distribute learning opportunities more equitably' (McDonnell 1995: 308). As a consequence, OTL has received considerable attention and is now widely recognised as 'a policy relevant curriculum variable' in a number of national education systems (Floden 2003: 253).

Despite evidence of a positive association between OTL and student achievement in country level comparative studies, until now the use of OTL in studies in developing countries has been limited. Few studies of academic achievement have incorporated explicit measures of OTL, and most studies have relied on indirect ones, such as total days worked in the school or teacher subject-matter knowledge (Marshall & White 2001). In South Africa, we have little information on the effects of OTL. The numerous small-scale case studies that have been conducted have not really been concerned with the curricular content made available to students and have largely focused on pedagogy.

Application of OTL in the comparative study

For the purposes of our current study, the attained curriculum was defined as gains in students' mathematics knowledge and skills. The principal OTL research interest in the study was in the implemented curriculum, although we also measure other types of variables that could influence OTL more indirectly, such as student, teacher, and principal reports of teacher absenteeism and student, teacher, and principal reported violence in the classroom and school. The intention of our direct measure of OTL, however, was not to assess how closely the content in the implemented curriculum was to the content outlined in the official (intended) curriculum. Rather, the focus was on establishing:

- the extent to which students had the time and opportunity between the pre- and post-test to learn the content tested and the mathematics topics and sub-topics associated with the content in the test items, and
- the relationship between students' general exposure to mathematics between the pre- and post-test, and pre- to post-test gains in achievement.

The study drew on key dimensions of OTL associated with student achievement in large-scale international studies and other studies within developed countries. The measures employed to reflect OTL in the study include 'content coverage by cognitive demand', 'content emphasis' and 'content exposure.'

Content coverage by cognitive demand

Content coverage refers to the extent to which mathematics topics and sub-topics associated with the test items were covered or taught in the classes that were tested in 2009. Cognitive demand is used to refer to the cognitive or conceptual level at which the students in each of the classes were engaged with the mathematic content covered (Gamoran et al. 1997 cited in Floden 2003; Husen 1967 cited in Pelgrum 1989; Porter & Smithson 2001; Schmidt et al. 2001; Thompson & Senk 2001). In the IEA's TIMSS frameworks, this dimension relates to the notion of 'performance expectations'. The five main categories for this in the mathematics frameworks were: knowing, using routine procedures, investigating and problem-solving, mathematical reasoning, and communicating (Schmidt et al 1996: 207).

Content emphasis

Content emphasis refers to the relative amount of time each class spent on each of the various topics and sub-topics that relate to the content of each of the test items (Wang 1998).

Content exposure

Content exposure refers to the overall amount of time students spent engaged in doing mathematics (Berliner et al. 1978 cited in Floden 2003; Carroll 1963; Lee 1982; McDonnell et al. 1990 cited in Wang 1998; Porter & Smithson 2001; Rosenshine & Berliner 1978; Schmidt et al. 2001). John Carroll's (1963) model of school learning has been identified as a possible source for this dimension of OTL. Carroll formulated a learning model that introduced the importance of opportunity to learn as 'time on learning' (Wang 1998: 137).

Instrument design

The first requirement for designing an instrument for measuring content coverage and content emphasis is identifying and constructing a content framework that ensures that data collected across classes and countries is comparable (Porter & Smithson 2001; Rowan 2002). For this, our study adapted the framework constructed by Reeves (2005) for use in her study in South Africa. The basis

of the content in this framework is the South African Department of Education's National Curriculum Statement Mathematics Learning Area Assessment Standards, which outline content that should be covered in Grades 4–6 (South Africa's Intermediate Phase). The framework 'clusters' mathematics topics and sub-topics under the following five learning outcomes (main content areas):
- numbers, operations and relationships,
- patterns, functions and algebra,
- space and shape (geometry),
- measurement, and
- data handling.

The content framework is fairly fine-grained in content complexity. It outlines grade level content across three grades, thus allowing for a specific analysis of content covered at different levels rather than simply providing broad content categories. For example, for the outcome 'numbers, operations and relationships', sub-category 'whole numbers,' the framework specifies whether coverage involved 3- or 6-digit whole numbers. Rather than simply recording evidence of general coverage of 'multiplication', researchers needed to record specific information on whether students had opportunities to work with 'multiplication of 2-digit by 2-digit whole numbers' or '3-digit by 2-digit numbers', etc. Table 3.1 is an extract showing some levels of topic complexity.

Reeves' original framework was designed to assess coverage of the South African curriculum. However, the main OTL interest in our study was not in establishing whether the implemented curriculum matched the intended curriculum as reflected in the official curricula of each country. Rather, the focus was on assessing the extent to which students in classrooms in South Africa and Botswana had access during the school year prior to post-testing to the content of items in the student test instrument. Hence, Reeves' framework was edited so that only the topics and sub-topics that relate to the content in the test items were listed. To do this, the specific content areas in the tests first had to be identified so that the framework used contained only those elements associated with each of the test items (i.e. the topics listed in the framework were confined to those associated with the items on the test given to students).

Data collection

We drew a sample of 60 schools in North West Province and another 60 schools in Botswana. The sample focused on low-income schools in districts within 50 kilometers of the Botswana border: in South Africa generally in the Zeerust/Mahikeng area, and in Botswana in the area between Gaborone, Lobatse and the south of Lobatse. The next chapter details the sampling strategy used.

We administered learner questionnaires and an initial largely Grade 5 mathematics test in March 2009 to more than 3 800 Grade 6 learners in North West Province schools plus more than 1 700 Grade 6 learners in Botswana. The test comprised some items from other sources, but most were developed

TABLE 3.1 *Example of topic complexity in the framework*

Using operations appropriate to solving problems involving:
Rounding off to the nearest
10
100
1 000

Source: Compiled by authors

by mathematics education experts from South Africa, Botswana, and the United States. These items were based on the curriculum used in South African and Botswana schools. Many of the test items had been used in our 2007 pilot study in Gauteng and the test as a whole was tried in several South African Grade 6 classrooms in 2008. In addition, we investigated teacher background and content and pedagogical content knowledge in questionnaires that we successfully administered to 120 Grade 6 teachers teaching mathematics in 126 Grade 6 classrooms in the two countries. We would have liked to have been able to test multiple Grade 6 mathematics teachers in most schools in order to test for within-school variation in teaching quality, but this proved to be difficult, since few schools in either country had more than one teacher teaching mathematics in Grade 6.

We videotaped almost all the teachers in our two samples teaching at least one mathematics lesson (some did not want to be videotaped), and about half the teachers were videotaped twice. We completed two detailed analyses of several of the best student notebooks in each class during the year to determine the number of mathematics lessons taught and the content of those lessons. We also administered a principal questionnaire.

Five instruments were prepared, namely:
- a learner questionnaire and test,
- a teacher questionnaire and test,
- a principal questionnaire,
- an OTL instrument to record notebook contents, and
- a video analysis instrument.

The learner questionnaire included questions pertaining to biographical, language, family education and socio-economic status and school violence. The teacher questionnaire had two components: a general component and mathematical knowledge component. The general section included biographical, socio-economic status, education and training, home language, curriculum coverage, supervision, school violence and absenteeism questions. The knowledge component required teachers to diagnose common errors made by children in primary mathematics.

We only surveyed teachers' mathematics knowledge at the grade level taught and somewhat above the 6th grade level. That test was developed by the same mathematics education experts in South Africa, Botswana, and the United States who developed the learner instrument. The OTL instrument has already been described. The principal questionnaire included questions linked to those asked of teachers about language, curriculum coverage, school violence, absenteeism and supervision.

Since we planned to administer the learner test initially in the beginning of the Grade 6 academic year, the test contained mostly Grade 5 level questions and some Grade 6 level questions, all based on the national curriculum. The initial learner test was applied in late March 2009 (a form needed to be signed by each participating child's parent before the test could be administered and districts, school governing bodies, principals and teachers needed to be informed and their consent gained). Learners were given the chance of taking the learner questionnaire/test in the language they spoke at home. All learners took the test either in English (or Afrikaans in South Africa, whichever was the language used in the school to teach mathematics). In retrospect, this is logical, since mathematics lessons are taught in those two languages, depending on the school. We collected data on the learners' language spoken at home (a very high percentage spoke Setswana) and we were able to analyse whether home language is correlated with test performance, once parents' education levels and other student characteristics are accounted for.

The teacher and principal questionnaires, the first videotaping, and the first round of notebook analysis using the OTL instrument were completed in late June and early July, 2009. The process was aided by the sharing of experiences from videotaping and administering similar teacher questionnaires in other countries and in the Gauteng pilot study completed in 2007 (Carnoy et al. 2007, 2008) during a short training period in February 2009.This process engaged participants from UB, the HSRC and UKZN.[3]

The same test (with content variation in some questions and changes in the position of a number of questions) was administered in all the sample schools in late October and early November 2009, very near the end of the academic year. This was largely successful. Only two classrooms of the initial 128 were not willing to repeat the test. We also repeated videotaping and the OTL analysis using learner notebooks. Several teachers who had been videotaped earlier refused to be videotaped again, and several teachers would not allow second round OTL analysis. For the latter, we were able to impute data based on first round OTL results.

OTL data collection

The measurement of OTL is fairly complex and it is worth providing greater detail on the procedure used. The most accurate approach to collecting data on content coverage and emphasis is to track topics that are dealt with during the year through direct classroom observation. Obviously, this is not practical for a large-scale study. Studies such as TIMSS usually survey teachers and/or students asking them whether particular topics were taught before the test date and how much time they spent on the topics. However, reliance on teacher or student judgement could reflect socially desirable responses rather than the actual curriculum made available to students (McDonnell 1995). In the South African context, self-reported data are not generally considered reliable (Taylor & Vinjevold 1999), and we have no real knowledge of levels of agreement between teachers' and researchers' reports of information on the content of instruction (Reeves & Muller 2005). For these reasons, we decided to use information gathered from an examination of work in a sample of three student workbooks or work files in each of the classes tested. We tended to focus on the 'best' students' notebooks in order to obtain a more accurate set of data on content coverage in each class. Since we were concerned with measuring how often the teachers taught and what was covered in the classes, we only needed to look at a limited sample of student notebooks in each class – preferably the notebooks of students who were likely to be absent infrequently – and to prepare complete versions of what the teachers asked students to write in their books.

The adapted version of Reeves' (Reeves 2005) framework formed the basis for the OTL instrument used to review students' mathematics workbooks. The first section of the instrument was designed to capture content coverage and emphasis. Researchers used the framework to simply indicate whether or not there was evidence that a topic or sub-topic had been covered (for content coverage), and then to record the estimated amount of time actually devoted to a topic or sub-topic in terms of the number of lesson periods (to gauge the relative emphasis given to a topic or sub-topic). This data allowed us to estimate how many lessons each class spent on topics related to each of the test items. Data collection for this second dimension of the OTL construct, content emphasis, involved using dates of daily work done in students' workbooks to estimate the number of mathematics lessons that were spent on each of the topics or sub-topics listed in the content framework. This process was challenging mainly because classes sometimes covered a number of topics in one lesson. Nevertheless, researchers tried to provide the best estimates they could. The instrument also provided for estimates of 'less than one lesson'.

---

3   The University of KwaZulu-Natal is conducting an independently funded parallel study in that province using an identical methodology.

Detailed data on content coverage and content emphasis was collected only on topics and sub-topics associated with the content of the test items and listed on the content framework on the OTL instrument. A limitation of using the framework was that the method excluded topics covered that are not included on the framework. Details of mathematics topics covered in class that were not related to the test content were not collected in content coverage or emphasis. Our main interest here was in the overlap between content taught and content tested.

The measure of one OTL dimension, content exposure – the count of the number of daily lessons in students' workbooks – was used to provide an indication of the overall time students spent engaged in 'doing mathematics' in class as opposed to the amount of time officially allocated in policy documents or in school timetables for mathematics instruction and incorporated content covered but not tested. Although the length of the South African and Botswana academic school years is comparable to that of other countries, evidence is that considerable teaching time is lost during the year in many schools, for example, through a late start to the school day, and non-instructional activities, such as staff meetings and staff training, taking place during official teaching time (Taylor & Vinjevold 1999; Fleisch 1999; Reeves 2001; Taylor 2001). Officially allocated teaching time is thus not considered a reliable measure of the total amount of time devoted to mathematics instruction.

For content exposure, researchers counted the dates of daily class and/or homework in students' workbooks to estimate the total number of mathematics lessons in which each class had done written class and/or homework in their workbooks. This 'time on task' or 'engaged time' measure thus incorporated overall time spent on doing mathematics, and included time spent on topics or sub-topics not covered in the OTL instrument's content framework even though they were not 'tested.'

As far as the variable cognitive demand is concerned, previous work by Reeves (2005) had shown that student workbooks could not be used to reliably establish the cognitive levels at which various topics of sub-topics are covered. This was mainly because copies of the actual worksheets or textbook material with the problems/exercises/questions used are not generally available in students' workbooks. The method for level of cognitive demand for OTL was to use the coding derived from Stein et al.'s (2000) rubric for classifying higher and lower cognitive demand from the videos of teachers' lessons. As shown previously, classifications include Memorisation, Procedures without connections, Procedures with connections, and Doing mathematics .

Table 3.2 on page 50 provides a summary of the OTL dimensions, variables, data sources, time of data collection, and the data collection instruments.

Coding and cleaning the data

Coding and cleaning the test and questionnaire data was completed in Botswana and South Africa by September 2010. The videotapes were analysed by a group of researchers in Botswana, South Africa and the U.S. Similarly, researchers in all three countries analysed learner and teacher questionnaire results and the OTL instruments.

Data collection issues

In general, the study was successful in collecting the data it set out to collect, and was able to do so in a reasonably short period of time. The data collection was well organised and generally, the HSRC, UB and the data collectors had complete cooperation from principals and teachers. Teachers and principals were forthcoming, and were generally willing to take the time to fill in the questionnaires and tests. The second round of videotaping and OTL data collection was slightly more problematic

TABLE 3.2 *South Africa and Botswana: OTL dimensions, variables, data sources, time of data collection and data collection instruments*

OTL dimension	Variable	Measure	Data source	Time of data collection	Instrument
Content coverage by cognitive demand	Content coverage	Number of mathematics topics/subtopics associated with the test items covered	Randomly selected samples of three students' mathematics workbooks (class work and/or homework books) from each class tested	Twice during the school year: once in June/July 2009 and once in October/November 2009	OTL instrument: Review of mathematics workbooks
	Cognitive demand	A rating based a point scale of five levels of cognitive demand	The videos of two mathematics lessons of each class tested		Rubric from Stein et al.'s (2000) classification of higher and lower cognitive demand
Content exposure		Number of mathematics lessons where students in the class did written class and/or homework in their workbooks	Random sample of three students' mathematics workbooks (class work and/or homework books) from each class tested (using dates in workbooks and/or the amount of written exercises/work each day)		OTL instrument: Review of mathematics workbooks
Content emphasis		Estimated number of lessons spent on each of the topic/subtopic/ content areas that relate to the content of each of the item tests			OTL instrument: Review of mathematics workbooks

Source: Compiled by authors

than the first, and in some cases, data collectors had to return to the school several times in order to find the relevant teacher and do the data collection.

Ultimately, we were able to match – in the North West Province sample – almost 3 500 students of the 3 745 students who took the second round of the test in late October/early November with the 3 868 students who took the first round of the test in late March, for a matching rate of 90 per cent. In Botswana, the matching rate was even higher, at 93 per cent, with a final match of 1 666 students.

We had some issues with data collection that are described in more detail in the chapters that follow. The second test application in North West Province (described in Chapter 4) was particularly problematic as in several classrooms it was apparent that teachers helped the students with at least some of the questions. We also had to revisit schools in both Botswana and North West to capture teacher and principal questionnaires that data collectors had missed in July. In some North West Province schools, OTL data were not collected in the second round (November), so second round data were imputed for those schools (see Chapter 8), and in a number of classrooms in both country samples, data collectors were not able to get videotaped lessons in the first round in July (in North West Province, one camera was not recording properly), and in other classrooms in the second round (in November). In theory, we should have made 252 videotapes (two lessons per teacher), but only collected 183 overall (discussed in Chapter 7). A final, more generic problem, was that, particularly in Botswana, several teachers left for other schools during the year and were replaced by other teachers in the sampled classrooms. We tested whether these classrooms had smaller learner gains, but found no significant difference.

Despite these problems, the process of collecting such a large amount of data achieved its goals and the process also provided important lessons for future research: with proper planning and training, it is possible to gather great quantities of useful data about students, teachers, and schools in a relatively short period of time. Timing of the data collection is crucial, and lead-time for the provincial governments and the schools is always longer than expected. Further, despite considerable communication with each school in the sample, several were not prepared for the researchers when they arrived. Principals were sometimes absent, and other principals had not discussed the study with their teachers. Such lack of communication between principals and teachers served as one piece of information about conditions in the school. But even where teachers had been informed, and the purpose discussed with them beforehand, considerable reassurance was needed that the research or its results would not be used against them. Finally, a key lesson is that supervision of data collectors is essential, and, unfortunately, teachers should not be responsible for supervising learner testing – a data collector must be present during test taking. Learners and teachers also need to be urged to take the test seriously and to try to answer all items.

CHAPTER 4

The school profile in the Botswana and North West samples

In this and the next chapter, we focus on three ways of looking at the school context. First we compare the broader national socio-economic and educational contexts of the schools in Botswana and South Africa. Next, we provide a picture of the location and specific contexts of the schools we sampled in North West Province and in South East Botswana, Finally, we elaborate a more detailed understanding of possible differences in the schools' institutional settings by analysing the principal questionnaires we collected there. These supply the underlying background for our estimates of student mathematics achievement differences on the two sides of the border and our estimates of the relation between teacher skills and student learning.

Whereas national-level economic and educational data is readily accessible in South Africa, this is not the case for Botswana. For this reason, and in order to ensure comparability of national socio-economic and educational information, we draw on United Nations Development Programme (UNDP) and World Bank. Both draw on UNESCO Institute of Statistics data provided to it by national governments.

National socio-economic and educational contexts

Botswana is a far less populous country than South Africa. With a population of only 2 million, little comparison seems possible with a country that is 50 million strong. Yet, there are strong socio-economic similarities and differences that are manifested and embedded in the local school contexts. With a bigger and more diversified economy than Botswana's, and with strong government institutions and civil society, South Africa is often viewed as the economic powerhouse of and gateway to Africa. And yet, as shown in Table 4.1, Botswana has a higher GDP per capita than South Africa and saw a phenomenal average of 8.2 per cent economic growth rate over three decades after achieving independence in 1966 (for the most recent period since South Africa's democratisation, see Figure 4.1). Unlike South Africa, whose economic development slowed significantly in the 1980s, Botswana is widely acknowledged as a 'star performer,' 'miracle' and a 'developmental state' in the African context.

Botswana's sustained growth was built on the discovery of diamonds in 1967, establishment of a joint government-mining house partnership in which the government of Botswana and de Beers each had a 50 per cent share in the industry, commitment to regular free and fair elections since 1966 and an approach to development within a framework of national unity. Recent strikes in health and education as well as challenges to the national leadership portend a more conflictual future akin to the history of South Africa (Good 2009; Manatsha & Maharjan 2009).

TABLE 4.1 *Botswana and South Africa: Income inequality comparisons*

	Botswana	South Africa
GDP per capita (2008 PPP$)	13 204	9 812
Income Gini coefficient	61.0	57.8

Source: Compiled from the 2010 UNDP Human Development Report, Table 1: The Human Development Index and its Components.[1]

FIGURE 4.1 *Botswana and South Africa: Gross domestic product per capita, 1995–2009*

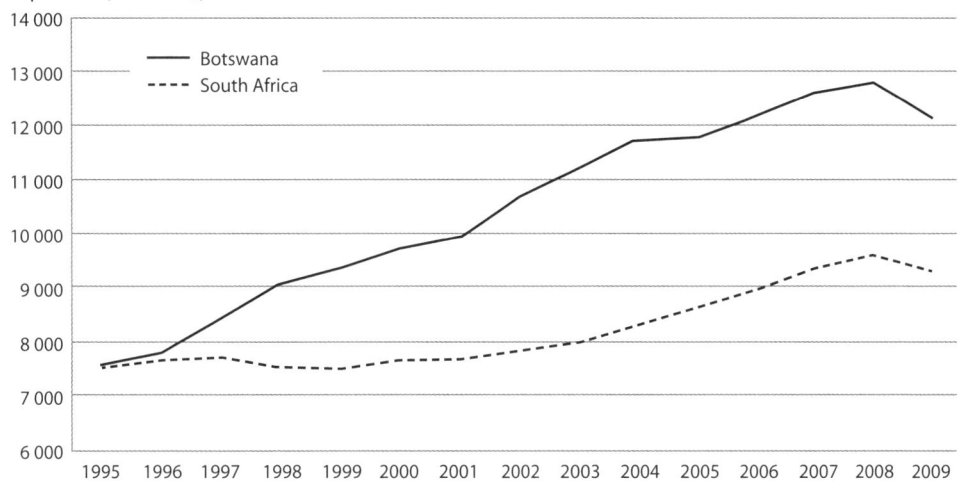

Source: Compiled from the World Bank, World Development Indicators database.[2]

Despite these differences, Botswana and South Africa share the uncommon honour of being middle-income countries in a continent consisting largely of low-income countries. They also shares jobless growth, high rates of inequality and poverty, high youth unemployment and are among the countries with the highest incidence of HIV/AIDS in the world.

Do differences in living standards, income inequality, quality of life, and the amount of resources these two countries devote to education cast any broader light on the subject of our enquiry – namely, achievement differences between Botswana and South African learners? How one answers this question depends on what one measures and how one measures it.

The data in Table 4.2, supplemented with more detailed education indicators from the World Bank, provide some insight into the relative inequalities between Botswana and South Africa. All these data rely on United Nations statistics provided by national governments. Although Botswana's income distribution is somewhat more unequal than in South Africa, with a Gini coefficient of 61 compared to

---

1 Table 1 from the 2010 UNDP Human Development Report is available at http://hdr.undp.org/en/media/HDR_2010_EN_Table1_reprint.pdf
2 The World Development Indicators database is available at http://data.worldbank.org/data-catalog/world-development-indicators. The data in Figure 4.1 are available at http://data.worldbank.org/topic/education

South Africa's 57.8 (both have among the most unequal income distributions in the world),[3] suggesting even bigger gaps between the rich and poor in Botswana than in South Africa, Botswana ranks higher on the United Nations' HDI. Inspired by the work of Amartya Sen, which views income per capita and growth as inadequate measures of human development, the UNDP has developed a set of indices that measure human development, inequality, poverty and women's empowerment.[4] As shown in Table 4.2, the UNDP's HDI places both Botswana and South Africa at the medium level as opposed to the very high, high or low index.

Botswana ranks 98th and South Africa 110th in the human development rankings. This is because Botswana has a higher life expectancy at birth than South Africa, its children spend more years in school, there is higher income per capita than in South Africa, and the peoples of Botswana live in a more secure society. Official unemployment rates are generally underestimates, and the estimates here are conservative. However, the UNDP reports Botswana's unemployment rate at 17 per cent. This is high, but lower than South Africa's 22.6 per cent. This figure is substantially higher among younger age cohorts. In 2008, unemployment in South Africa, for example, stood at 46.6 per cent among 15 to 24 year olds and 26.2 per cent among 24 to 35 year olds (National Planning Commission, NPC 2011: Table 1.1). Expressed differently, despite being more unequal than South Africa, Botswana has somewhat greater wellbeing and more highly developed human capabilities than South Africa. To some extent, socio-economic context might be reflected in the resources the two countries devote to education. Both Botswana and South Africa's governments spend heavily on education, and since they are middle-income economies, they spend more per pupil in school than most African countries. However, as evidenced in Table 4.3, their patterns of spending are quite different. Botswana tends to spend a higher fraction of its government budget on secondary and especially higher education, while South Africa spends more on primary education.

TABLE 4.2 *Botswana and South Africa: Human Development Index and its components*

Country	HDI	Life expectancy at birth	Mean years of schooling	Expected years of schooling	Gender inequality Index	Net savings rate	Non-income HDI value
Botswana	0.633	55.5	8.9	12.4	0.663	37.2	0.613
South Africa	0.597	52.0	8.2	13.4	0.635	−3.5	0.581

Source: Compiled from the 2010 UNDP Human Development Report, Table 1: The Human Development Index and its components.[5]

---

3   One of the best-known indicators of economic inequality is the Gini coefficient. A Gini coefficient is a number between 0 and 1 measuring national income inequality where 0 corresponds to perfect equality (where everyone has the same income) and 1 corresponds to perfect inequality (where one person has all the income and the rest have none). We have multiplied the Gini index by 100 in Table 4.1.

4   Over the years the Human Development Report has introduced new measures to evaluate progress in reducing poverty and empowering women. But lack of reliable data has been a major constraint. The Human Development Index measures a long and healthy life, access to knowledge and a decent standard of living. The Index is available at http://hdr.undp.org/en/statistics/indices/

5   Table 1 from the 2010 UNDP Human Development Report is available at http://hdr.undp.org/en/media/HDR_2010_EN_Table1_reprint.pdf

TABLE 4.3 Botswana and South Africa: Public spending on education as a percentage of total government spending and proportion of government spending on education by level of education, 2003–2009

	2003	2005	2007	2009
Botswana				
Education (% of TGS)	–	21.5	21.0	16.2
Primary (% of GSE)	–	30.0	27.5	17.8
Secondary (% of GSE)	–	39.6	44.2	32.7
Higher (% of GSE)	–	27.9	27.5	41.5
South Africa				
Education (% of TGS)	19.3	18.6	18.4	17.9
Primary (% of GSE)	41.7	42.9	41.5	41.1
Secondary (% of GSE)	35.2	32.8	32.8	31.4
Higher (% of GSE)	14.4	15.6	13.4	13.0

Source: Compiled from the Unesco Institute of Statistics database.[6]

Abbreviations: TGS, total government spending; GSE, government spending on education.

Even so, because Botswana's public spending is a higher fraction of GDP than is South Africa's (Botswana has been spending about 8 per cent of GDP on education in recent years, and South Africa, about 5 to 5.4 per cent) and Botswana's GDP per capita is higher, Botswana ends up spending more per pupil in primary education and much more on those in secondary education (Table 4.4).[7] This has helped Botswana achieve somewhat better conditions in schools than those in South Africa. However, Botswana's primary school spending advantage seems to be disappearing as expenditure on primary school pupils has been falling. If we take into account that private spending per pupil on primary schooling is certainly greater in South Africa than in Botswana because of the existence of fee-paying public schools in South Africa, the total spending per pupil on primary education could now be higher in South Africa than in Botswana.

Primary school pupil-teacher ratios are smaller in Botswana (an average of 26 students versus 31 in South Africa) and the proportion of certified teachers in primary schools is higher in Botswana (97 versus 87 per cent in South Africa in 2009). Table 4.4 also shows that Botswana invests more per pupil than South Africa in secondary education, even accounting for fee-paying public schools. Although we have not analysed secondary education differences, this may contribute to a higher quality of secondary graduates in Botswana, hence higher quality candidates for teacher education, hence higher quality new teachers.

---

6 The Unesco Institute of Statistics database is available at www.uis.unesco.org/Education/Pages/education-finance.aspx
7 Botswana spends a very high amount per university student, about PPP$36 000 in 2005, and PPP$32 000 in 2007. Although we do not have comparable figures for South Africa, this is probably about ten times what South Africa spends per university student.

TABLE 4.4 *Botswana and South Africa: Public spending per pupil in primary and secondary education, 2003–2009*

	2003[a]	2005	2007	2009[b]
Botswana				
Public spending per primary pupil as % GDP/capita	16	16	12	12
Public spending per secondary pupil as % GDP per capita	40	40	38	38
Public spending per primary pupil (2005 PPP$)	1 793	1 884	1 512	1 458
Public spending per secondary pupil (2005 PPP$)	4 483	4 709	4 790	4 619
South Africa				
Public spending per primary pupil as % GDP/capita	13	14	14	14
Public spending per secondary pupil as % GDP per capita	19	17	17	16
Public spending per primary pupil (2005 PPP$)	1 039	1 204	1 311	1 345
Public spending per secondary pupil (2005 PPP$)	1 519	1 461	1 592	1 537

Source: Compiled from the World Bank, World Development Indicators database.[8]

[a] For Botswana, spending as % of GDP per capita assumed equal to 2005.
[b] For Botswana, spending as % of GDP per capita assumed equal to 2007.

In summary, Botswana has a higher income per capita than South Africa, but an even more unequal income distribution. It has traditionally put a lower fraction of its resources into primary education, but having more resources, has spent more per pupil in primary schools, and has had somewhat better conditions in primary schools in terms of teacher pupil ratios and the proportion of certified teachers. Primary education spending differences seem to have been declining between the two countries in the past decade.

Location and profile of schools in the South East Botswana and North West Province samples

The schools in our sample are located along the border of South East Botswana and North West Province, where the shaded area of the map at Figure 4.2, on the South African side, shows the location of the former Bantustan, Bophuthatswana. Schools were selected from the northern shaded stretch in South Africa and from across the border in Botswana.

The sampled schools in Botswana are spread across four districts: Gaborone, South East, Southern and Kgatleng districts, shown in the map. The schools are located close to the capital city of Gaborone and the town of Lobatse, and are within a radius of about 80 kilometers. Both Gaborone and Lobatse are near the border posts of Tlokweng and Mahikeng. The four districts include government, government-aided, and private primary schools. These schools are located in rural, semi-urban and urban centres.

---

8 The World Development Indicators database is available at http://data.worldbank.org/data-catalog/world-development-indicators. The data in Table 4.4 are available at http://data.worldbank.org/topic/education

FIGURE 4.2 *Border Area: Botswana-South Africa including boundaries of former Bophuthatswana*

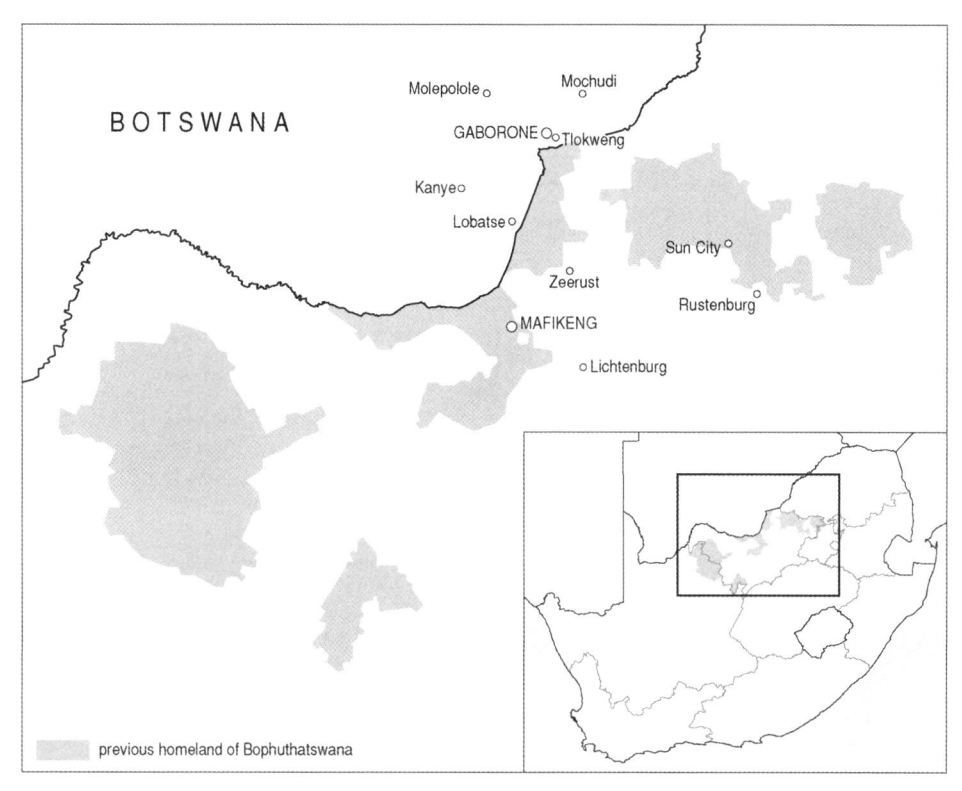

Source: Map created by authors from HSRC GIS data. Old SA provincial boundaries and Homeland (Bophuthatswana) boundaries based on the 1991 Census (StatsSA); Botswana Towns from PC Atlas; North West Province Towns from the 2003 HSRC GIS SA Towns shapefiles.

Note: The map only shows the part of the North West Province involved in the natural experiment.

A sampling frame from the Ministry of Education in Botswana depicts all these primary schools in the study area, constituting a total population size of 8 118 Standard 6 pupils in all the primary schools with their respective class stream within a school. Private schools and Standard 6 classes with enrolments of less than 20 were excluded from the sample. The exclusion criteria enables the elimination of disparities in the distribution of resources in the form of teacher-student ratios, facilities, computing equipment and other inputs which may be superior in private schools or classrooms with unusually small enrolments. Nineteen schools were therefore excluded. A population of 107 schools with enrolment of 6 835

TABLE 4.5 *Botswana: Distribution of sampled schools, by location and district, 2009*

Districts					
Location	South East	Kgatleng	Southern	Gaborone	Lobatse
Rural	2	7	4		
Semi-urban	7	8			
Urban				25	5
Total	9	15	4	25	5

Source: Compiled by authors from Botswana School Survey, 2009

FIGURE 4.3 *Political map of Botswana showing districts*

Source: Redrawn from Compare Infobase Limited, 2007.

Standard 6 pupils constituted the sampling base. Sixty schools were sampled. Of these 60 schools, 58 schools agreed to participate in the study. Table 4.5 shows the distribution of sampled schools, by location and district, 2009. Figure 4.3 is a political map of Botswana showing the districts.

The sampling frame available allowed for stratification by location and district. Due to the moderate number of schools involved, a simple random sample without replacement was drawn from each of the strata cells. The objective of this strategy was two pronged in that it randomly selected the school, hence allowing for generalisation of results on Standard 6 pupils amongst the government and government-aided schools in the concerned districts, and allowed for computation of selection probabilities. Thus a stratified simple random sampling method was used with proportional allocation weighted by the number of schools in both the district and location.

Our North West Province sample schools are spread across two municipalities in North West Province, namely Mahikeng and Zeerust. Many schools in the stretch between Mahikeng and Zeerust and to the north of Zeerust lie in what was the former Bantustan, Bophuthatswana. These are the more rural and impoverished areas in the province. Bophuthatswana was administered from the then-Mafikeng until

1966. It became the capital of the Bantustan, and is now the capital of the North West Province. Zeerust is an enclave of conservative Afrikaner commercial agriculture.

As in the Botswana sample, the district municipalities of Mahikeng and Zeerust cut across urban and rural neighbourhoods and schools and include schools in both middle-income and poor schools.

In 2009, when the study was conducted, North West Province had a small population of some 3.5 million out of South Africa's total population of almost 49 million. The vast majority of those living in North West Province are African, accounting for over three million, or 91.5 per cent of the population, with the minority populations making up less than half a million – 6.7 per cent whites, 1.6 per cent coloureds and 0.3 per cent Asians.

All provinces that include former Bantustans and rural populations within their borders are considered poorer than the more urban provinces. But even though North West comprises a former Bantustan within its borders, it was not as poor as other provinces with similar histories. Within the province, the former Bantustan areas are poorer than those that were not in the Bantustan.

Ninety-eight per cent of schools in North West Province are public schools.[9] The past 15 years have also seen increased enrolments nationally at the upper (wealthier students) and lower (poorer students) ends of the schooling system. Teachers comprised both state-employed and school governing body-employed educators. For the majority of schools in our sample, where schools could not afford to pay for additional teachers, class sizes were accordingly larger than the average. This contrasted sharply with the average learner-educator ratio of 15:1 in private schools in North West.

North West Province has 1 201 schools with Grade 6 classes. Twenty per cent of these schools are in urban areas, 51 per cent in census-designated Tribal Areas and 29 per cent in rural areas. The information provided by the South African Department of Education included the learner population in these schools, 66 134 Grade 6 learners, and the number of classes by school. The field 'Classes by Grade' had a considerable number of missing records.

In South Africa, all schools are demarcated according to socio-economic criteria on a scale from 1 to 5, where 1 constitutes extremely poor schools and 5 the most affluent and well-resourced schools. This type of demarcation of schools was excluded as criteria from the sampling methodology because it is not applied in the Botswana Ministry of Education. All public schools with Grade 6 learners were included, irrespective of class size or number of classes (stream). North West Province is a fairly large province and approximately one-third of Grade 6 schools are small schools with a class size below 20 learners. Because these schools encompass a large proportion of Grade 6 schools and learners, we included them in the sample.

A two-level stratified random sampling methodology was applied to public schools with Grade 6 learners. Schools were sampled in the Mahikeng and Ramotshere Moiloa local municipalities, which border Botswana and encompass two of the major urban centres in the province, Mahikeng and Zeerust. A total of 155 schools with a learner population of 9 157 constituted the sampling frame, with 12 per cent of schools urban, 72 per cent Tribal Area and 16 per cent Rural Formal (Table 4.6). The categories Tribal Area and Rural Formal were combined into one area, Rural.

---

9 In 2009, North West had a total school learner enrolment of 777 285. Ninety-eight per cent of these were in public schools. Out of a total of 1 768 schools, 52 were private and the remaining 1 716 were public schools. A total of 26 697 (or 96 per cent) of North West's teachers taught in public schools, while 935 (or 4 per cent) were teaching in private schools.

TABLE 4.6 *Distribution of schools by geography in the Mahikeng and Ramotshere Moiloa local municipalities, 2009*

Geography	Schools	%	Learners	%
Rural Formal	25	16	566	6
Tribal Area	111	72	6 739	74
Urban Formal	19	12	1 852	20
Total	155	100	9 157	100

Source: Municipal data from the HSRC GIS 2005 Municipal Boundaries; schools from the Education Management Information Systems 2010 Public Ordinary Schools Masterlist (includes GIS coordinates).

The Mahikeng and Ramotshere Moiloa local municipalities were not individually sampled but were combined into one stratum. All urban schools in the sampling frame were retained, constituting 20 per cent of the sample. A simple random sample, without replacements, was drawn from the remaining schools, all rural, to make up the remaining 80 per cent of the sample.

Our sample was drawn to include schools with characteristics of the majority of schools in South Africa whilst maintaining comparability with Botswana. In order to maintain a level of comparability between North West and Botswana schools in terms of location or geography, the urban or town schools in the sampling frame were retained, based on our understanding that between 30 per cent and 40 per cent of the schools in the South East education districts of Botswana were in urban towns.

Conclusion

This chapter has considered and compared the national socio-economic and educational contexts of the schools sampled for the study. It shows that whereas Botswana has higher income per capita than South Africa, and higher levels of inequality, it nonetheless ranks higher on human development indices. Its spending on education is higher overall than in South Africa but spending on primary education in recent years has evened out and is more comparable.

Our sample of schools was selected from a strip along the border on the south-east of Botswana and north-west of South Africa. The sample was selected to ensure comparability of urban and rural as well as within-country representation. On the South African side, many of the schools were rural, but many were also in or near the towns of Mahikeng and Zeerust. This is an area with a rich political and educational history and includes areas that once were reserve or Bantustan territory. As such, even though North West Province has recently benefited from the wealth of platinum mines further away towards Rustenburg, this region and its schools still carry the marks of household poverty and labour migration that began in the late nineteenth century and gained momentum during the apartheid period in the latter half of the twentieth century. On the Botswana side of the border, about one-fourth were rural, one-fourth semi-urban, and one-half in and around Gaborone and Lobatse. This region, too, has benefited indirectly from Botswana's mineral wealth. Yet, as in North West Province, there is much poverty in the south-east of Botswana. In both Botswana and South Africa a stratified simple two-level random sampling method was used.

In the next chapter we consider the way principals in Botswana and South Africa responded to our questions and the insight this provides into school leadership – another critical feature shaping the context of teaching and learning.

CHAPTER 5

The school context: Characteristics of principals and instructional leadership

We can get a closer look at the school context of our study, particularly how school conditions and school leadership in our two school samples on either side of the border compare, through our principal questionnaires. We asked principals a series of questions about their profiles. We also asked them to tell us what their main tasks were in running their schools and how they viewed the main problems of their schools. We found a number of differences in profiles and differences in the way the principals reported using their time. We also got a sense that principals (and teachers) in Botswana were more willing to be realistic about some the problems their schools face. We think that this is a revealing difference in the instructional context of the two countries.

Comparing principals' profiles

Principals in the North West Province and Botswana samples were similar in age, with around half of each sample over 50 years old and about 90 per cent over 40. However, the gender composition differed dramatically between the samples. In North West Province, more than half of the principals in the sample were male (57 per cent), while nearly three-quarters (74 per cent) of the principals in Botswana's schools were female.

A comparison of educational attainment between the two groups of principals is more difficult to make due to a misinterpretation of the question in Botswana, and to differing educational systems. However, the data do suggest that principals in the North West Province had attained higher levels of education: 40 per cent of the North West principals in the sample reported having obtained an honours (4-year) degree, a masters degree, or higher, and another 27 per cent of the principals had achieved at least a three-year degree or diploma. Of the North West principals who had not completed a college degree, 15 per cent had some college level training, while 8 per cent reported having only attained a primary school level of official education. In contrast, only 3.5 per cent of principals in Botswana had obtained an honours degree or higher, and about 50 per cent of the principals in Botswana had not progressed past a senior secondary level education or the equivalent. Almost 60 per cent of the principals in Botswana did not have more than a post-O-level teaching degree (three years of teacher training college after the O-level secondary certificate), which was the standard teaching degree before the early 1990s.

As principals often spend many years teaching before they become principals, the questionnaire asked about both years of experience as a principal and years of teaching experience prior to becoming a principal. As Figures 5.1a and 5.1b show, the number of years of experience of the principals was

FIGURE 5.1a *North West Province: Length of tenure as principal, 2009*

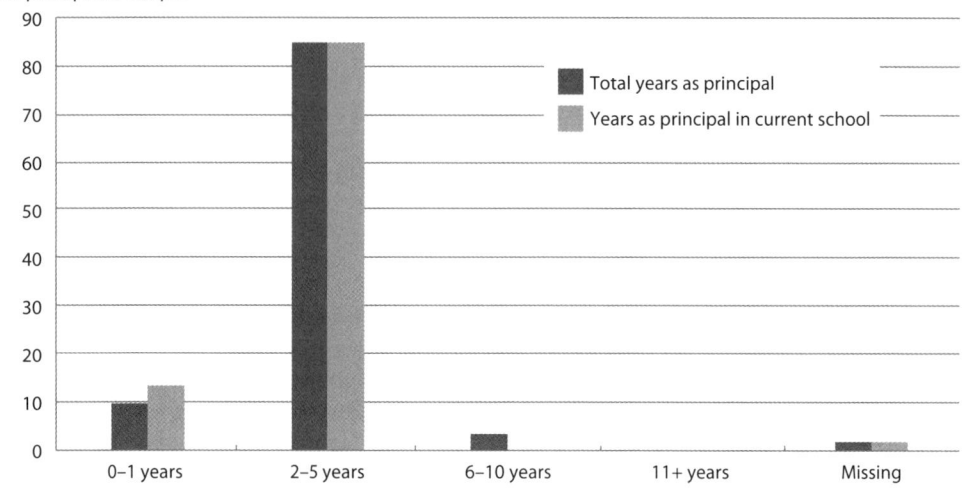

% of principals in sample

[Bar chart showing Total years as principal and Years as principal in current school:
- 0–1 years: ~10%, ~13%
- 2–5 years: ~85%, ~85%
- 6–10 years: ~3%, 0%
- 11+ years: 0%, 0%
- Missing: ~2%, ~2%]

Source: North West Province School Sample, 2009.

FIGURE 5.1b *Botswana: Length of tenure as principal, 2009*

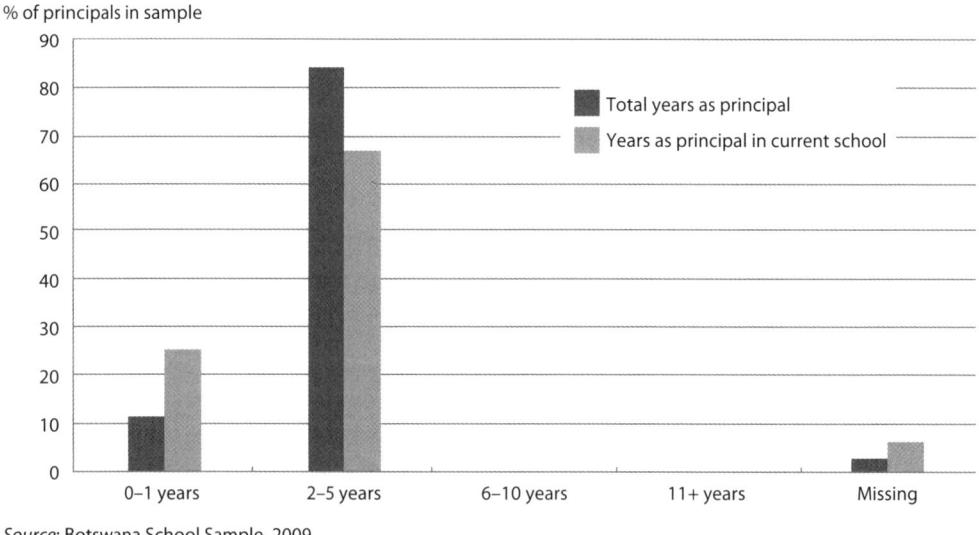

% of principals in sample

[Bar chart showing Total years as principal and Years as principal in current school:
- 0–1 years: ~12%, ~25%
- 2–5 years: ~84%, ~67%
- 6–10 years: 0%, 0%
- 11+ years: 0%, 0%
- Missing: ~3%, ~6%]

Source: Botswana School Sample, 2009.

strikingly similar across the two samples, and suggests that most principals are relatively new to their position, with about 95 per cent of principals in each sample having been a principal for less than five years. In Botswana, no principals had more than 5 years of experience, while 3 per cent of North West Province principals had between 6 and 10 years of experience.

Botswana principals appear to move between schools more often. While a fairly similar proportion on each side of the border had been principal for one year or less (10 per cent in North West and 13 per cent in Botswana), 13 per cent of North West principals and 25 per cent of Botswana principals had been at their current school for a year or less. Only 3 per cent of North West Province principals were in their second or higher post, while this was at least the second post for nearly 13 per cent of principals in Botswana.

Although the number of years of experience as a principal is similar in the two samples, the years of teaching experience of principals prior to becoming a principal differs. Becoming a principal in Botswana generally seems to be a later career move than in South Africa. In the North West Province, while the overall average for years of teaching experience was 14.6, there was a great deal of variance in the principals' reported number of years of teaching experience. The most commonly reported level of teaching experience was between 6 and 10 years (32 per cent), while 20 per cent had 21 or more years of experience, 15 per cent had between 16 and 20 years and 22 per cent had taught for between 11 and 15 years before becoming a principal. In Botswana, the trajectory from teacher to principal seems have less variance: nearly 60 per cent of principals had 16 or more years of teaching experience before becoming a principal, and only 10 per cent had 10 or fewer years of teaching experience before taking the job.

Overall, both groups of principals are older and relatively new to both the role of principal and to being principal at their current school. It appears that principals in Botswana are more likely to be female and to have lower level qualifications but more years of teaching experience than their counterparts in North West Province. The Botswana principals also appear to move from school to school more often.

What are the key characteristics of the schools in which these principals work?

We now explore some of the key characteristics of the schools in which these principals work.

Teaching and learning

The vast majority of principals in both country samples reported that English was the main language of instruction in their school (83 per cent in North West and 90 per cent in Botswana). In North West Province, 8 per cent of teachers reported using Afrikaans as the primary language of instruction in mathematics and 5 per cent said teachers taught mainly in Setswana. In Botswana, none of the schools used Afrikaans as a medium of instruction, 3 per cent used Setswana and 7 per cent used a mix of Setswana and English.

In both countries, principals were fairly realistic about the lack of curriculum coverage. We measure curriculum coverage in Chapter 7 and find it to be less complete than the principals were willing to admit, particularly in North West Province. Most North West principals felt the mathematics curriculum was covered only partially (68 per cent) or not at all (3 per cent). Only 25 per cent thought it was completely covered by the end of the school year. According to the Botswana principals, 76 per cent of the schools completed the mathematics curriculum partially and 3 per cent, not at all. Only 17 per cent of teachers were thought to have completed the mathematics curriculum over the academic year. In terms of in-school support and monitoring teachers, more than 40 per cent of the North West principals reported they either rarely (27 per cent) or never (15 per cent) observed the mathematics lessons of their teachers, while nearly 37 per cent said they did so sometimes and 20 per cent said they observed lessons often. Botswana principals reported nearly the reverse, with over 90 per cent of principals reporting they either often (43 per cent) or sometimes (48 per cent) observed mathematics lessons, with only 5 per cent reporting they either only rarely or never did.[1]

In terms of district or provincial support, all of the principals in both samples reported a mathematics curriculum specialist had visited their schools at least once. In the North West Province, most (63 per cent) said they had received one visit, while 25 per cent said they were visited two or three times in the past year and 7 per cent had been visited four or five times. In Botswana, 88 per cent had been visited once, and 9 per cent had been visited twice – none reported having more than two visits. Since the inspectorate system seems to be more functionally operative in Botswana, it is interesting that North West principals were likely to report a greater number of visits than in Botswana. We have no way of checking these statements, but this may be further evidence of principals in North West Province painting a more rosy picture relative to reality than Botswana principals.

Social issues

Feeding programmes appear to be slightly more prevalent in Botswana than in North West Province in the samples for this study, and those feeding programmes tended to cover all instead of most of the learners in the schools. In the North West Province, 92 per cent of the principals reported that their school provided a daily school feeding programme for learners, 2 per cent said their school feeding programme ran two to three times per week, and 5 per cent said their schools did not have any feeding programme for learners. In terms of inclusion, 87 per cent of the principals said all of their learners participated in the feeding programme, while 5 per cent reported only one-quarter of their learners participated. In Botswana, all schools that answered the question (99 per cent) reported having daily school feeding. Over 90 per cent of the principals reported that 100 per cent of pupils participated in those programme, and only 2 per cent reported one-quarter or fewer students were beneficiaries of the programme.

Interestingly, more principals in the North West Province than in Botswana reported that HIV/AIDS was not a major issue for most schools. A majority of North West principals (62 per cent) said HIV/AIDS did not affect their school at all, while 15 per cent said it affected learner absenteeism, 13 per cent felt it affected their school in other ways, and only a few felt it affected the school through learner illness (5 per cent) or teacher absenteeism (2 per cent). In Botswana, 43 per cent of principals reported HIV/AIDS did not affect their school and 15 per cent said it affected learner absenteeism. Whereas the North West principals did not think it affected their teachers in terms of illness or absenteeism, 7 per cent of Botswana principals felt it affected teacher absenteeism, and 3.5 per cent said it affected teacher illness.

Reported violence in schools

According to the sample of North West province principals, violence did not appear to be an important factor in their schools, but was reported as more of a problem in Botswana. In the North West sample it appears principals believe learners are often the perpetrators of any violence against other learners, and that violent acts against learners are generally only rarely, if ever, committed by teachers or outsiders to the school. Similar percentages of principals in Botswana reported learners threatened other learners 'often' or 'sometimes' as in the North West (about 60 per cent), but 21 per cent of

---

1 North West teachers' reports on principal teaching observations were even more positive than their principals': 28 per cent said they were observed often and 41 per cent sometimes. Only 30 per cent said rarely or never. On the other hand, Botswana teachers were slightly more likely to say that principals rarely or never visited their classrooms – 15 per cent rather than the 5 per cent reported by principals.

FIGURE 5.2a *North West Province: Principals' perceived frequency of violence against learners, 2009*

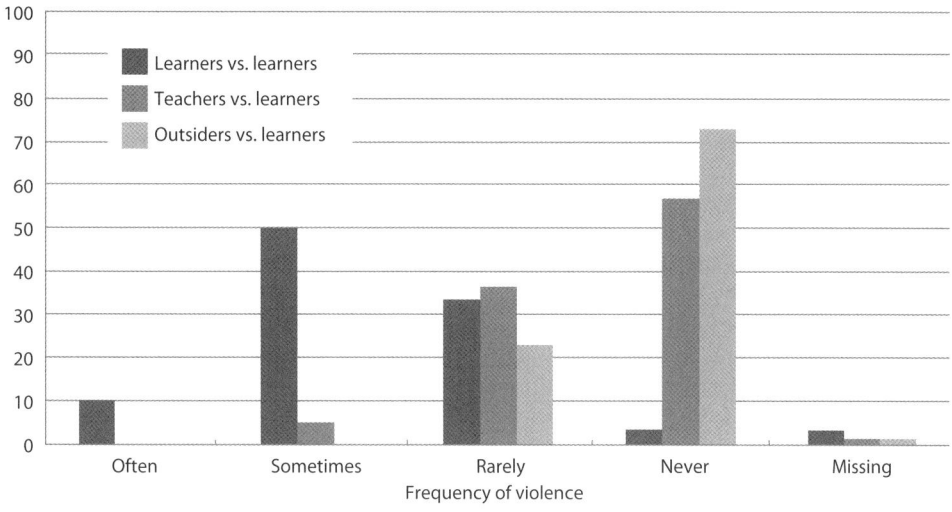

Source: North West Province Schools Sample, 2009.

principals in Botswana said teachers threaten or hurt learners 'sometimes', and 55 per cent said this happens 'rarely,' while in the North West these figures are 5 per cent and 37 per cent, respectively. Only 22 per cent of principals in Botswana say teachers never threaten or hurt learners, while 57 per cent of principals in the North West Province claimed this. Figures 5.2a and 5.2b compare the frequency with which North West and Botswana principals felt violence against learners was occurring, as committed by other learners, by teachers or by outsiders.

FIGURE 5.2b *Botswana: Principals' perceived frequency of violence against learners, 2009*

Source: Botswana Schools Sample, 2009.

In addition, as we show later, 20 per cent of North West Province principals and 25 per cent of Botswana principals listed disciplining students as one of the issues that they spend the least time attending to (although 17 per cent of Botswana principals reported that learner against learner violence occurred often in their schools). So, neither North West nor Botswana principals consider violence a major issue in schools.

Nevertheless, principals' opinions about violence vary from school to school in each sample. We also have information from teachers and pupils in our sample answering the same questions about violence among learners, between teachers and learners, and between outsiders and learners. From this information, we were able to construct a 'violence index' for each classroom/school (several of the schools in our sample had more than one mathematics classroom included in the surveys). We constructed the index by weighting the 'often' answer by 3, 'sometimes' by 2, 'rarely' by 1, and 'never' by 0. We added up the weighted responses to the three types of violence – learners on learners, teachers on learners, and outsiders on learners – from learners, teachers, and principals. The highest level of violence score for each of the three respondents (learners, teachers, principals) would garner a score of 9. The highest score for a classroom/school (if all three respondents answered 'often' for each of the three types of violence) would be 27. The lowest level of reported violence would be a score of 0. The reported level of violence in our samples of North West Province and Botswana schools is relatively low, with a mean index of 8.7 in North West Province and significantly higher in Botswana, at 11.6. This suggests that respondents, on average, observe violence 'rarely' in North West Province, and somewhat more than 'rarely' in Botswana. Even at the extreme end of the distribution, the average observed violence is slightly less than 'sometimes' in North West Province and 'sometimes' in Botswana. Figure 5.3 shows the distribution of classrooms/schools by our violence index in the two samples.

Whether this is accurate or not depends on the willingness of respondents to be open about a subject that might reflect on their own management abilities. The statistically significantly higher level of

FIGURE 5.3 *Botswana and North West Province: Distribution of sampled classrooms by level of reported violence index, 2009*

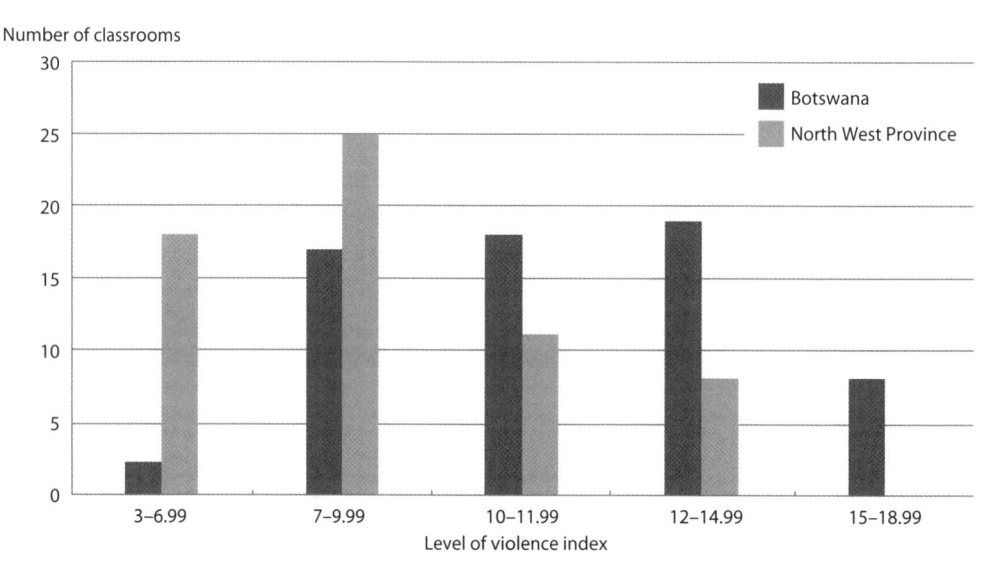

Source: Botswana and North West Province Schools Sample, 2009.

violence reported by principals in Botswana could reflect a reality that there is more violence in Botswana schools, although it should be noted that in both countries the reported levels suggest fairly low levels of school violence. But our observations and discussions with teachers in the two countries provide little support for the notion that Botswana schools are marked by more threats to students by other students, teachers, or outsiders. Rather, we believe that these differences in principals' perceptions provide more evidence that teachers and principals in North West tend to downplay any negative aspects of conditions in their school and classrooms more than in Botswana. In our follow-up teacher interviews in the two countries, we also noted that North West Province teachers painted a much rosier picture of their work and their students' performance than the teachers we interviewed in Botswana.

It is telling that in both samples a higher fraction of learners report feeling scared that someone (other learners, teachers, or outsiders) will hurt them 'sometimes' or 'often' than teachers and principals reporting violence at these levels. Furthermore, the reported violence by students in North West Province is considerably higher than reported by either teachers or principals, whereas in Botswana, the students' reported level of violence averages only slightly higher than reported by teachers (Figure 5.4). Students in North West Province report an average index of 3.8 out of a possible 9, considerably higher than the overall violence index of 8.7 out of a possible 27. This suggests that teachers and principals in North West Province are more likely to tend to under report the level of violence than teachers and principals in Botswana. Yet, it is also true that students in North West Province report a somewhat (but statistically significantly) lower lever of feeling scared than in Botswana.

There could be important implications of these results. On the one hand, the reported opinions of North West teachers and principals could reflect an unwillingness to present a pessimistic picture to outside interviewers – a typical effect found in such surveys. On the other hand, teachers and principals could be less willing to face up to a series of unpleasant realities about their schools and classrooms. If it is the latter, it could be more difficult in North West than in Botswana to convince school personnel that serious change is needed.

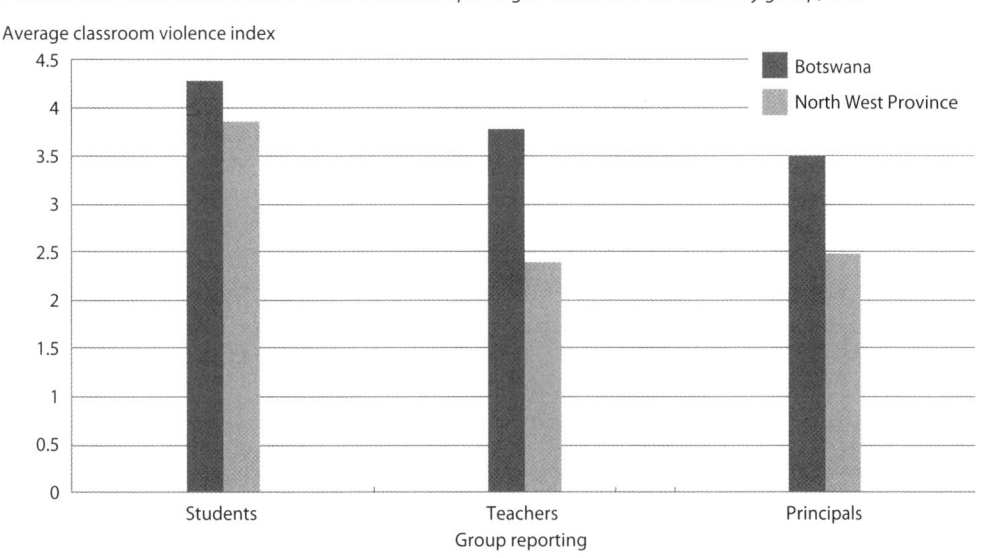

FIGURE 5.4 *Botswana and North West Province: Reporting of violence in the school by group, 2009*

Source: Botswana and North West Province Schools Sample, 2009.

What do North West principals perceive to be the time-consuming issues in their schools?

The majority (57 per cent) of North West Province principals reported administration and departmental reporting took up the majority of their time, while 27 per cent felt oversight of teaching and curriculum was their most time-consuming task; few felt any of other tasks were their main focus. In contrast, only 10 per cent of Botswana principals regarded administrative and departmental reporting as the most time-consuming task they faced. Most principals in Botswana reported that overseeing teaching and curriculum and supervising teachers took up most of their day. This is consistent with the percentages of principals who reported observing lessons in each country. Figures 5.5a and 5.5b show the percentage of time that principals in North West Province and Botswana felt they spent on various time-consuming tasks.

FIGURE 5.5a *North West Province: Tasks on which principals report spending most time, 2009*

- Missing 3%
- Other 5%
- Supervising teachers 3%
- Administration and departmental reporting 59%
- Disciplining learners 3%
- Financial management (including fundraising) 0%
- Co-ordinating the school board, governing body 0%
- Overseeing teaching and curriculum 27%
- Liaising with parents 0%

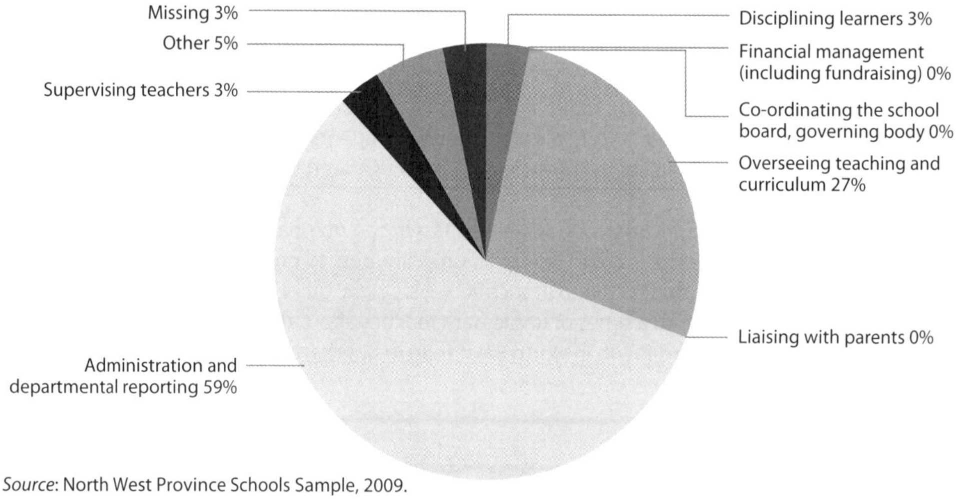

Source: North West Province Schools Sample, 2009.

FIGURE 5.5b *Botswana: Tasks on which principals report spending most time, 2009*

- Missing 6.9%
- Supervising teachers 20.7%
- Administration and departmental reporting 10.3%
- Co-ordinating the school board 0%
- Disciplining learners 0%
- Meeting with parents 0%
- Financial management 0%
- Overseeing teaching and curriculum 62.1%

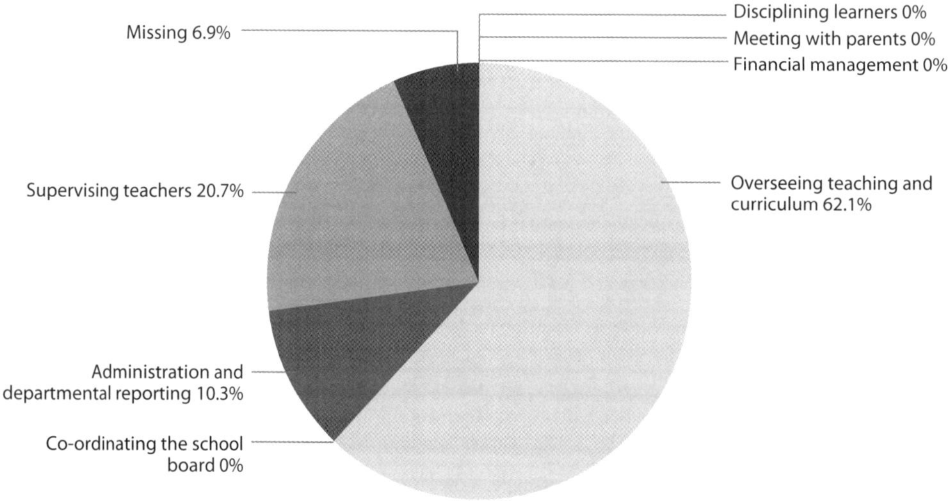

Source: Botswana Schools Sample, 2009.

As is shown, North West Province and Botswana principals were more evenly divided on which tasks took up the least of their time than which took up the most. In North West Province, only 8 per cent and 7 per cent felt administration or teaching oversight took the least of their time, respectively, while about 20 per cent onf the principals chose each of coordinating the school governing body, liaising with parents and disciplining learners as their least time-consuming task. While very few (3 per cent) of the principals felt disciplining learners was their most time-consuming task, and 20 per cent felt it was their least time-consuming task, over 18 per cent of principals reported having to deal with issues of learner discipline several times per day, and about half of the principals reported having to discipline learners at least several times per week (Figure 5.6a).

FIGURE 5.6a *North West Province: Management issues on which principals report spending least time, 2009*

- Other 1.7%
- Missing 3.3%
- Administration and departmental reporting 15%
- Supervising teachers 8.3%
- Co-ordinating the school board 21.7%
- Disciplining learners 20%
- Liaising with parents 18.3%
- Financial management (including fundraising) 5%
- Overseeing teaching and curriculum 6.7%

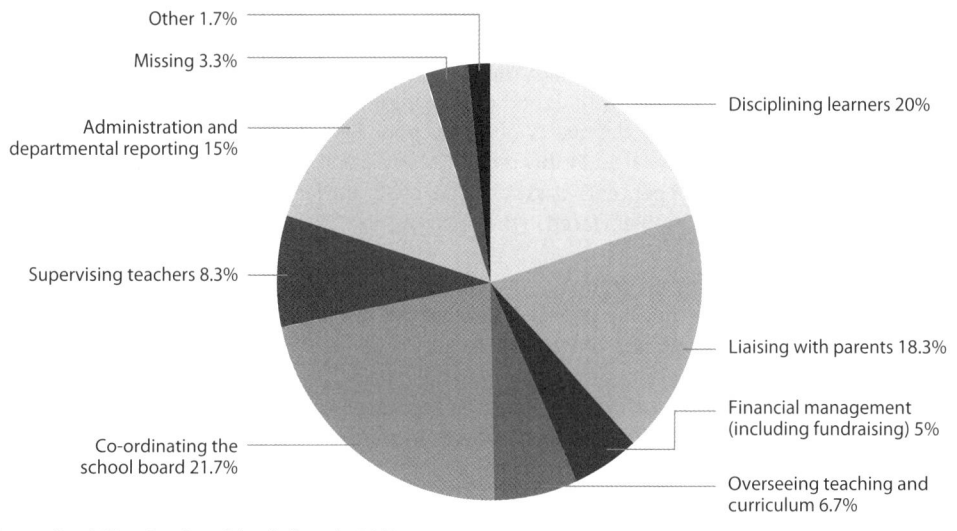

Source: North West Province Schools Sample, 2009.

FIGURE 5.6b *Botswana: Management issues on which principals report spending least time, 2009*

- Other or missing 3%
- Supervising teachers 3%
- Administration and departmental reporting 5%
- Co-ordinating the school board 17%
- Overseeing teaching and curriculum 3%
- Disciplining learners 25%
- Meeting with parents 17%
- Financial management (including fundraising) 27%

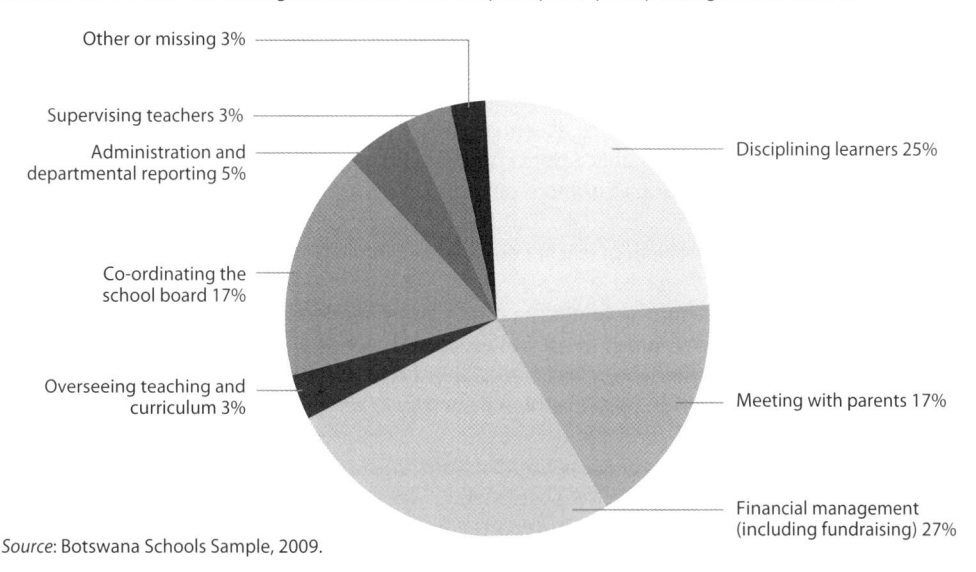

Source: Botswana Schools Sample, 2009.

In Botswana, while few of the respondents thought that administrative and departmental reporting occupied the most of their time, they seemed divided on whether financial management (27 per cent), disciplining students (25 per cent), meeting with parents (17 per cent) or coordinating the school board (17 per cent) were the least important tasks in terms of time requirements (Figure 5.6b).

The principals in both countries were fairly consistent in reporting that student discipline consumes very little of their time. Only 10 per cent indicated that they have to discipline learners more often than several times a week, and more than a third suggested that they do so less than once a week.

Main obstacles to improving the school

North West Province principals' answers about management tasks were fairly consistent with what they reported most inhibited them from making their school a 'good school'. Twenty per cent of the principals felt their administrative workload was the most important problem they faced in trying to improve their school, while nearly one-third of principals (28 per cent) felt a dearth of resources impeded their ability to improve the quality of their school. Few (7 per cent) felt learner discipline was the biggest problem they faced in this regard. A similar proportion of principals named the introduction of new policies (8 per cent), class size (7 per cent), and lack of parental involvement (7 per cent) as the most important problem faced in their school.

For Botswana principals, their perception of the main obstacles were very different. The three main problems at the school level (for the principal) were lack of resources (23 per cent), lack of parental involvement (17 per cent), and lack of learner interest (13 per cent). Only 10 per cent of Botswana principals indicated that administrative workload was their major issue at the school level, while only 8 per cent indicated lack of good quality teachers as their major problem. There was much more unanimity concerning the main problems they had with learners: 31 per cent of principals thought that lack of parental motivation was the biggest issue with learners, and another 27 per cent indicated that lack of learner interest was the main issue. Only 8 per cent said that learner discipline was a major problem.

While teacher absenteeism is sometimes mentioned in the literature as a major issue in South African schools, over 90 per cent of North West Province principals in the sample felt it was either not a problem (55 per cent) or only a problem for a few teachers (38 per cent) in their schools. This is consistent with the fact that none of the principals felt teacher absenteeism was the most important problem in their school, and only 5 per cent felt it was the most important problem they faced when dealing with teachers.

In Botswana, on the other hand, teacher absenteeism was reported to be a more widespread issue. As shown in Figure 5.7, although only 5 per cent of the principals in our sample said that teacher absenteeism was a problem for half or more of the teachers in their schools, another 66 per cent admitted that it was a problem for a few. This is a far higher percentage than the South African principals reported for the problem of teacher absenteeism in the North West Province sample.

Reasons for teacher absenteeism, according to principals, were more consistent across the samples than the degree to which they agreed that it was an issue. Over half of the principals in both samples felt the main reason for teacher absenteeism was illness. The next highest specified reason in both samples was domestic responsibilities, which was named by 22 per cent of North West and 10 per cent of Botswana principals (14 per cent of Botswana principals reported some 'other' reason for teacher absenteeism). It is interesting that only 2 per cent of North West principals and 7 per cent of Botswana principals felt HIV/AIDS affected teacher absenteeism, when they agree that teacher absenteeism is caused by illness, and HIV/AIDS is often reported in the literature as one of the main causes of

FIGURE 5.7 *Botswana and North West Province: Perception of principals on whether teacher absenteeism is a problem, 2009*

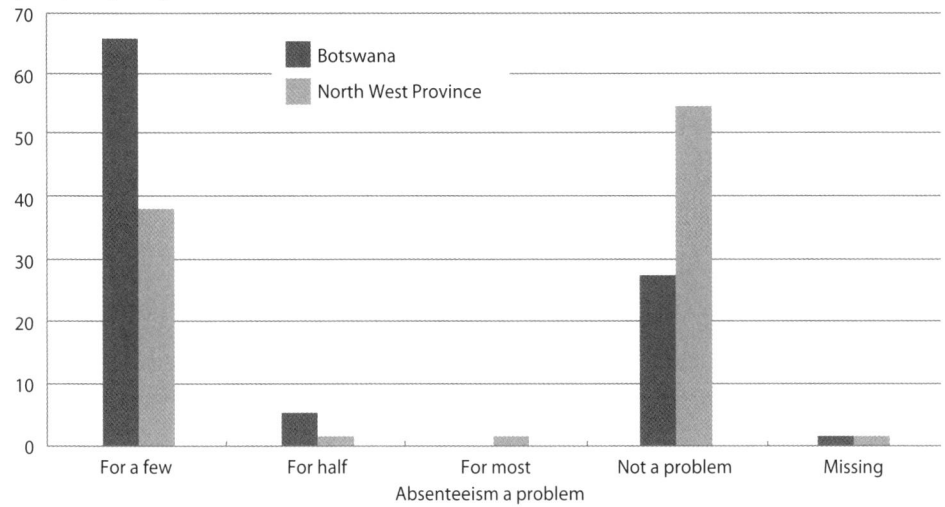

% of principals agreeing

[Bar chart showing percentage of principals agreeing on whether absenteeism is a problem, comparing Botswana and North West Province across categories: For a few, For half, For most, Not a problem, Missing]

Source: Botswana and North West Province Schools Sample, 2009.

longer-term illness in southern Africa. Figures 5.8a and 5.8b show the breakdown of principals' perceived reasons for teacher absenteeism.

Overall, it seems that principals in North West Province spend more time on administrative tasks and less on the oversight of teaching and learning than their Botswana counterparts, and that they are more likely to feel their administrative work gets in the way of improving their schools. Over a quarter of principals in both samples felt that a lack of resources impeded their ability to improve their schools. The two samples were also very different in the extent to which they felt teacher absenteeism was an issue, with principals in the North West reporting it was not as significant an issue as reported by principals in Botswana, though both groups felt illness was the main cause of teacher absenteeism.

Conclusion

The principals in our schools were mostly male, over the age of fifty, and reasonably well qualified. Most were relatively new to the post and to the school and had spent an average of ten years teaching prior to becoming a principal. While aware that the majority of teachers covered the curriculum only partially, a fraction reported observing lessons often (more in Botswana), saying that administration and departmental work took up most of their time, constituting their biggest problem in trying to improve their school. They did not consider teacher absenteeism a major problem (more did in Botswana), and where it did exist, explained it as being due to ill health and domestic responsibilities.

Given our estimates from direct observations of student notebooks about the number of lessons taught in these classrooms/schools, principals' (and teachers') apparent perception of (or at least, their willingness to discuss) the absenteeism problem is troubling. One possibility is that teachers are not absent, but do not teach mathematics lessons even when in school. It is, however, more likely that principals and teachers do not consider 'legitimate' absences, such as union meetings, professional

FIGURE 5.8a *North West Province: Principals' perceived reasons for teacher absenteeism, 2009*

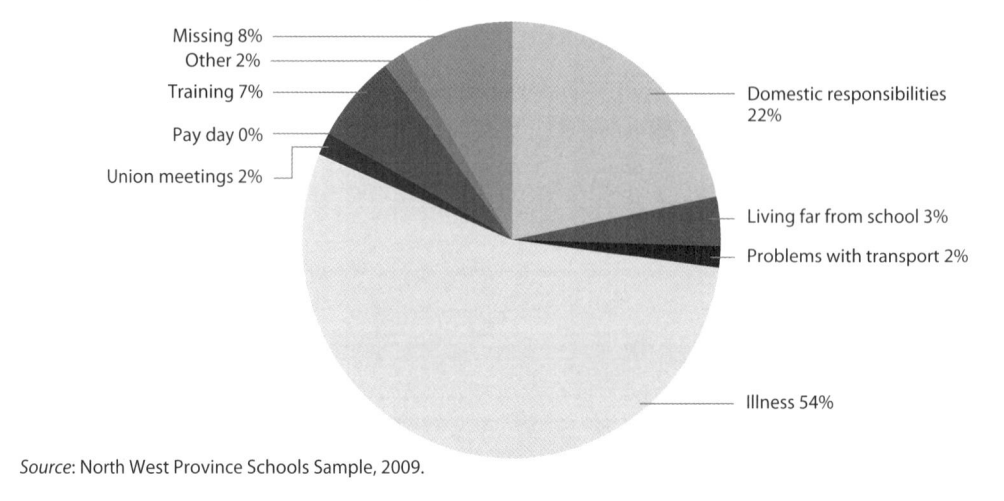

- Missing 8%
- Other 2%
- Training 7%
- Pay day 0%
- Union meetings 2%
- Domestic responsibilities 22%
- Living far from school 3%
- Problems with transport 2%
- Illness 54%

Source: North West Province Schools Sample, 2009.

FIGURE 5.8b *Botswana: Principals' perceived reasons for teacher absenteeism, 2009*

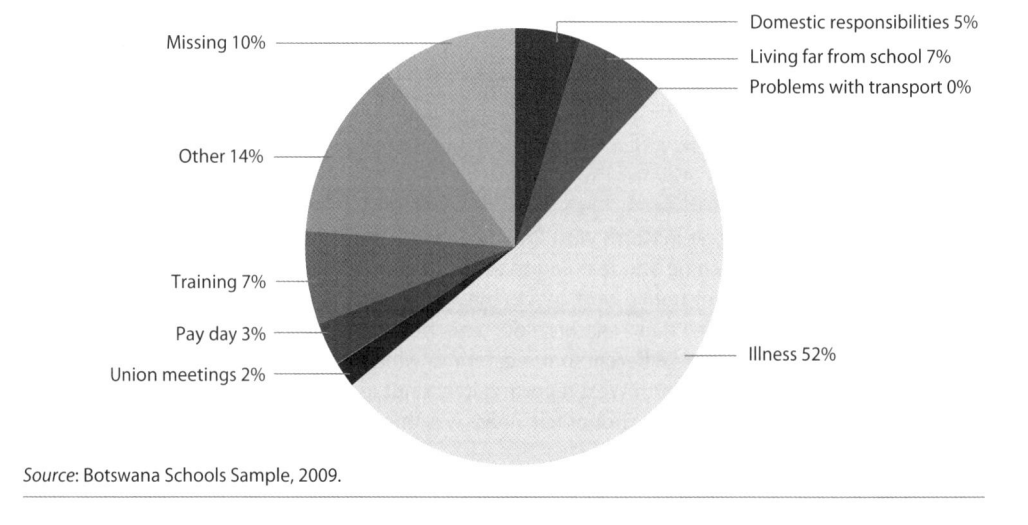

- Missing 10%
- Other 14%
- Training 7%
- Pay day 3%
- Union meetings 2%
- Domestic responsibilities 5%
- Living far from school 7%
- Problems with transport 0%
- Illness 52%

Source: Botswana Schools Sample, 2009.

training, departmental meetings, or illness, as absences. Further, in North West Province, much more than in Botswana, there is a considerable gap between the school violence reported by students, their principals and teachers. Again, this suggests a perception by school authorities in North West that seems very different from other versions of reality.

Therefore, what we observe from the questionnaires is that the school environment is perceived by principals (and teachers) as being much more favourable to learning than it is, and that this gap between reality and perceived reality is much greater in the administrative offices and among teachers in North West Province than in Botswana. This raises important policy questions regarding the climate for educational change, particularly in South Africa. If key actors view the current situation to be much better than it is, changing it may not be easy.

CHAPTER 6

Learner knowledge of mathematics

The basis for much of our comparative analysis of schooling in Botswana and North West Province is an assessment of students' mathematics knowledge. The assessment was designed to measure the knowledge that students in our sample of schools should have by the stage they reach in Grade 6. The items on the learner test were drawn from the existing South African NCS, which requirements align with other international mathematics curricula. It is likely that the fundamental mathematical concepts to be covered will not change significantly in the latest curriculum reviews presently underway in the two countries we studied.

The learner test

Students took the test in late March and again in late October. In the second test application, we changed the numbers in some of the problems and the problems were presented in a different order. The overall content of the test remained the same, so that gains that students made in the seven-plus months between test applications should represent how much mathematics knowledge they gained in a major portion of the 2009 academic year. Since we are controlling for the mathematics knowledge they had near the beginning of the year, that gain should also represent the contribution of conditions inside and outside the classroom to their mathematics learning. The initial test was taken by 3 868 students in 64 classrooms in 60 schools in North West Province, and 1 774 students in 64 classrooms in 58 schools in Botswana. The follow-up test was taken by 3 745 students in North West Province and about 1 700 in Botswana.

In North West, students in two of the original classrooms where we applied the initial test did not take the second test (about 90 students), and, of the remaining students, we were able to match 3 490 of them to the initial test. This means we 'lost' about 290 students for whom we could not match test scores. For one of the two classrooms where students did not take the second test, we did not impute scores because we had no data on the teacher. But for the other classroom, we did impute scores by using the overall relationship between the follow-up test and the initial test.[1] In Botswana, we were

---

1 In total, second round test scores had to be partially or totally imputed for eight of the North West sample of classrooms/schools. As mentioned, the post-test score was imputed for one classroom because students did not write the post-test. For four of the classrooms, post-test scores were imputed for all test items because post-test results showed unusually and suspiciously (very) large gains on all/most items. These were all classrooms where data collectors were not present when students took the test. Results for three other classrooms showed evidence of suspiciously large gains only on some questions, suggesting partial cheating in the post-test; therefore, for students in these classrooms, second round test scores were imputed only for the 'questionable' items. These imputed scores for schools in which there were questionable or missing second round scores were used in the subsequent analyses of student gain scores.

FIGURE 6.1 *North West Province and Botswana: Average of individual learner initial mathematics test score by test item, late March, 2009*

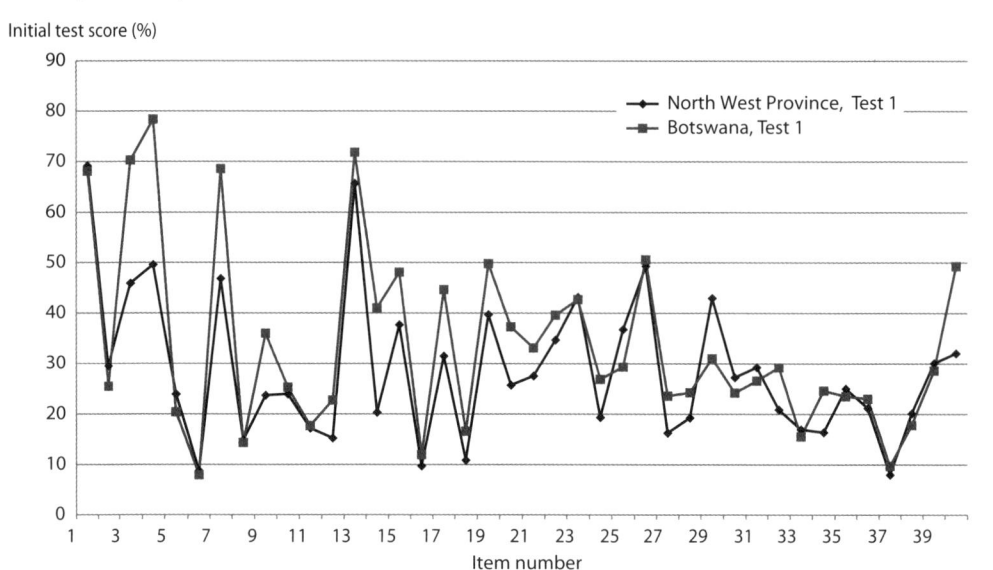

Source: North West Province and Botswana Schools Sample, 2009.

able to match an even higher percentage (93 per cent) of those taking the second test to those who had taken the initial test, to end up with 1 666 learners for whom we had both scores. Furthermore, we had no issues regarding second round test scores in Botswana.

Students in our sample of Grade 6 mathematics classrooms began the year (actually almost two months into the academic year) with a rather low level of the mathematics knowledge they were supposed to have at the start of the Grade 6. This is consistent with other studies of how southern African learners have performed in system tests (Howie & Plomp 2002; Van der Berg & Louw 2006) as well as various provincial systemic testing programmes that have been carried out in South Africa, particularly in Western Cape and Gauteng.

The average test score in our sample of more than 3 800 students in North West Province who took the initial test was 28.6 per cent, with a standard deviation in the first round test of 12.2. The average test score in our sample of 1 774 Botswana students who took the initial test was 34.6 per cent (omitting items 27 and 37, which had printing issues in the Botswana version of the test that made them difficult to read) with a standard deviation in the first round test of 12.4.[2] Thus, the difference in test score was a minimum of 5 points (including question 27 and 37 for both countries), a statistically significant difference. There was also great variation in the score from test item to test item in both countries. Figure 6.1 shows this variation.

Items on which the students, on average, did particularly poorly were, for example, questions 16 and 18, which were simple fractions problems, and question 37 (only valid in North West), which

---

2 If we include items 27 and 37, the average score on the initial test for Botswana learners was 33.6 per cent, with a standard deviation of 12.

asked the student to estimate the area of a simple shape. We should remind readers that this was largely a 5th grade test in terms of the South African and Botswana curricula.

The gains that students made between March and October also varied greatly, with the gains on some items coming out reasonably large and positive and others, negative (see Figures 6.2a and 6.2b).

FIGURE 6.2a *North West Province: Average of individual learner pre-test and post-test mathematics score by test item, late March and late October, 2009*

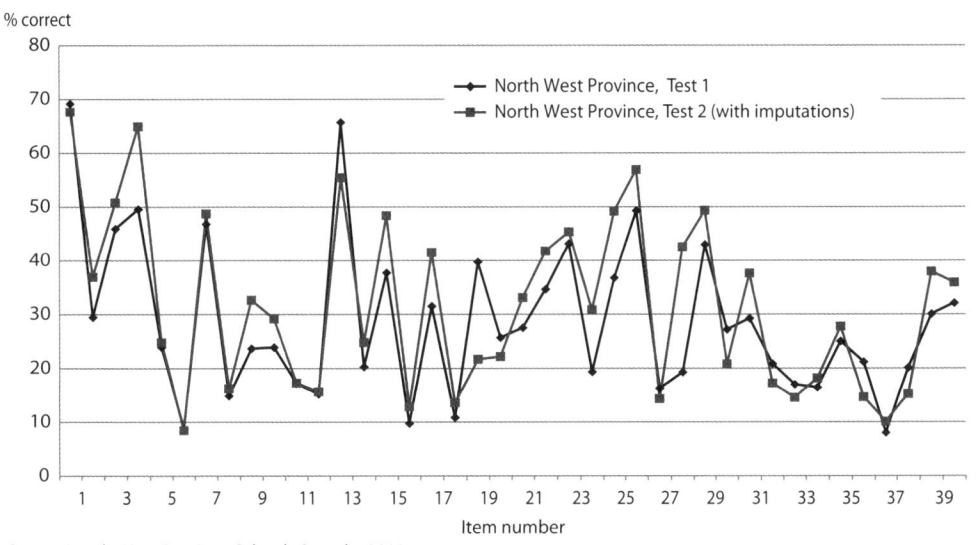

Source: North West Province Schools Sample, 2009.

FIGURE 6.2b *Botswana: Average of individual learner pre-test and post-test mathematics score, by test item, late March and late October, 2009*

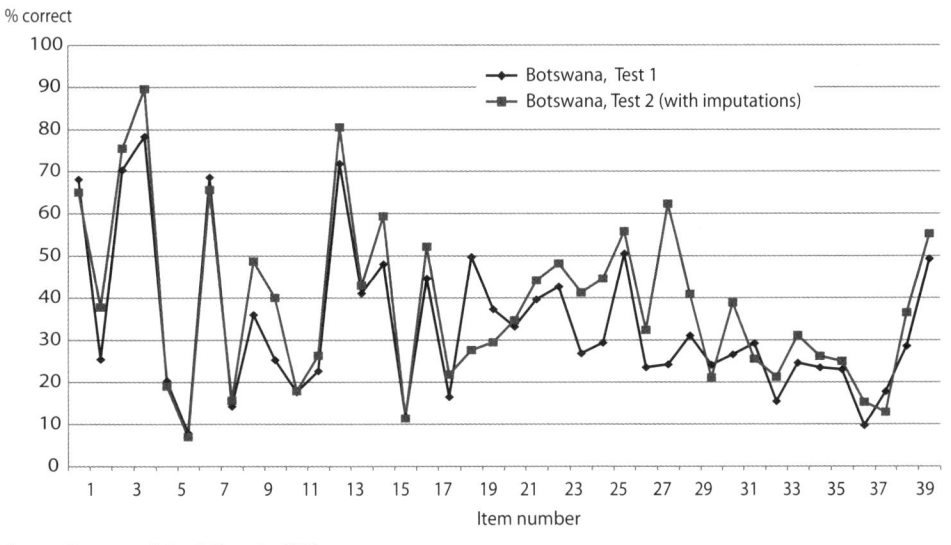

Source: Botswana Schools Sample, 2009.

Learner knowledge of mathematics | 75

In the North West sample, as we have pointed out, we needed to impute second round test scores for eight of the classrooms mainly because of possible cheating on some or most items in the second round. When these imputations are made (based on the regression estimate of test 2 scores on test 1 scores of the other schools in the sample), the average score on the post-test (round 2) for the sample as a whole was 31.6 per cent, with a standard deviation of 12.4. The average gain for the 3 485 students we could match in North West Province was therefore 3 points, with a standard deviation of 11.2 points. So the gain has a high variation among individual students, which suggests that it might be difficult to explain with variables such as teacher inputs that are likely to vary much less.

In Botswana, the gain was larger than in North West. The average score on the post-test (round 2) for the sample as a whole was 38.6 per cent, with a standard deviation of 14. Again, the difference between the average score in Botswana and North West was statistically significant. The average gain for the 1 666 students we could match was 4.0 points (excluding gains on question 27 and 37), with a standard deviation of 10.2 points. The one point difference in gain is also statistically significant at the 1 per cent significance level.

From pre- to post-test there were some general signs of improvement. For example, in North West, learners scored between 40 and 49 per cent on 6 items in the pre-test and on 8 items in the post-test, and above 50 per cent on 2 items in the pre-test and 5 items on the post-test. In Botswana, learners scored between 40 and 49 per cent on 8 items in the pre-test and on 10 items in the post-test, and above 50 per cent on 8 items in the pre-test and 10 items on the post-test. But these improvements are minimal and at face value indicate very poor overall performance. If one looks beyond the 'poor performance' to item gains on particular items, one can distil information that could be useful to the teacher of mathematics in Grade 6 (or at other levels). As is evident in Figure 6.2a, in North West Province learners showed overall negative gains in 10 of the 40 items on the learner test, with the biggest negative gain of about 18 per cent on item 19. As shown in Figure 6.2b, Botswana learners showed overall negative gains in 7 of the 40 items on the learner test, with the biggest negative gain of more than 20 per cent also on item 19. That common fall in test score on item 19 resulted from a simple change in the problem, from a plus sign to a minus sign in an algebraic expression, suggesting that learners did not really understand the underlying mathematics of the expression.

Analysis of selected items on the learner test

A closer examination of the distractors selected by learners in the pre- and post-tests gives insight into the misconceptions of a large majority of North West Province and Botswana learners. Table 6.1 on page 77 shows the analysis for North West students, but it is similar for those in Botswana. The items selected for the discussion below were those where a majority of learners selected an incorrect distractor in favour of the correct answer. Embedded in the distractor is a misconception that is common, not only to learners in the North West, but internationally, as has been shown in other research in mathematics education. The table summarises this information for some key items.

To get a better idea of how students did on various types of items, we divided the test questions into five parts of the curriculum. Those parts, or content areas, are number, patterns, shapes, measurement, and data handling.

TABLE 6.1 *North West Province: Analysis of average learner test score and common distractors in selected mathematics test items, 2009*

Item number on pre-test (post-test)	% correct on pre-test	% selecting distractor with common misconception	Mathematical concept(s) involved	Mathematical misconception demonstrated in selection of distractor
5 (6)	24%	53%	Multiplication of a fraction with a whole number, in a problem context	When you multiply a fraction by a whole number you simply write them next to each other. For example: $5 \times \frac{1}{3} = 5\frac{1}{3}$ (The answer should be $\frac{5}{3}$)
16 (19)	13%	55%	Addition of fractions Purely numeric statement of question	When you add fractions you add the numerators and the denominators. For example: $\frac{3}{4} + \frac{2}{5} = \frac{5}{9}$ (The answer should be $\frac{23}{20}$)
19 (20)	21%	39%	'BODMAS'	When you operate on a string of numbers you work from left to right. For example: $5 + 3 \times 2 = 16$ (The answer should be 11)
20 (28)	23%	34%	Difficult number pattern question	Learners need to know how to identify and work with number patterns.
33	14%	45%	Data handling – calculating the median given a set of numbers (not quite sorted)	Learners simply chose the middle number of the given set of numbers without sorting them.
38 (40)	9%	39%	Calculation of area of a shape – difficult (multistep)	Learners calculated the area of one of the shapes making up the shape instead of calculating the area of the whole given shape.

Source: North West Province Schools Sample, 2009.

Figures 6.3a, 6.3b, 6.4a and 6.4b on the following two pages give more detail of the item means and the gains per content area in North West Province and Botswana. They indicate that the learner gains in each country were spread across the content areas with some variation. Each blue or red dot in the graphs represents a test item. In Figures 6.3a and 6.3b, the means (violet and pale green) are for the pre- and post-test scores.[3] The highest scores are in numbers patterns and shapes, those parts of the curriculum which South African and Botswana teachers are possibly best prepared to teach. The

---

3   Trimmed means are estimated in these graphs by cutting the highest and lowest scores in each category and recalculating the mean.

lowest scores are in measurement and data, which they are apparently least well prepared to teach. The pattern of scores and of gains are strikingly similar in the two countries except that learners in Botswana do considerably better than students in South Africa in shapes.

Achievement could also be linked to the content reflected in the items, if, for example, the shapes questions were particularly simple, learners would do better on such items. The item content level may explain these higher means in certain content areas, but generally these content areas do get more

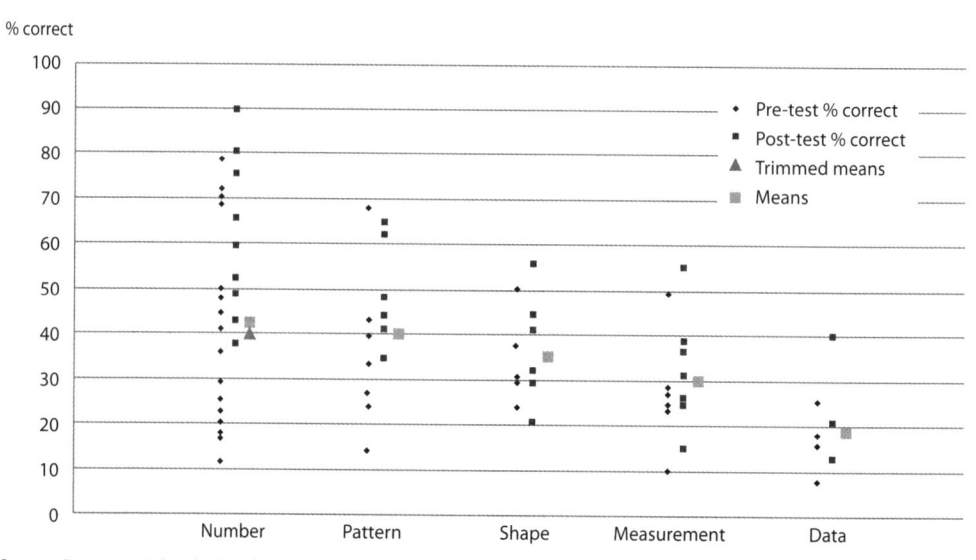

FIGURE 6.3a *North West Province: Pre- and post-test scores by item and curriculum category of items, 2009*

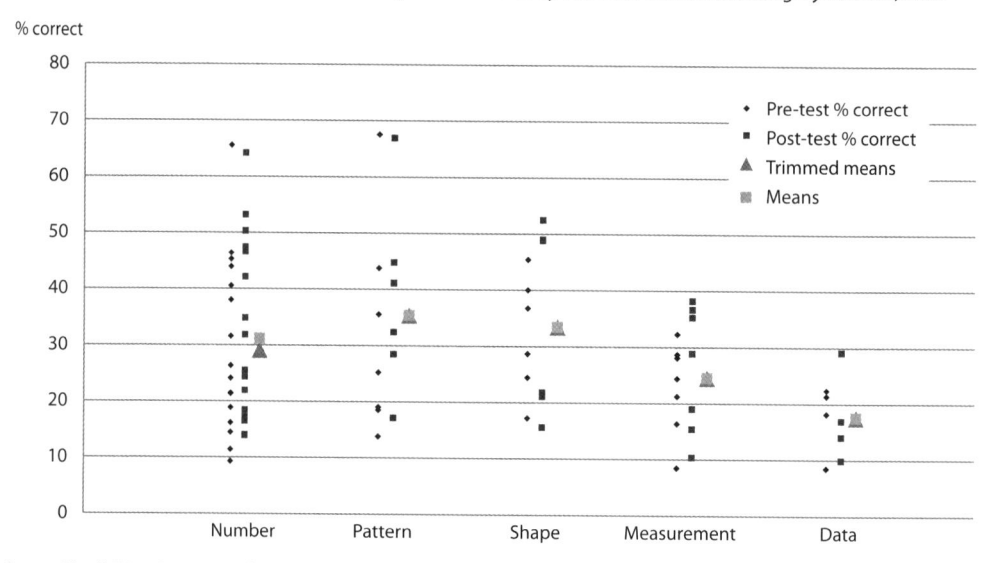

Source: North West Province Schools Sample, 2009.

FIGURE 6.3b *Botswana: Pre- and post-test scores by item and curriculum category of items, 2009*

Source: Botswana Schools Sample, 2009.

FIGURE 6.4a *North West Province: Test score gains by item and curriculum category of items, 2009*

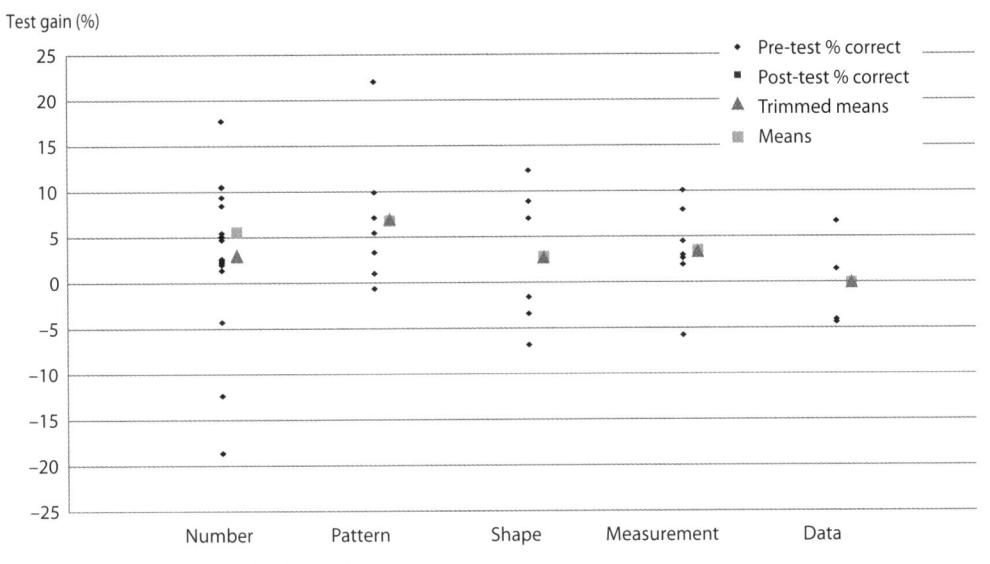

Source: North West Province Schools Sample, 2009.

FIGURE 6.4b *Botswana: Test score gains by item and curriculum category of items, 2009*

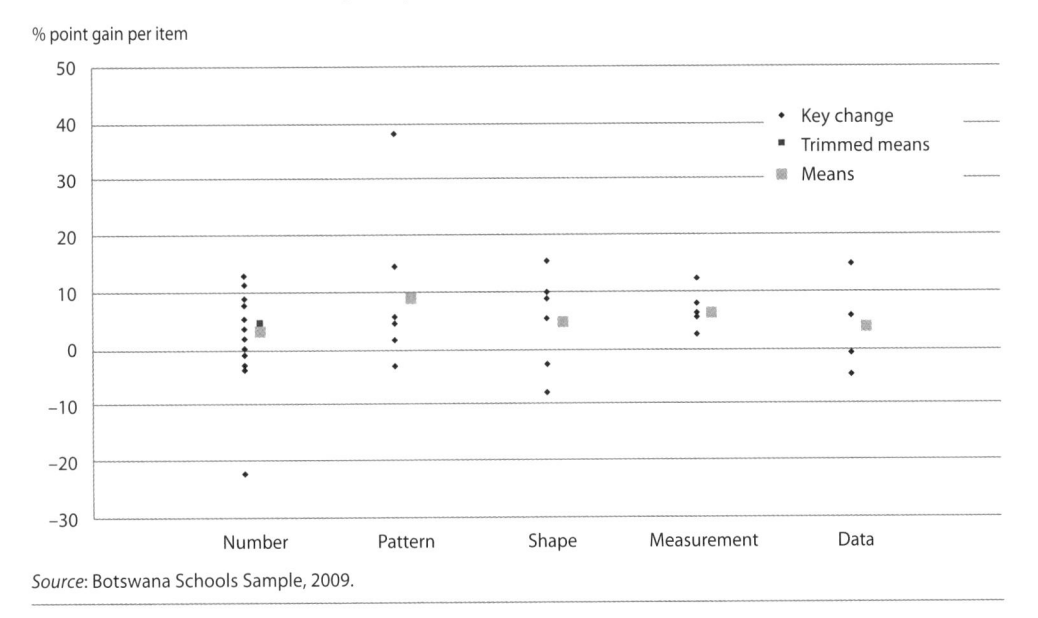

Source: Botswana Schools Sample, 2009.

coverage and learners do better here, which again relates to OTL. Further, if it were a question of the ease of the items, then it is hard to explain why students in Botswana do better in shapes (clearly one case in which they do much better on the same test items than students in South Africa).

In Figures 6.4a and 6.4b, the blue points represent the gains on each item, and the red squares are the means of the gains. The largest gains in North West Province are in patterns and numbers and the smallest, not surprisingly, in data. In Botswana, the largest gain is in shapes, followed closely by patterns and numbers. One result that stands out is the large variation of the gains, with eight items for each set of learners showing negative gains. The reasons for these negative gains are hard to explain at this point and need more detailed item analysis.

Other measurements included in the study and discussed later, such as videotaped lessons and analysis of learners' notebooks, may provide explanations for these differences in performance by content area. In our videotaped lesson observations, for example, we saw very few data lessons actually being taught. This could indicate that poor scores in data may result from insufficient OTL. Measurement is also an area where learners internationally score poorly since they are often taught to memorise conversions and formulae which they struggle to apply correctly without adequate conceptual understanding of the core concepts. The lessons we observed being taught in measurement in both countries were largely procedural, allowing little opportunity for learners to develop a mathematical understanding. Teaching a rule is no guarantee that the rule is learnt.

Another example of such a data breakdown is found in the Joint Education Trust's Western Cape Education Department's (WCED) baseline study for the Literacy and Numeracy Intervention in South Africa. The spread of items in these tests was heavily dominated by number items, based on the understanding that numbers is given the most teaching time in the majority of South African schools. In spite of this, the results reflect the usual poor general knowledge of mathematics that is currently evidenced in South African schools. In the WCED study, achievement was not consistent across content areas nor grades in the Foundation Phase, and so one could not say that any one content area is generally better understood than another (Taylor & Pereira 2010).

Given the data presented here it can be concluded that learners in Botswana and South Africa generally have insufficient knowledge across all curriculum mathematics content areas, although they do show some competence on about eight items in North West and 11 items in Botswana (those on which the average score was 45 per cent or higher on the second test). Four (five) of those are in numbers and two in patterns in both countries, two in shapes in North West Province and four in shapes in Botswana. Eventually, it would be important to analyse the item results for the kinds of errors that students made and begin to understand the error patterns. This diagnostic could be used as the basis for improving teacher pre-service and in-service training for teaching mathematics in South African primary schools.

Learner achievement and socio-economic background at the classroom level

The learners in our sample of North West and Botswana classrooms/schools varied considerably by an index we constructed of socio-economic background using learner-reported items in the home. The average SES also varied between classrooms, and average learner achievement score on the pre-test was highly correlated with this SES measure (Figures 6.5a and 6.5b). The R-squared of the regression estimate of average classroom learner pre-test score as a function of average classroom learner SES is 0.54 in North West Province and 0.20 in Botswana, much lower than in North West Province suggesting that test scores vary less across schools in Botswana. We confirm this in more detail in Chapter 11.

The slope of the regression line in our sample of Botswana schools is also much smaller than that in North West Province, indicating that the relative average achievement of students in higher SES classrooms in North West Province was much higher than the relative achievement of students in higher SES classrooms in Botswana. In Botswana, for one standard deviation increase in classroom SES

FIGURE 6.5a *North West Province: Learner achievement on pre-test and average learner socio-economic background by classroom, 2009*

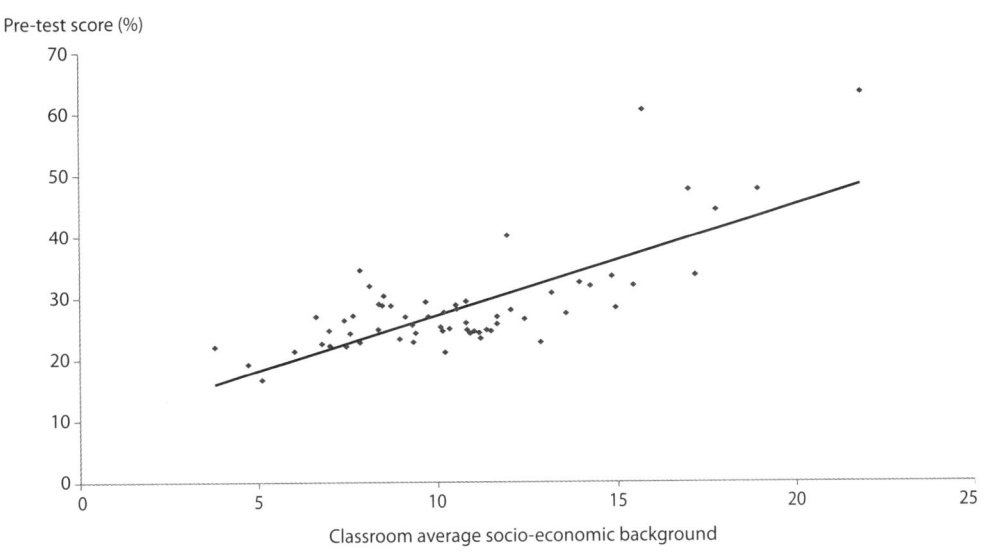

Source: North West Province Schools Sample, 2009.

FIGURE 6.5b *Botswana: Learner achievement on pre-test and average learner socio-economic background, by classroom, 2009*

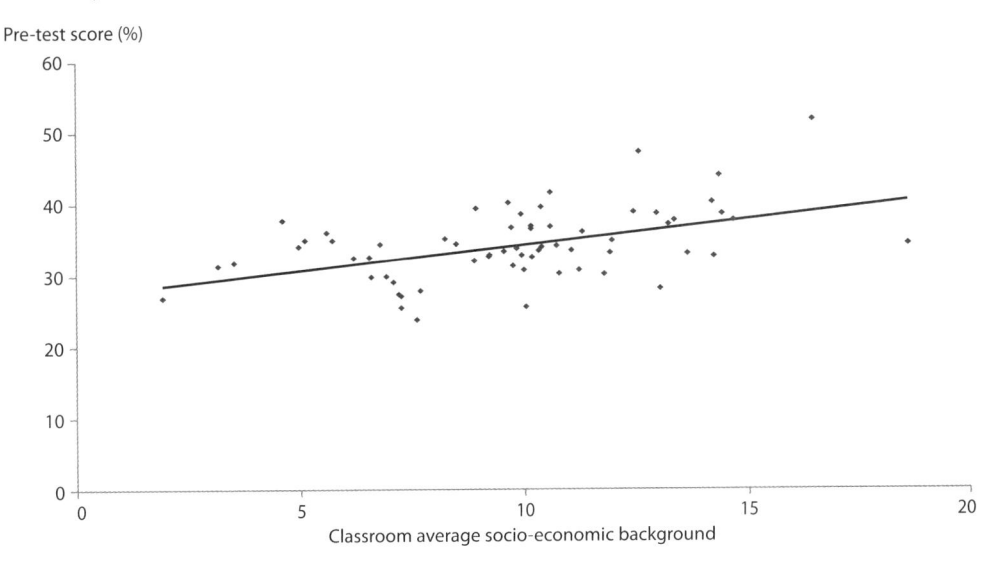

Source: Botswana Schools Sample, 2009.

(3.3), average initial classroom test score rises 2.4 points, or about 0.2 standard deviations. In North West Province, the corresponding increase in average classroom initial test score associated with a one standard deviation higher classroom SES is more than 0.5 standard deviation increase in average classroom initial test score.

Learner knowledge of mathematics | 81

TABLE 6.2 *North West Province: Learner scores by fees of school, 2009*

Fees (rand)	Pre-test	Post-test
0	0.28	0.32
<500	0.29	0.42
500–2 000	0.34	0.38
> 000	0.48	0.51
Urban	0.34	0.36
Rural	0.26	0.31

Source: North West Province School Sample, 2009.

In both North West Province and Botswana, students in urban schools have significantly higher scores than students in rural schools but the achievement gains of urban students were much smaller than those of rural students. In addition, some public schools in North West Province (as in the rest of South Africa) charge fees. The pre- and post-test scores of learners in the 13 per cent of schools in our sample that charged fees are higher than in the no-fee schools, but students in fee-paying schools did not necessarily make greater gains. Of the North West learners in the sample, 87 per cent attended no-fee schools, 3.6 per cent attended schools that charge less than R100 annually, 4.4 per cent schools that charge between R500 and R600, and 4.7 per cent were in schools that charge more than R2 000 annually. As shown in Table 6.2 (which reflects the figures for schools in North West) learners in the higher fee paying schools scored significantly higher.

Language and learner achievement

A major issue in South African and (to a lesser extent) in Botswana classrooms is the language capacity of students and teachers. Beginning in 4th grade in South Africa and 5th grade in Botswana, mathematics is taught in English (or Afrikaans, in South Africa). A very high proportion of the lesson is in English or Afrikaans in the classrooms we observed, although we did record considerable code switching by some teachers. Teachers insisted that we give the test to the students in English (or Afrikaans) even though we made it available in African languages. At the same time, we observed that most students in the North West Province classrooms we surveyed spoke English (the language of instruction in almost all our surveyed classrooms) with difficulty. Therefore, language could certainly be an issue in how well learners did on the mathematics test we gave them.

A comparison of the scores of the vast majority of learners whose mother tongue was Setswana with those whose mother tongue was English or Afrikaans, shows that the Afrikaans speakers scored 16 per cent higher on the pre-test and those with English home language scored 9 per cent higher than the Setswana speakers. The post-test shows similar results, although with smaller differences (9 per cent and 7 per cent higher, respectively). It is, however, important to recognise that speaking Afrikaans as a home language or being taught in Afrikaans may be correlated with other student or school background characteristics that affect learning, and therefore language may not be the primary causal factor in the production of these higher scores.

In terms of code switching, learners whose teachers rarely used Setswana or another African language in addition to English or Afrikaans scored higher than learners whose teachers code switched more often. The test score gains for those with teachers who rarely code switched also appear to be larger. This goes against the prevailing idea from other research which indicates that learners whose teachers use code switching in their classrooms should do better, and warrants further investigation (Adler & Pillay 2007; Setati 2005; Setati & Adler 2001).

Another way to look at the language issue is to rate each test item by its difficulty in language and mathematics. Based on this item classification rating the language and mathematical difficulty of the items in the HSRC/UB/Stanford test, we generated the results in Figures 6.6a, 6.6b, 6.7a and 6.7b. The dots present items classified into four categories: eLeM – easy language, easy mathematics; eLhM – easy language, hard mathematics, hLeM – hard language, easy mathematics, and hLhM – hard language, hard mathematics.

FIGURE 6.6a *North West Province: Pre- and post-test scores by item and mathematics and language difficulty of item, 2009*

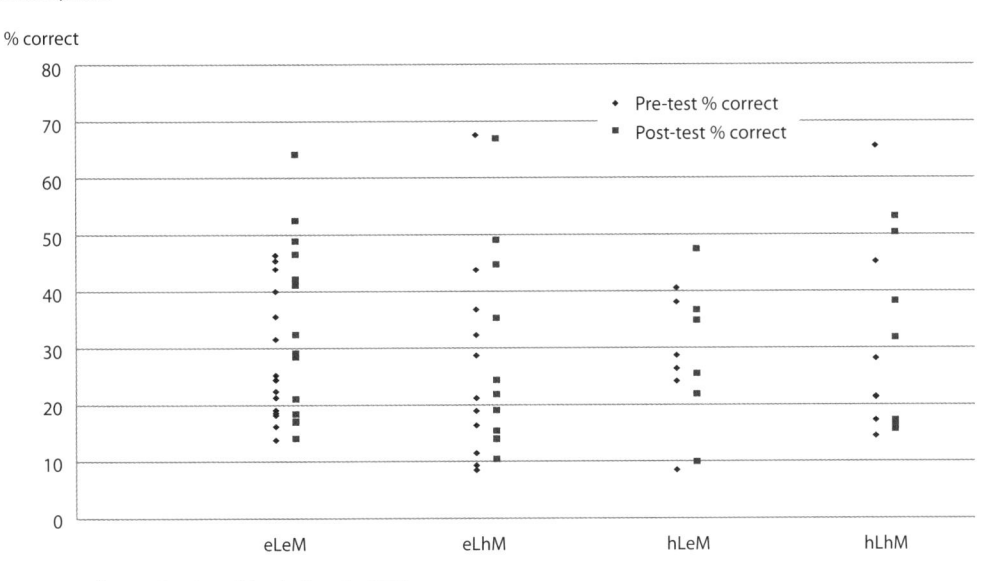

Source: North West Province Schools Sample, 2009.

FIGURE 6.6b *Botswana: Pre- and post-test scores by item and mathematics and language difficulty of item, 2009*

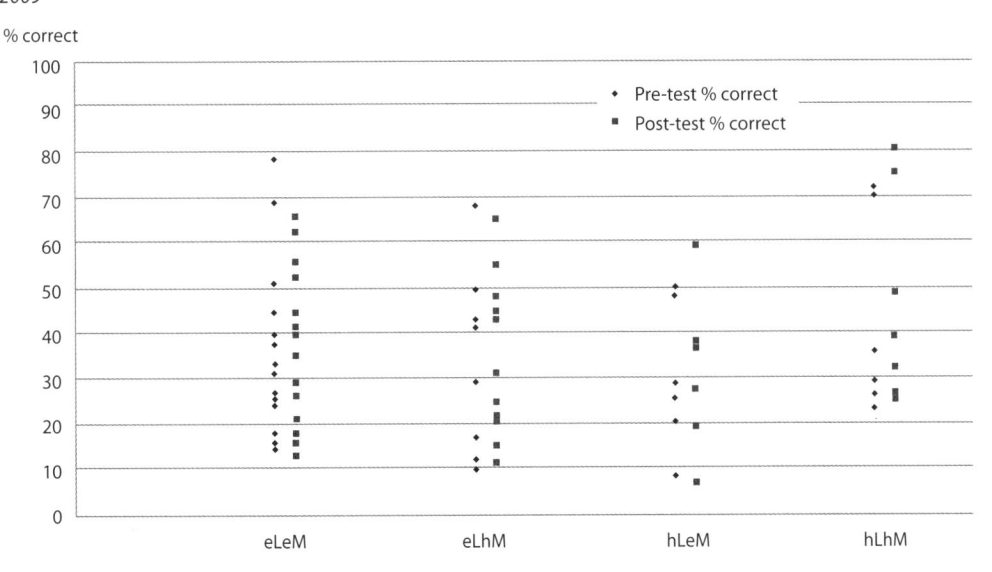

Source: Botswana Schools Sample, 2009.

In Figures 6.6a and 6.6b, each blue or pink dot in the graph represents a test item. In both country samples, on the easy language items learners scored lower on the harder mathematics items, and on the hard language items learners actually seemed to do better on the harder mathematics items, but lower overall than on the easy mathematics items. The initial test score mean on the hard language/hard mathematics items was higher than the other three, although that was not the case for the trimmed means. However, this difference is not statistically significant. The main difference between the North West Province and

FIGURE 6.7a *North West Province: Test score gains by item and mathematics and language difficulty of item, 2009*

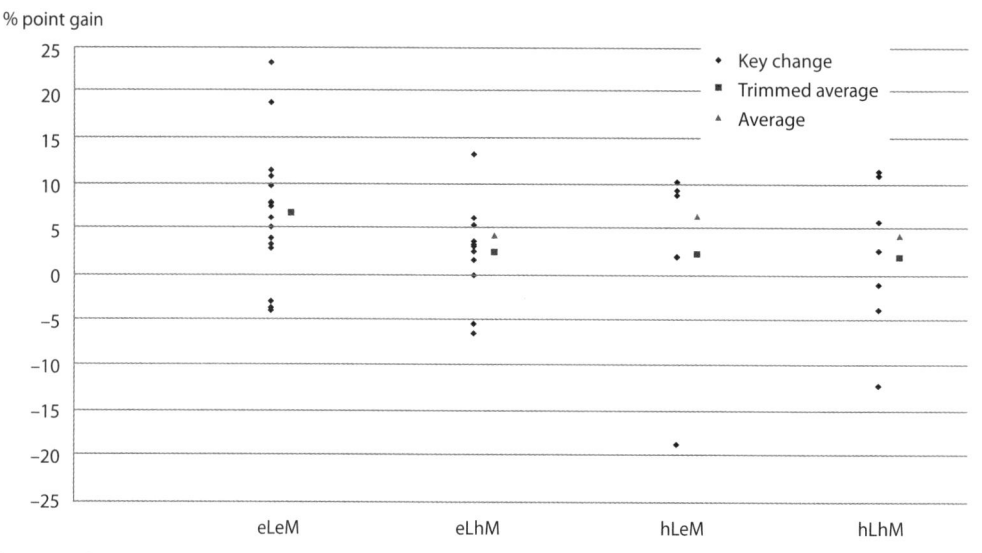

Source: North West Province Schools Sample, 2009.

FIGURE 6.7b *Botswana: Test score gains by item and mathematics and language difficulty of item, 2009*

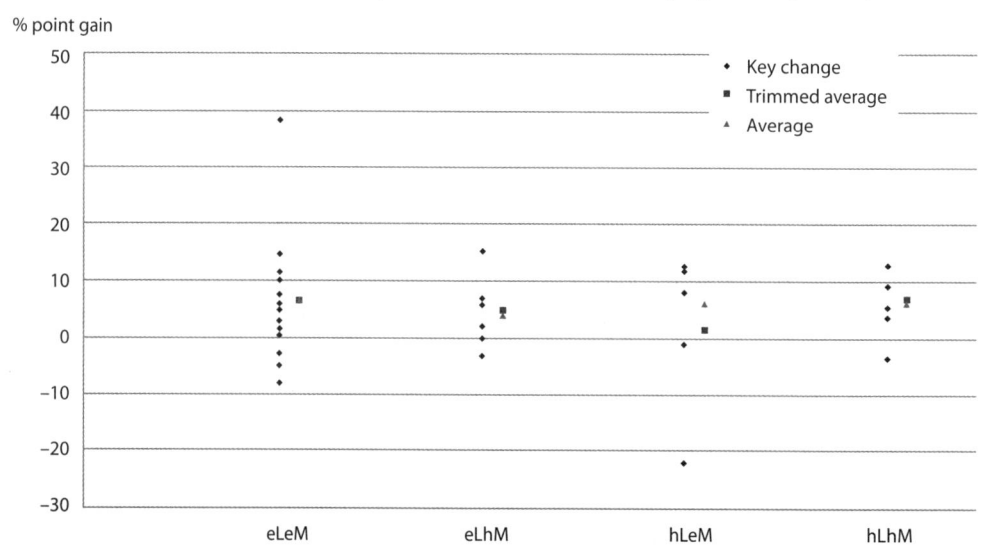

Source: Botswana Schools Sample, 2009.

Botswana scores is the somewhat lower variation in Botswana scores within the various categories of test items. However, the patterns of distribution on the items are very similar.

In Figures 6.7a and 6.7b, we see that the gains in both countries on the 'easy mathematics' items are somewhat larger (6 per cent in North West Province and 7.8 per cent in Botswana) when we use the

FIGURE 6.8a *North West Province: Pre- and post-test scores by item and by alternative specification of mathematics and language difficulty of item, 2009*

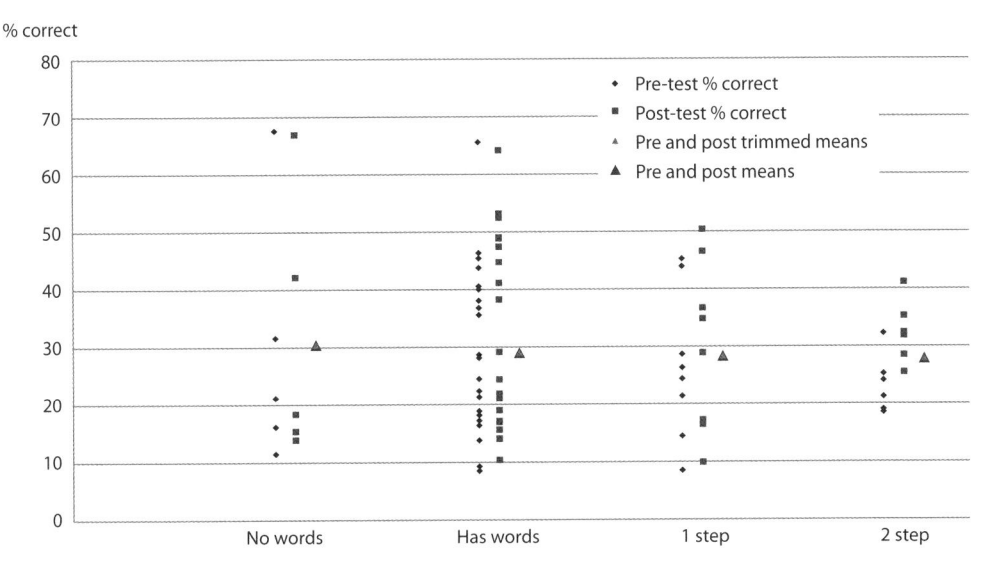

Source: North West Province Schools Sample, 2009.

FIGURE 6.8b *Botswana: Pre- and post-test scores by item and by alternative specification of mathematics and language difficulty of item, 2009*

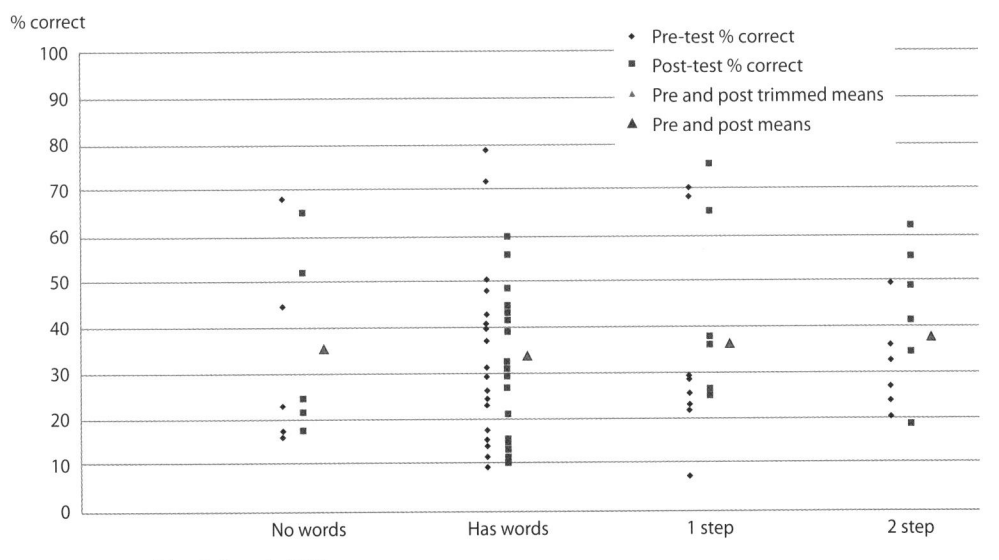

Source: Botswana Schools Sample, 2009.

Learner knowledge of mathematics | 85

trimmed gains (denoted by triangles) and smaller on the harder mathematics items, regardless of language. Thus, language difficulty does not seem to be that important. However, the largest gains when outliers are not removed is in the easy language/easy mathematics category of items, and the biggest negative outliers occur on hard language items (although there are only two of them). This could indicate that language does matter.

FIGURE 6.9a *North West Province: Test score gains by item and by alternative specification of mathematics and language difficulty of item, 2009*

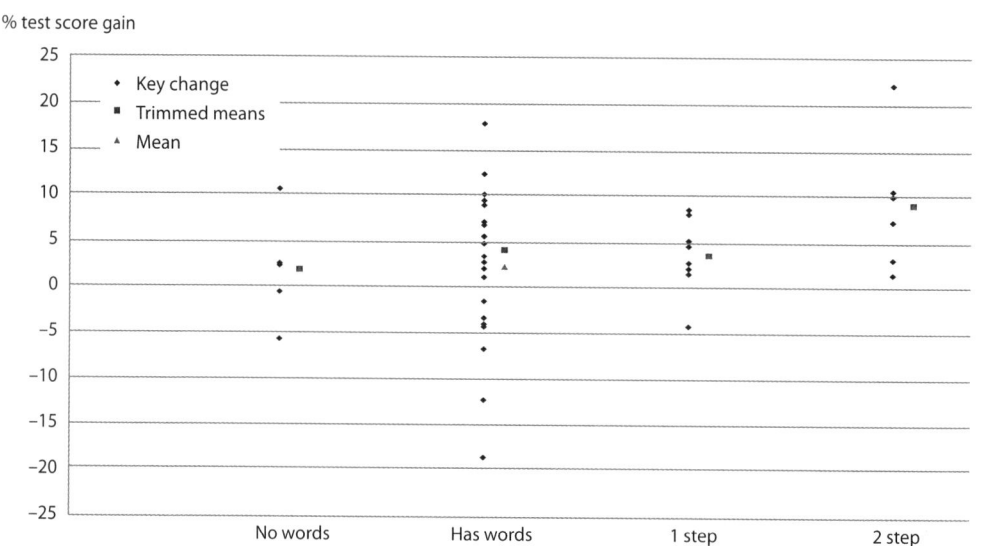

Source: North West Province Schools Sample, 2009.

FIGURE 6.9b *Botswana: Test score gains by item and by alternative specification of mathematics and language difficulty of item, 2009*

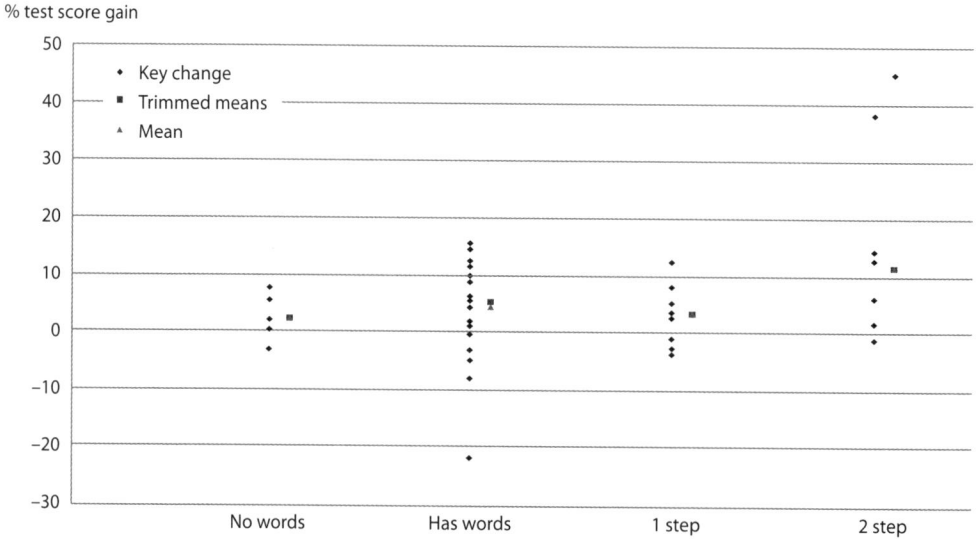

Source: Botswana Schools Sample, 2009.

The most significant outlier in both countries is related to an item that tests the learners' understanding of the concept of 'order of operations'. This is a complex rule, often stated using a rhyme or acronym: brackets of division multiplication, addition and subtraction (BODMAS). This is easy to pronounce but clearly not as easy to apply. An error analysis of the item reveals that there was a move to ignore the brackets and just to proceed left-to-right. The language embedded in this 'rule' (BODMAS) is complex. Presentation of this content in materials needs to be carefully considered.

The next pair of graphs presents an analysis based on a different classification of the language and mathematics complexity of the items. This classification rates the numeric, symbolic, and language complexity of the items in the HSRC/UB/Stanford test. The items were classified according to the following four categories:
- no words – included all items that contained only numeric or symbolic information,
- has words – included simply worded questions which give word instructions in combination with numeric and symbolic information,
- 1 step – included all single-step word problems, and
- 2 step – included word problems with more than one step.

In Figures 6.8a and 6.8b, we present the results for the pre- and post-test item distribution by category for the two countries. Each blue or red dot in the graph represents a test item. The means (magenta triangles) include both pre- and post-test scores.

The means (trimmed and untrimmed) show very little difference in mean achievement among these categories. The mean score on the two-step word problems, which tend to be more difficult, was somewhat, but not significantly lower, than the others.

Figures 6.9a and 6.9b present the test score gains based on the item classification rating the numeric, symbolic, and language complexity of the items in the HSRC/UB/Stanford test. Each green dot in the graph represents a test item. The pattern of the gains suggests that the 'no words' category shows the smallest gains while '2 step' shows the highest gains. This goes counter to the expectation that complexity according to the language and mathematics should be the most difficult items and hence those on which we would expect the lowest gains.

Both of the different classifications we have discussed here seem to suggest language does not necessarily make things harder for learners. This needs further investigation, but the item results on this 40-item test suggest that the main difficulties students experience is with the mathematics, not with the language. Nevertheless, item and error analysis could be done in detail to unpack the meaning of these statistics generated from our learner tests.

Conclusion

The large majority of the 3 800 North West Province students and the 1 750 Botswana students in our original sample were from poor families and attended fee-free schools where the language of instruction was English. Although their home language was mostly Setswana, only a minority were taught in Setswana.

The average initial test scores were 28.6 per cent in North West Province and 33.6 per cent in Botswana (when all items are included – even those that were not clear on the Botswana version of the test). Thus, at the beginning of Grade 6, Botswana students scored significantly higher on this test than students in North West Province, and students in both samples scored rather low on a largely Grade 5 test. Improvements between the pre-and post-test scores were also minimal – 3 points in North West Province and 4 points in Botswana – yet, also significantly higher in Botswana. In many cases, learners in both countries answered test items incorrectly because it did not appear that they had been taught the mathematics correctly. Answers were frequently based on misconceptions that are shown in the literature to be common in other mathematics education research. Whereas learners scored poorly overall, the highest scores were in patterns, shapes and numbers, and the lowest in measurement and data. In the following chapters we will show that this may be linked to low teacher knowledge in mathematics, inadequate levels of mathematics teaching skills and insufficient coverage and exposure. Lesson observations also show that learners are taught to memorise without conceptual understanding.

Our findings on the relationship between mathematics and language are also significant and run counter to much of the conventional wisdom on language in mathematics teaching and learning in southern Africa. Even though teachers insisted we give the student test in English, we observed that the majority – particularly in South Africa – spoke English with difficulty. Students whose mother tongue was Afrikaans, who were taught in Afrikaans and who wrote the test in Afrikaans, scored substantially higher than English or Setswana speakers. Learners whose teachers code-switched did worse than those learners whose teachers consistently spoke one language, either English or an African language. When we assessed how well learners did on test items that were scored according to how difficult the mathematics and English was, we found that language difficulty did seem to be important. On another classification of test items according to the numeric, symbolic and language complexity of items, there was also very little difference in achievement, suggesting again that language does not necessarily make things harder for learners.

CHAPTER 7

Teacher knowledge of mathematics

In this chapter, we analyse the characteristics of the Grade 6 mathematics teachers in our samples of North West Province and Botswana schools who filled out the teacher questionnaire and took the mathematics knowledge test. We also analyse whether teachers who did better on the test teach in schools with students of higher socio-economic background and in schools where students scored higher on the initial (pre-) test. There are several reasons why it is important to know whether teacher mathematical knowledge is distributed in a way that advantages students who are already more academically favoured. First, since most analyses of student achievement use only one test, not pre- and post-tests, to estimate the relation between student achievement and teacher skills, if teacher skills are distributed in favour of higher achieving students, this would suggest a systematic bias in such estimates (we will test this proposition in a later chapter). Second, from the standpoint of equity, a systematic assignment of more mathematics knowledge to already higher scoring students could mean that the gap between lower and higher achieving students increases over time. This equity issue is important if teachers with more mathematics knowledge are shown to produce greater student learning. We also test this proposition in a later chapter.

Who are the teachers in North West Province and Botswana and what are their mathematics skills?

In both North West Province, where we surveyed 62 teachers teaching in 64 classrooms in 58 schools, and in Botswana, where we surveyed 58 teachers in 62 classrooms (four teachers taught multiple classes) in 58 schools, one-third of the teachers were men and two-thirds women. In North West Province, the teachers were, on average, considerably older than those in Botswana, where they averaged 39 years old – not particularly old as teacher labour forces go. The age distribution of teachers in Figure 7.1 reflects that in North West Province, 46 of the 62 teachers were forty years old or older, and almost one-third of them were over fifty years old, whereas in Botswana, 30 of the 58 teachers were forty years old or older, but only 3 per cent were fifty years old or older.

Another important difference between our teacher samples in the two regions is that although teachers on both sides of the border had a lot of teaching experience, Botswana teachers were much more likely to have been in their current school a relatively shorter time. This is consistent with the policy of the Botswana government to allow and even encourage teachers to move around to different schools in the country. As other data on where teachers were trained suggests, teachers in Botswana are relatively mobile and move from one part of the country to another, but teachers in North West Province are not. Figure 7.2a shows that teachers in the North West Province sample overwhelmingly (90 per cent)

FIGURE 7.1 *North West Province and Botswana: Sampled teachers by age, 2009*

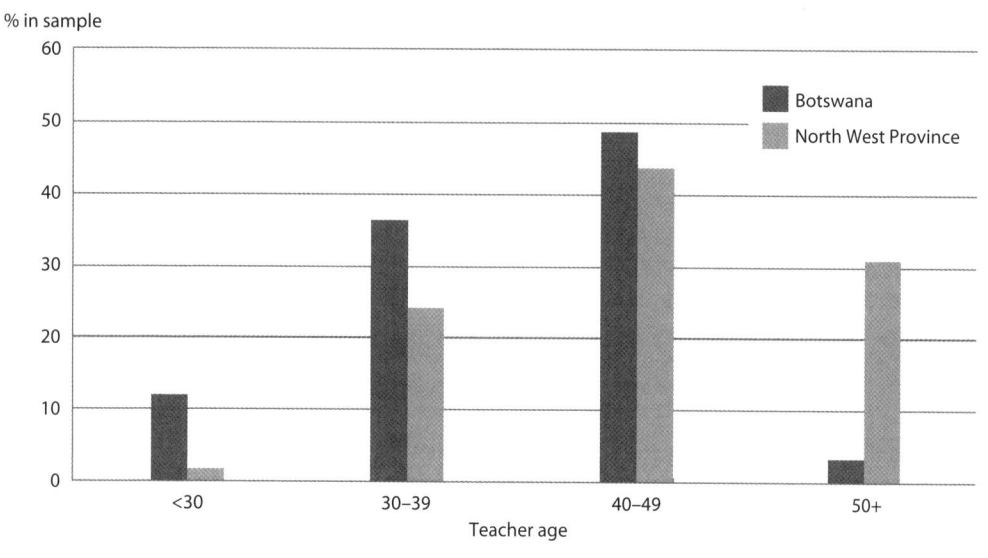

Source: North West Province and Botswana Schools Sample, 2009.

had more than 11 years teaching experience, the majority of them had taught more than 11 years in their current school and had taught mathematics for more than 11 years overall during their career. Figure 7.2b shows that in Botswana, most teachers in the sample (75 per cent) had more than 11 years teaching experience, about 60 per cent had taught mathematics for more than 11 years overall during their career, but only one in four had been at their current school for more than five years.

FIGURE 7.2a *North West Province: Percentage of teachers by years of teaching experience, years teaching in current school, and years teaching mathematics, 2009*

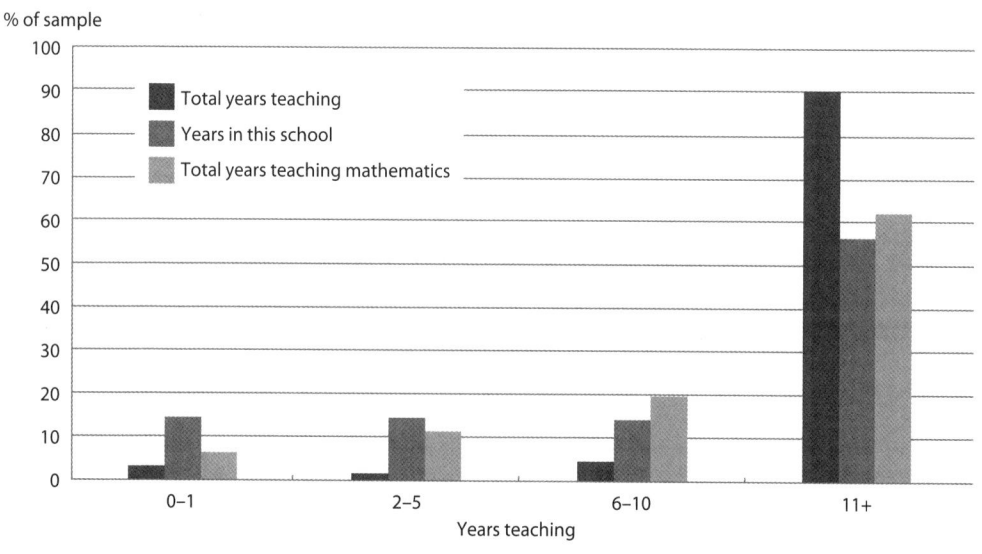

Source: North West Province Schools Sample, 2009.

TABLE 7.1 *North West Province and Botswana: College at which teachers in sample trained, 2009*

North West Province		Botswana	
Teacher training college	Number in sample trained	Teacher training college	Number in sample trained
Taung College	9	Lobatse	11
Batswana College	9	Serowe	19
Lehurutshe College	12	Tlokweng	18
Tlhabane College	7	Francistown	7

Source: North West Province and Botswana Schools Sample, 2009.

Teachers on both sides of the border were almost all trained in nearby teacher training colleges. All but three of the teachers in North West Province attended primary schools in North West Province (most in the area where they were now teaching). This is consistent with data in the United States, which shows that more than 80 per cent of teachers in New York State, for example, teach in schools less than 20 miles from the high school that they attended (Lankford et al. 2002).

All but nine teachers were trained in local North West Province teacher training colleges (before the late 1990s, when these colleges were integrated into universities and technikons). Of the 62 teachers who filled out our questionnaires, 37, or almost 60 per cent, attended four of those teachers' colleges, as shown in Table 7.1. Only three teachers had university degrees (two from North West University, one from the University of South Africa, UNISA). In Botswana, all but one of the teachers attended primary schools in Botswana, but they were more likely to come from various parts of Botswana to teach in their current schools. All but two were trained in Botswana's four teacher training colleges (but some as far away as Francistown on the other side of the country), and the two were trained at UB.

FIGURE 7.2b *Botswana: Percentage of teachers by years of teaching experience, years teaching in current school, and years teaching mathematics, 2009*

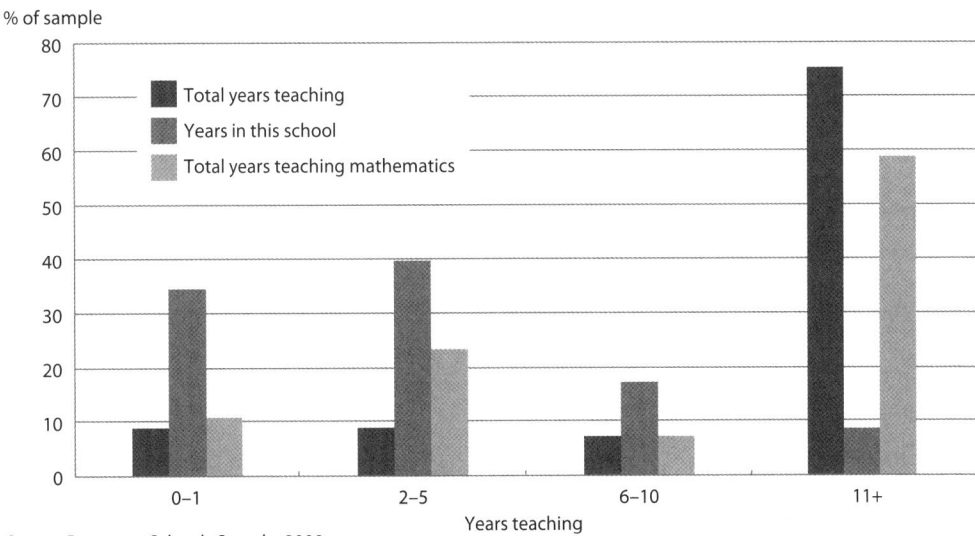

Source: Botswana Schools Sample, 2009.

Teacher knowledge of mathematics | 91

All the teachers in our North West Province sample (but two) had been teaching for more than ten years, 80 per cent of them more than 15 years, and 60 per cent more than 20 years. In other words, only one out of five began teaching after the apartheid era, and three out of five began teaching during a period in which schools were an important point of resistance against the apartheid government. The teachers in our Botswana sample had also been teaching for many years – a third for more than 20 years – so a majority were trained under the previous system, where the requirement to enter into a teacher training college was the equivalent of the passing the O-level examination (roughly the 10th grade). This was one more year of schooling required than for teacher training in pre-1997 South Africa.

Today, in Botswana, entry into a teacher training college requires the Botswana equivalent of passing the British A-level examination (about 40 to 45 per cent in our sample have been trained at this higher level), and in South Africa, primary school teachers require a university degree. The big difference between the two countries is that in the 15 years since the reform of the South African teacher training system, primary school teachers in Botswana have been trained in the same teacher training colleges as before but at a higher level of training; whereas in South Africa, local teacher training colleges no longer exist. Those who want to become teachers need to attend a university (in North West Province, the local university is North West University, with three campuses, the closest of which to the region where we sampled is at Mahikeng).

We asked teachers what degree they had received, and the vast majority, 85 per cent in North West Province and 96 per cent in Botswana, had undergone at least three years of training. It should be remembered, however, that the teacher training colleges that almost all teachers in North West and a majority of teachers in Botswana attended were upper secondary school level education in terms of the mathematics they were exposed to (with that mathematics exposure less than students in academic secondary schools).[1] Only 15 of the 44 teachers in our Botswana sample who reported finishing secondary school or more (Form 5 or above) had entered teaching before 1992. Nevertheless, that the teaching force in Botswana is relatively younger means that their mathematics preparation before entering teacher training tends to be associated with completed secondary school education, thus a higher level of mathematics training than in our North West teacher sample. Tables 7.2a and 7.2b on page 93 show the distribution of teacher education in the two countries.

Thus, a high percentage of the teachers in both our samples are local and trained in local teacher training colleges before the early 1990s. In North West Province, this means that they started teaching during the apartheid era. The teachers in our North West sample are, on average, older than in Botswana and more likely to have had only some upper secondary school level training in mathematics. In both regions of the study, teachers average three to four years of teacher training.

Teachers in our samples were asked what mathematics topics they had covered in their training, and those in Botswana appear to have had more mathematics training than those in North West. The vast majority of those who answered this question (86 per cent in North West Province and 98 per cent in Botswana) said that they had covered numbers (including fractions and word problems). Around 75 per cent in North West and 88 per cent in Botswana said that they had covered geometry; 75 per cent in North West and 96 per cent in Botswana indicated that they had covered measurement (mass,

---

1   In addition, in North West Province, although the teachers we interviewed were all teaching mathematics to Grade 6 students, and in many schools were responsible for all Grade 6 mathematics teaching in the school, only about one out of five named mathematics as their primary subject of specialisation during their teacher education. We also asked them which level of schooling they had been trained to teach. Again, and not surprisingly, a vast majority had been trained for the Foundation Phase of primary, or for senior primary, or for general primary. A few had been trained to be junior secondary teachers.

TABLE 7.2a *North West Province: Highest degree of training for teachers in the sample, 2009*

Highest level of training attained by teachers	Number in sample with this level
Teacher's Certificate – 2-year initial training	2
Diploma in Education – 2- or 3-year upgrading	7
Teacher's Diploma – 3- year initial training	18
Further Diploma in Education (FDE) or Diploma in Special Education (DSE) or Post Professional Certificate or Higher Diploma in Education – 1 year after initial teaching certificate/diploma	6
Higher Diploma in Education – 4- year initial training	8
Advanced Certificate in Education (ACE) – 1 year after initial teaching diploma/degree	15
Postgraduate Certificate in Education (PGCE) or Higher Diploma in Education postgraduate – 1-year training after degree	1
4-year BEd	7

Source: North West Province Schools Sample, 2009.

TABLE 7.2b *Botswana: Highest degree of training for teachers in the sample, 2009*

Highest level of training attained by teachers	Number in sample with this level
Form 3 + three years teacher education	11
Form 5 + three years teacher education	31
BGCSE + three years teacher education	3
Other secondary school degree + three years teacher education	6
4-year BEd	4

Source: Botswana Schools Sample, 2009.

capacity, length, volume, etc.); only two-thirds in North West but 84 per cent in Botswana said that they had covered algebra; and about half in North West but 61 per cent in Botswana reported having covered data handling.

Teacher mathematics knowledge

After administering the mathematics pre-test in our sample schools in March 2009, researchers from the UB, HSRC, and Stanford administered three additional instruments in the same sample of schools in July 2009. These three instruments were:
- a teacher questionnaire, which included a test of teacher Grade 6 level mathematics knowledge,
- a principal questionnaire, and
- videotaping a Grade 6 mathematics lesson taught by the teachers who filled out a questionnaire.

In North West Province, 64 teachers filled out questionnaires and 61 took the mathematics test that we gave to assess how much mathematics knowledge the teachers had retained and were bringing to their teaching. In Botswana, 58 teachers filled out the questionnaire and 57 took the test.[2] The questionnaire focuses on basic operations: multiplication-division, fractions, geometry, and percentages. There were 24 questions on the questionnaire, and about one-half of the questions had multiple parts.[3] We graded the test in two ways: (A) including the multiple parts, the test had 63 possible answers, and every answer counted as 1 – the per cent correct was the number of right answers divided by 63; and (B) we estimated the percentage correct of each of the multiple answer questions and gave that score to each of the 11 multiple answer questions – the sum of the correct answers on the single answer questions and the internal score of each of the multiple answer questions were added and divided by 24.

The first test score rewarded teachers more who did well on the multiple answer questions; the second way of scoring gave each of the 24 questions the same weight, whether multi-part or not. The two test scores are highly correlated, with a correlation coefficient of 0.88. We generally use test score (grading system A), but undertake some alternative estimates of the relation between test score (using grading system B) and other variables to check whether there is sensitivity to the way teacher test score is calculated.

In either case, teachers in North West Province did not do particularly well on average in this assessment of their mathematics knowledge. Teachers in Botswana did significantly better but still scored fairly low. The percentage for teachers using scoring method (grading system A) was 46.5 per cent in North West and 53.5 per cent in Botswana, and using grading system B, 40 per cent in North West and 47.7 per cent in Botswana. This could be the result of not taking the questionnaire very seriously (it had absolutely no consequences for them), or that after many years (the majority of teachers were over 40 years old) they had forgotten much of the mathematics they had learnt, or had not had a good initial base of mathematics training. We should also point out that the teacher information part of the questionnaire that preceded the test part of the questionnaire was long and asked a lot of detailed information on their teacher training and opinions on various education issues. Thus, by the time they got to the test section, they may have been short of time or just tired of answering questions. This aspect of the testing could be important in explaining the results. In any case, the relatively low average scores suggest that they did not find the 24 mathematics and mathematic diagnostic questions – drawn almost entirely from the Grade 6 curriculum – easy.

The results varied greatly over items, as shown in Figures 7.3a (63-item test grading) and 7.3b (24-item test grading). However, the most notable feature of the teacher test results is how similar the variation was across items in the two countries, regardless of the way the test was graded. Teachers in Botswana did better on many items, but in general they did poorly and well on the same items as the teachers in North West Province. The mathematics knowledge teachers have in the two countries is surprisingly similar.

---

2   The 58th teacher took the questionnaire/test, but only attempted to answer a few questions, and only answered one correctly. We imputed his/her score as the mean score of the other 57 teachers.
3   Teachers were assured that these questions were for research purposes only, and were asked to complete items when they had left them blank. However, in some cases they chose not to respond to items. These blank items are marked as incorrect. This is justified by some preliminary statistical analysis that shows that teachers tended to leave harder items blank, and these same teachers tended to score lower on the remaining items that they did answer. However, if teachers were simply skipping some questions then this strategy will bias the overall averages downwards. This was only a serious problem in one of the questionnaires, since in the others, a small percentage (less than 6.7 per cent) of the knowledge questions were left blank.

FIGURE 7.3a *North West Province and Botswana: Teacher mathematics test results by test item, 63-item grading, 2009*

Source: North West Province and Botswana Schools Sample, 2009.

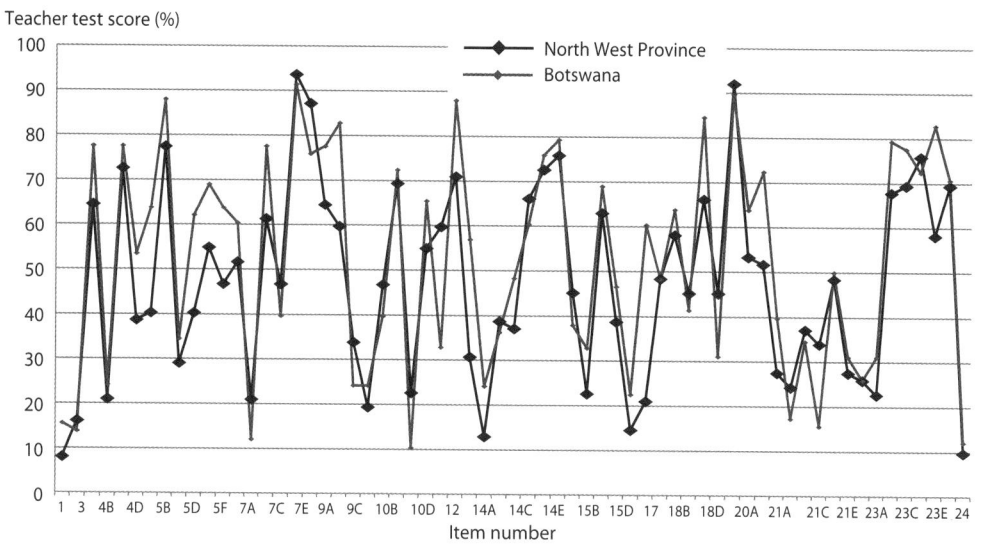

FIGURE 7.3b *North West Province and Botswana: Teacher mathematics test results by test item, 24-item grading, 2009*

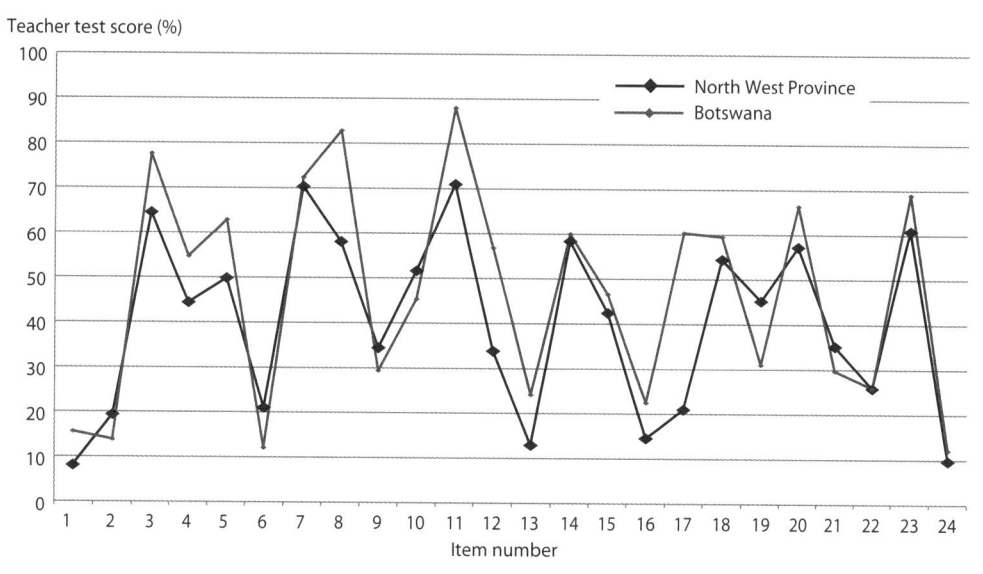

Source: North West Province and Botswana Schools Sample, 2009.

Despite doing poorly on eight of the 24 questions, teachers did reasonably well on some of the items. For example, on parts C and D of this item:[4]

Ms. Bahadur asked her learners to write expressions that, when evaluated, give an answer of 10. After reviewing her learners' work, she was pleased that many of her learners used more than one operation in their expressions. However, she was concerned that their notation was not mathematically correct. Determine if each expression, as it is written below, equals 10.

(Circle 1 or 2 to indicate EQUALS 10 or DOES NOT EQUAL 10 for each expression.)

Expression	Equals 10	Does not equal 10
A. $2 + 3 \times 2$	1	2
B. $8 + 9 - 5 + 2$	1	2
C. $15 - 2 - 3$	1	2
D. $80 \div 4 \times 2$	1	2
E. $6 + 2 \times 2$	1	2

Note that to obtain a correct answer for parts C and D of this item, the teacher simply operates from left to right without taking into account the order of operations. However, the other parts of the item requires the teachers to know that multiplication is performed first and then addition (part A and E) and that subtraction does not follow addition when parentheses or brackets are absent from the mathematical sentence (part B), and so the performance is much lower. Learners also had difficulty applying the order of operation rule (BODMAS) properly.

The teachers also did well on this one:

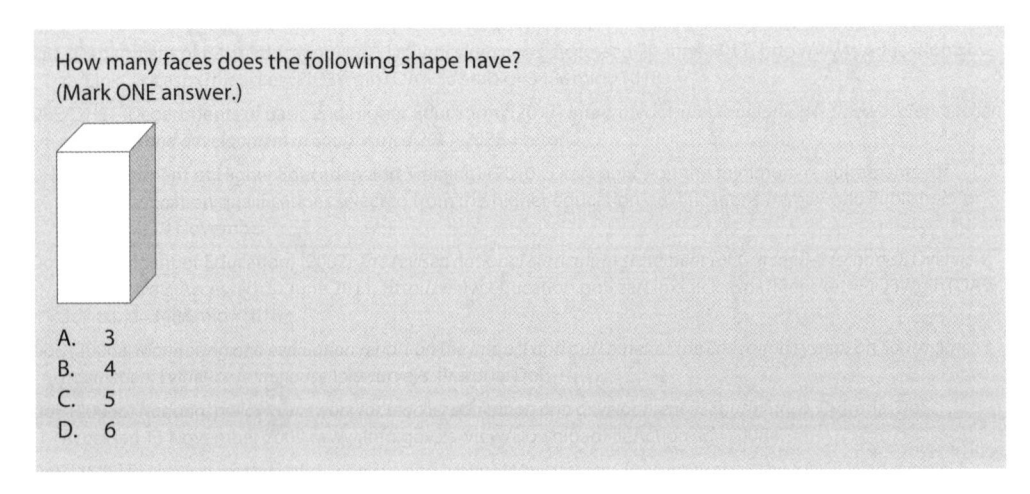

How many faces does the following shape have?
(Mark ONE answer.)

A. 3
B. 4
C. 5
D. 6

This simple shape item, testing basic knowledge of a 3-D shape, was also on the learner test, and learners also performed well on it.

---

4   This item is an adaptation of the original item used in the Learning Mathematics for Teaching (LMT) Project from the University of Michigan. The original item included mathematical expressions with negative numbers and exponents.

On the other hand, here is a question that very few teachers answered correctly:

> How many decimal numbers are there between 0.30 and 0.40?
> (Mark ONE answer.)
> A. 9
> B. 10
> C. 99
> D. An infinite number

This question calls on higher-level understanding of rational numbers. It is not surprising that teachers found it more difficult.

Similarly, few answered this one correctly:

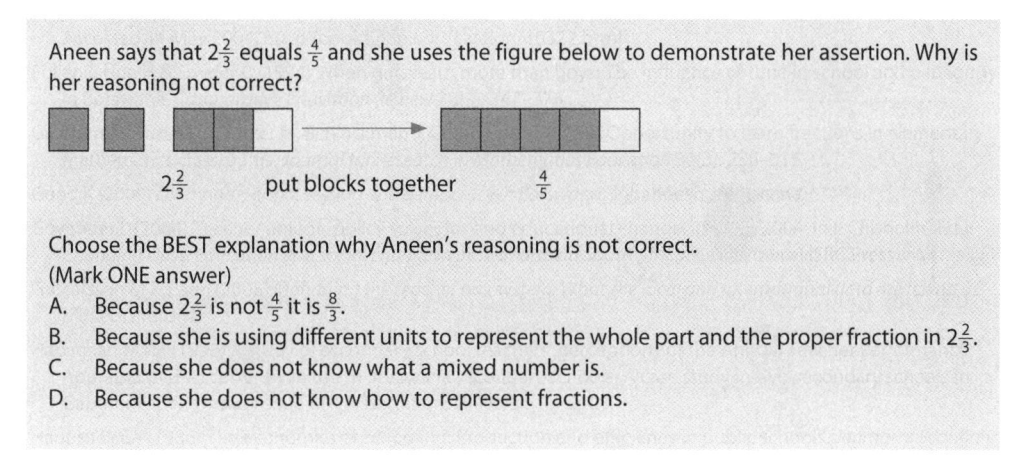

> Aneen says that $2\frac{2}{3}$ equals $\frac{4}{5}$ and she uses the figure below to demonstrate her assertion. Why is her reasoning not correct?
>
> $2\frac{2}{3}$ put blocks together $\frac{4}{5}$
>
> Choose the BEST explanation why Aneen's reasoning is not correct.
> (Mark ONE answer)
> A. Because $2\frac{2}{3}$ is not $\frac{4}{5}$ it is $\frac{8}{3}$.
> B. Because she is using different units to represent the whole part and the proper fraction in $2\frac{2}{3}$.
> C. Because she does not know what a mixed number is.
> D. Because she does not know how to represent fractions.

This item allowed teachers to demonstrate their pedagogic content knowledge.

Thus, teachers did well on most questions that dealt with basic arithmetic operations and simple geometry, but poorly on those questions of decimals and fractions and on those questions that required more underlying knowledge of mathematics and mathematics pedagogical knowledge, such as the multiplication problem shown.

We would expect that teachers with higher levels of education would have scored higher on this test. For the purposes of estimating this relationship, we defined the first two categories of teacher education in North West (Table 7.2a) as the lowest level (Level 1) of teacher training (9 observations), the next two categories as the next level (Level 2) of teacher training (24 observations), the next three categories as the third level (Level 3) of teacher training (24 observations), and the BEd degree as the highest level (Level 4) of teacher training (7 observations). In Botswana, we define the first category as the lowest level of teacher training shown in Table 7.2b (11 observations), the next category as the next two levels of teacher training (34 observations), the next category as the third level of teacher training (6 observations), and the BEd degree as the highest level (Level 4) of teacher training (4 observations).

Figures 7.4a and 7.4b on page 98 show the test scores by grading the level of teachers educated in North West Province and Botswana respectively. When we matched the average test score for teachers in North West with each of these levels of education, we found a negative but not significant relation between having higher teaching degrees and the average score on the test.

FIGURE 7.4a *North West Province: Teacher test score by Grading A, Grading B and level of teacher education, 2009*

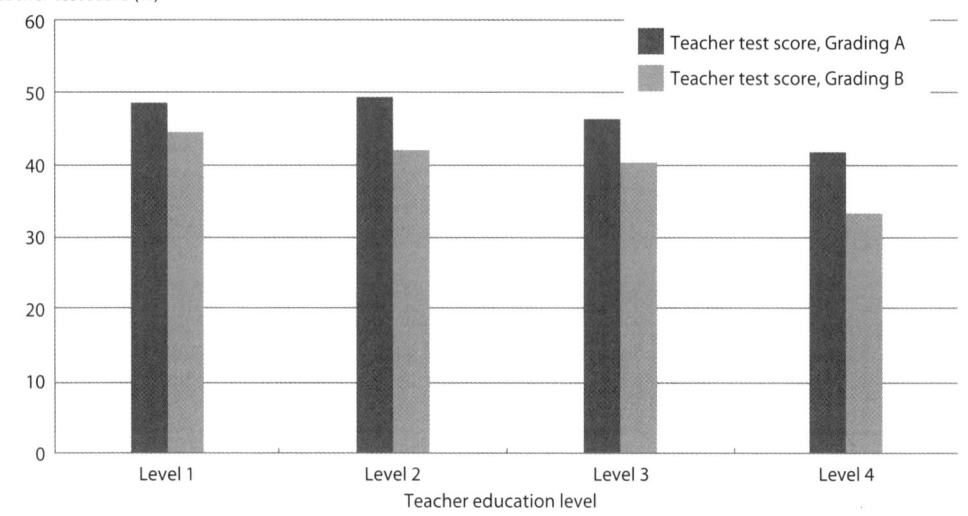

Source: North West Province Schools Sample, 2009.

Note: Level 1 – Teacher Certificate or Diploma in Education; Level 2 – Teacher's Diploma; Level 3 – FDE or DSE or PPC or Higher Diploma in Education or ACE; Level 4 – PGCE or BA in Education.

FIGURE 7.4b *Botswana: Teacher test score by Grading A, Grading B and level of teacher education, 2009*

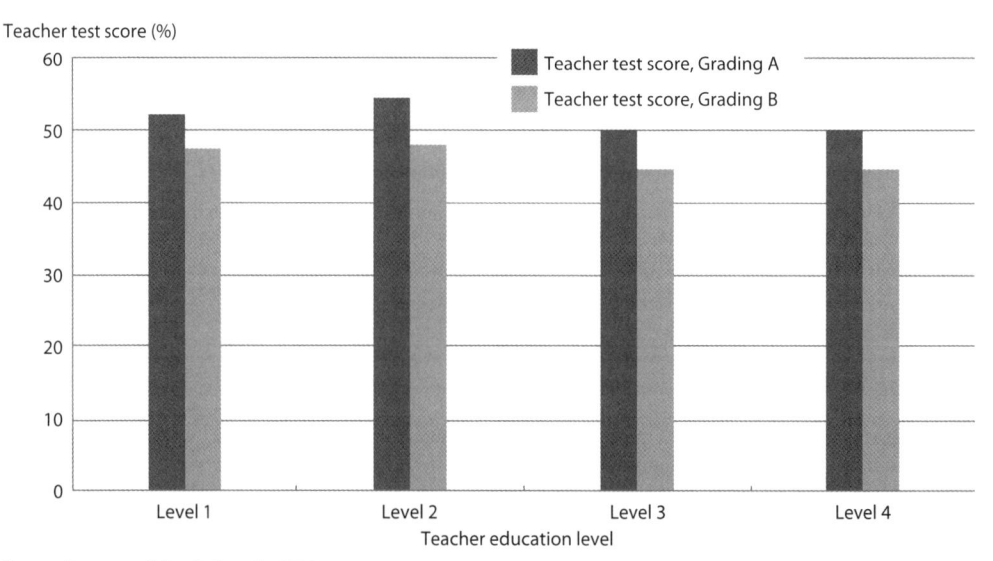

Source: Botswana Schools Sample, 2009.

Note: Level 1 – Form 3 plus Teacher Training College Diploma in Primary Education; Level 2 – Form 5 or BGCSE plus Teacher Training College Diploma in Primary Education; Level 3 – other secondary degrees plus Teacher Training College Diploma in Primary Education; Level 4 – Form 5 plus BA in Education.

Using both the A grading system (based on giving equal weight to each possible answer) and the B grading system (giving equal weight to each of the 24 questions) for the teacher test we found that teachers with different levels of training had essentially the same average score on the teacher questionnaire test. An exception was those who said they had a postgraduate certificate in education (PGCE) or a BEd degree – these teachers scored lower than the others (Figure 7.4a).

However, in Botswana, we found the opposite tendency: there is a positive but not significant relation between having probably had more mathematics (completing Form 5 rather than Form 3 before taking teacher training) and the average score on the test. However, the few teachers that reported having a bachelors degree in education did less well on the test (Figure 7.4b).

We need to be careful about drawing inferences from such a comparison because we specifically sampled schools in North West Province that were likely to be serving low-income students, and those with, say, bachelors degrees in education who teach in these schools may be self-selected in a negative way. In other words, teachers with BEd degrees who are much more proficient in mathematics are not very likely to be teaching in the schools we sampled. At the other extreme, those who only have Level 1 teacher training (as we defined it from the formal categories) who ended up teaching two decades ago were probably a local (largely female) elite who could only get professional jobs as teachers, so may have a higher level of mathematics knowledge than the average younger person in the province with only secondary school education. We should therefore not draw the conclusion from these results that formal education makes no difference in teachers' mathematics knowledge.

It appears that older teachers, who have taught more years both in total and spent more time teaching mathematics, did not do as well in the mathematics test as did the teachers with less experience. This is logical in one sense, since older teachers have probably not been exposed to mathematics training for a longer period of time. It suggests that the high average age of teachers in North West schools means that the mathematics knowledge of these teachers may be an issue. However, we have to be careful in drawing strong conclusions from the means in Table 7.3 since there are relatively few teachers in the 0 to 1 years of experience category in either measure of experience (overall and mathematics teaching).

We also need to be careful because there is not the same trend when we measure teaching experience by the number of years teaching mathematics. So those who have taught mathematics for more years do not have significantly lower mathematics test scores. We did the same analysis for the sample of Botswana teachers and found no relationship between teachers' years of experience teaching and their performance in the mathematics questionnaire/test we gave them. It is possible that older teachers have less education, so the two variables could confound the relation of their experience to

TABLE 7.3 *North West Province: Mean teacher test score (per cent) by overall mathematics teaching experience, 2009*

	Overall teaching experience		Mathematics teaching experience	
Years experience	Grading A	Grading B	Grading A	Grading B
0 to 1 years	61	67	57	67
2 to 5 years	52	63	41	52
6 to 10 years	47	58	51	64
>11 years	47	57	47	56

Source: North West Province Schools Sample, 2009.

their mathematics knowledge, but when we control for their education level, we still find no relation to their mathematics knowledge score.

Do teachers who know more mathematics teach students of higher socio-economic background and higher mathematics achievement?

One of the more important methodological problems researchers face in trying to disentangle the effect on student achievement of school inputs from the effect of resources in the home, such as more educated parents, more reading material and greater social capital, is that teachers are not likely to be randomly assigned to schools, and students may not be randomly assigned to teachers in the school. The first problem may be important, but the second problem is minimised in our sample of schools

TABLE 7.4 *North West Province and Botswana: Teacher mathematics knowledge and average student socio-economic background, by test grading method, 2009*

	North West		Botswana	
Variable	Teacher test Grading A	Teacher test Grading B	Teacher test Grading A	Teacher test Grading B
Average class SES	0.694*	1.088***	0.491	0.617
	(0.390)	(0.431)	(0.564)	(0.504)
Intercept	39.26***	28.83***	48.05***	40.88***
Observations	62	62	64	64
Adjusted R²	0.034	0.081	−0.004	0.009

Source: North West Province and Botswana Schools Sample, 2009.

* p<0.10, *** p<0.01.

FIGURE 7.5 *North West Province: Teacher questionnaire score and average classroom student socio-economic background, 2009*

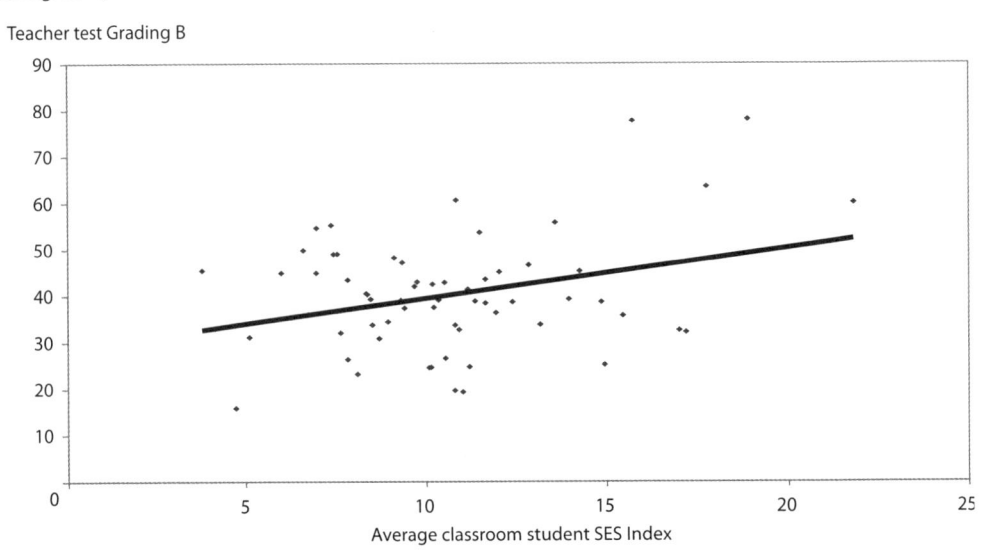

Source: North West Province Schools Sample, 2009.

because in almost all (all but three in North West) of the schools we sampled, only one mathematics teacher taught all the 6th grade classes. In Botswana, we have several cases of teachers teaching more than one class in the school, and we collected data on students' test scores, how many lessons were taught, class size, and other data in more than one class these teachers taught. In such cases we assigned the same teacher test score and teaching quality of the teacher to each of these classes, but used other class measures to capture variation between classes for the same teacher. Thus, as is shown

FIGURE 7.6a *North West Province: Initial student achievement score and teacher test score graded giving equal weight to each question (Grading B), 2009*

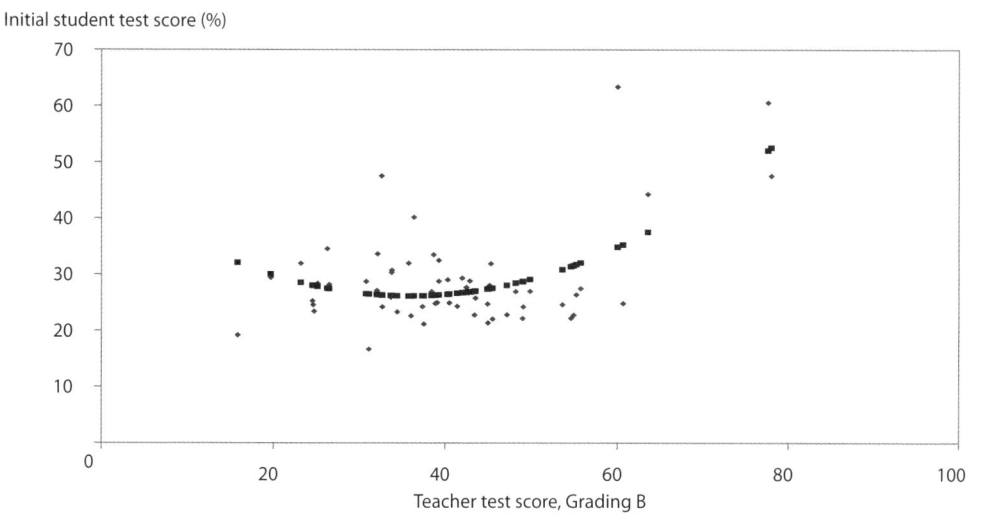

Source: North West Province Schools Sample, 2009.

FIGURE 7.6b *Botswana: Initial student achievement score and teacher test score graded giving equal weight to each question (Grading B), 2009*

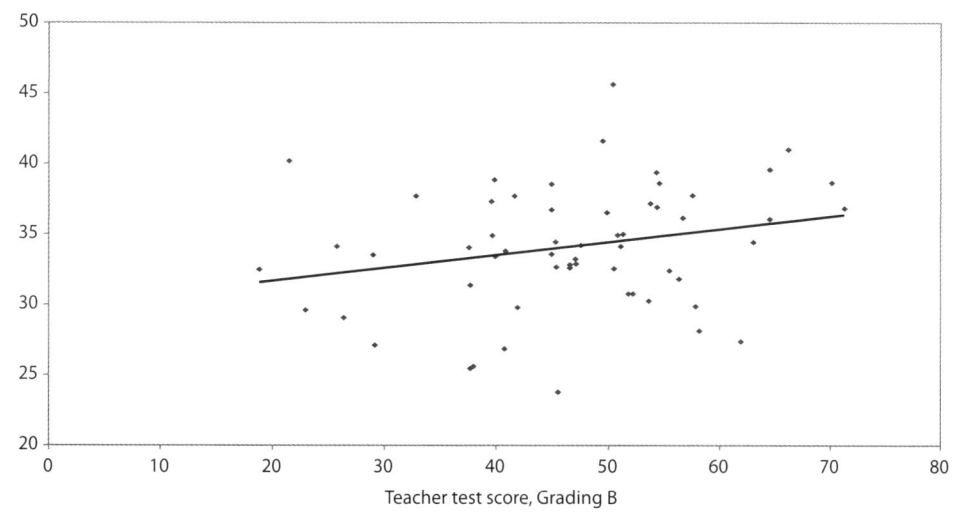

Source: Botswana Schools Sample, 2009.

Teacher knowledge of mathematics | 101

in Table 7.4, in North West, we have 62 teachers in 62 classrooms in 58 schools and in Botswana, we have a total of 58 teachers in 58 schools who took the test, but they teach a total of 64 classes.

The relationship between the average socio-economic background of students in each school and teacher test score in our two samples suggests that, in terms of their mathematics knowledge, teachers appear to be randomly assigned to schools in Botswana but not in North West. In North West, for both methods of grading the teacher's score on the questionnaire, we find a positive and statistically significant relationship between teacher score and the average socio-economic background of students in the teacher's class, but not in Botswana.

Figure 7.5 shows this relation in North West.

However, the teacher test score in Botswana is positively and, in the case of the Grading B teacher test score, statistically significantly, correlated with the average classroom student pre-test score (Figure 7.6b). In North West, this is also the case no matter how the teacher test was graded. Figure 7.6a, which shows the relation for Grading B (each teacher test question given equal weight), suggests that

TABLE 7.5a North West Province: Initial student achievement score and teacher test score, 2009

Variable	Model 1	Model 2	Model 3	Model 4
Teacher test score, Grading A	0.276***	−0.871		
	(.093)	(.606)		
Teacher tests score, A squared		0.012*		
		(.0063)		
Teacher test score, Grading B			0.282***	−0.989***
			(.080)	(.333)
Teacher test score, B squared				0.014***
				(.0036)
Intercept	15.75***	41.66***	17.18***	43.34***
Observations	62	62	62	62
Adjusted R²	0.11	0.15	0.15	0.32

Source: North West Province Schools Sample, 2009.

* $p<0.10$, *** $p<0.01$.

TABLE 7.5b Botswana: Initial student achievement score and teacher test score, 2009

Variable	Model 1	Model 2
Teacher test score, Grading A	0.057	
	(.044)	
Teacher test score, Grading B		0.092*
		(.048)
Intercept	31.00***	29.72***
Observations	64	64
Adjusted R²	0.012	0.044

Source: Botswana Schools Sample, 2009.

* $p<0.10$, *** $p<0.01$.

in North West this positive and highly significant relation is largely driven by teachers with higher mathematics knowledge in higher student scoring schools. We use the quadratic form of the equation because it gives a better fit, particularly in the case of Grading B of the teacher test.

Tables 7.5a and 7.5b corroborate that there is a significant and positive relation between teacher test score and student initial achievement in both countries, and that in North West, this positive relation is driven by higher levels of teacher mathematics knowledge in much higher scoring schools.

As we have discussed, this could mean that higher scoring teachers 'produce' higher student test scores, assuming that other teachers at these schools are also more knowledgeable in mathematics, or that these same teachers also teach mathematics in the 4th and 5th grades, for example. In the latter case, the argument would be more compelling that the initial student test score is the result of having several years of a more knowledgeable mathematics teacher. However, that these higher scoring teachers are teaching in higher student achievement classrooms could mean that the more knowledgeable teachers selected, or were selected, to be in these higher achieving classrooms/schools. Hence, higher scoring teachers did not 'produce' these higher test scores but were rather 'matched' in some way with higher scoring students.

The quadratic relation between students' initial test score and teacher test score that we used to estimate the relationship in North West Province suggests that if there is a systematic assignment of teachers with higher mathematics scores to schools with higher scoring students, this is mainly taking place in the higher scoring classrooms (above 45 per cent test score) and involves the much higher scoring teachers (above 60 per cent test score). Similarly, if we think that higher scoring teachers 'produce' higher student test scores, this too is true only for teachers that are at the higher end of the mathematics knowledge spectrum, above a 60 per cent score.

When we analyse student achievement gain scores, we show that achievement gains in our North West school sample are negatively related to teacher mathematics knowledge. This is due mainly to the negative relation between gain score and initial test score (students and classes that scored higher on the initial test tended to have smaller gains on the post-test). This gives some credence to the argument that at least in this range of mathematics knowledge, higher teacher mathematics knowledge is positively related to higher student test scores because teachers with more mathematics knowledge teach in schools with higher achieving students.

On the other hand, we show later that student achievement gains in our Botswana schools sample are indeed significantly related to teacher mathematics knowledge in the case of teacher test Grading B. When we control for average student socio-economic background in each class, it does little to change the positive relation between teacher mathematics knowledge and student test gains during the Grade 6 year. This suggests that the positive relation we find between teacher mathematics knowledge and students' initial achievement score in Botswana is probably not due to the slight tendency for higher scoring teachers in Botswana to be in higher scoring schools.

Summary

Most of the teachers in our North West Province and Botswana samples are over 40 years old and were trained in local teacher training colleges. The vast majority went to school near where they were trained and the schools where they now teach, although Botswana teachers are subject to greater mobility. Many of them have taken additional training in the years after they did their initial teacher education. Few are well trained in mathematics or even had mathematics as a principal subject in their teacher education or subsequent teacher training. Botswana teachers are somewhat better prepared in mathematics, mainly because they are younger and because the teacher training system in Botswana maintained its teacher training colleges and upgraded them in the early 1990s, so that entrance required five years of secondary school.

Since most have not done mathematics as a subject for many years, it is not surprising that, on average, they fared relatively poorly on the teacher mathematics knowledge questionnaire we gave them. A small group did well on the questionnaire: in North West, these teachers tend to teach in classrooms with somewhat higher socio-economic background students who, in turn, also scored higher on the initial mathematics test we asked them to take in March 2009 at the beginning of their Grade 6 school year. In Botswana, the relationship between teacher mathematics knowledge and student SES is not significant, and the relationship between teacher knowledge and student initial test score is also weaker than in North West.

Therefore, teachers with higher test scores on the teacher test in North West tend to teach in classrooms with higher social class students who score higher on the initial test we asked them to take early in the year. But this is not the case in Botswana. Thus, there is some reason to believe that teachers are not randomly assigned to classrooms in North West Province, so that we should not ascribe the higher student achievement we observe on the initial test to the greater mathematics knowledge of the teachers teaching higher achieving students. This implies that any analysis that uses cross-section (at a single point in time) tests to measure student learning could yield biased estimates of teacher effect. This is less likely to be the case in Botswana.

We test this possible bias in Chapter 10. We find that when we assess how teacher quality impacts gains in student mathematics performance controlling for student socio-economic background, we do get some positive and, in North West, large classroom effects. Part of this increased teacher quality may be mediated through the greater knowledge that better teachers have of the mathematics content of what they are teaching.

CHAPTER 8

Teacher proficiency to teach mathematics

This chapter is informed by data from the teacher classroom observation videos in both South East Botswana and North West Province. Using 183 videotaped mathematics lessons (83 from Botswana and 100 from South Africa) from a sample of 120 teachers in 116 randomly selected schools, we formulated the following questions:
1. To what extent is the mathematical content covered in the lessons different between the countries?
2. To what extent is the mathematical proficiency of the lessons different between the countries?
3. To what extent is the level of cognitive demand the learners engage in when the teacher implements the lesson different between the countries?
4. To what extent is the level of the observed mathematical and pedagogical knowledge of the teacher during the lesson different between the countries?

These four questions were used, in turn, to develop the components of the framework used to code the videos in North West and Botswana schools. Together, these four components make it possible to go beyond a simple reconstruction of each lesson and consider the deeper mathematical meaning of what is being taught. These elements also allow us to assess what the teachers know and how they apply this knowledge in the classroom. This in turn makes for some useful linkages between the lesson analysis and teacher questionnaires, as we have already shown in the previous chapter describing teacher performance on tests of mathematics content and pedagogical content knowledge.

The analysis that follows represents the findings of the video coding in relation to the questions stated above. The results summarise the observed lessons on four dimensions:
- content area teaching focus,
- the mathematical proficiency that the teacher gives learners the opportunity to acquire,
- the level of cognitive demand learners are engaged in during the lesson, and
- the observed teachers' knowledge while teaching.

The average observed class size for the sample of lessons combined in Botswana was about 27.8 learners with a standard deviation of about 5.6 learners, and in North West, a higher average of 36.4 learners and a much larger standard deviation of 13.2 learners. The length of classes we observed was from 30 to 40 minutes.

Typical mathematics lessons in terms of what teachers and learners do in both countries are very similar. About one-third of the lesson time is teacher-led, in which the teacher presents the content to the whole class, another one-third of the lesson time is taken by the teacher asking questions, which are answered by individual learners or in chorus, and about one-third is seatwork. Much of the

FIGURE 8.1 *Flow of the lesson in a typical Grade 6 lesson in both countries*

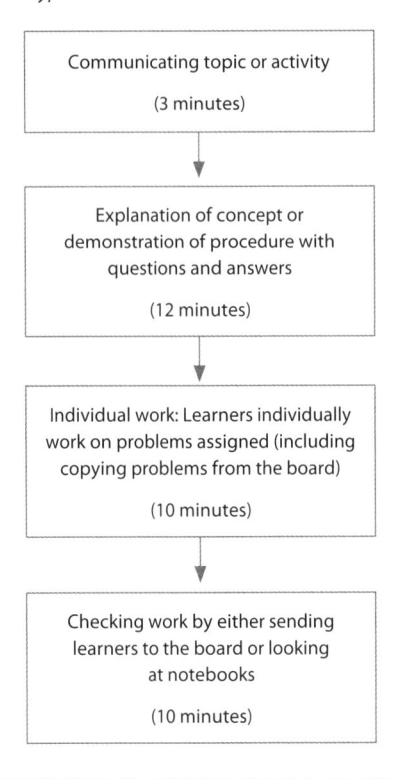

```
┌─────────────────────────────┐
│  Communicating topic or     │
│        activity             │
│        (3 minutes)          │
└─────────────────────────────┘
              │
              ▼
┌─────────────────────────────┐
│  Explanation of concept or  │
│ demonstration of procedure  │
│  with questions and answers │
│       (12 minutes)          │
└─────────────────────────────┘
              │
              ▼
┌─────────────────────────────┐
│ Individual work: Learners   │
│ individually work on        │
│ problems assigned (including│
│ copying problems from the   │
│ board)                      │
│       (10 minutes)          │
└─────────────────────────────┘
              │
              ▼
┌─────────────────────────────┐
│ Checking work by either     │
│ sending learners to the     │
│ board or looking at         │
│ notebooks                   │
│       (10 minutes)          │
└─────────────────────────────┘
```

Source: Compiled by authors

discussion time (individual learners and learner chorus responding to the teacher) is mixed in with the teacher-led talking about mathematical content. Figure 8.1 shows the flow of a typical mathematics lesson.

An important difference between the countries is that more teachers deviate from this typical Grade 6 lesson in North West Province than in Botswana. More teachers in the North West Province spent time on activities that engage the learner in conversations, discussions and active participation than in Botswana. As we will see later, although these are in general good practices, teachers did not use these techniques effectively, mainly because the content level was too low for Grade 6.

Mathematical content coverage

Figure 8.2 shows the distribution of the mathematical content observed in the lessons in both of the sample areas. The first result that stands out is the larger percentage of lessons covering numbers and operations and the smaller percentage of lessons covering algebra and measurement topics in North West Province compared to Botswana's lessons. Differences are less significant in the other content areas. The fact that more lessons in North West Province cover topics in numbers and operations and far fewer in algebra indicates that teachers are teaching at a lower level than Grade 6. The emphasis of content areas in mathematics varies according the grade level. The area of number and operations should be more predominant in early grades (1 to 4) and the areas of measurement and algebra should be more predominant in upper grades (5 to 6).

FIGURE 8.2 *North West Province and Botswana: Mathematical content of the lessons, 2009*

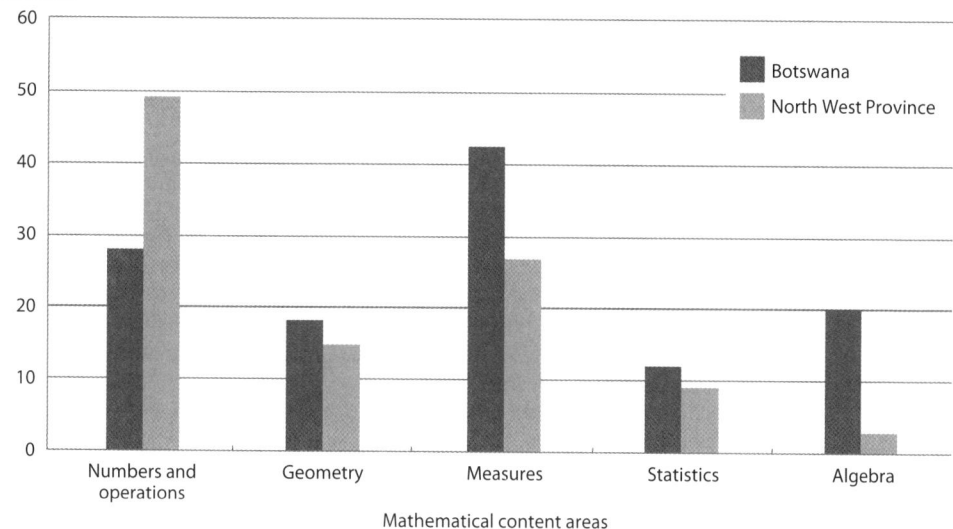

% of lessons

[Bar chart showing percentages by mathematical content area for Botswana and North West Province:
- Numbers and operations: Botswana ~28%, North West Province ~49%
- Geometry: Botswana ~18%, North West Province ~14%
- Measures: Botswana ~42%, North West Province ~26%
- Statistics: Botswana ~11%, North West Province ~8%
- Algebra: Botswana ~19%, North West Province ~2%]

Mathematical content areas

Source: North West Province and Botswana Schools Sample, 2009.

Mathematical proficiency

Mathematical proficiency is measured by the presence of the opportunity for the development of any of the five strands that form the mathematical proficiency variable, which according to *Adding It Up* (National Research Council 2001:116) are necessary to learn mathematics successfully. As outlined in Chapter 3, these are:
- conceptual understanding,
- procedural fluency,
- strategic competence,
- adaptive reasoning, and
- productive disposition.

In the context of evaluating one or two (short) lessons, it may be unrealistic to expect all five elements to be developed – even in a very good class. This argues for some flexibility in how we assess the mathematical proficiency of the lesson. The focus in this component is the mathematics available to the learner in the observed lessons. We are more concerned about the extent to which all strands are developed in the overall summary of multiple lessons. In other words, are there specific elements of proficiency that are largely absent from these classrooms as a whole?

The overall pattern of the proficiency in mathematics in both countries is very similar, except for the conceptual understanding strand where we see a significant difference (see Figure 8.3). The majority of the lessons in both countries provide opportunities for the development of procedural aspects of mathematics. Botswana has a higher percentage of lessons in that category. A smaller percentage of the lessons in both countries also includes development of conceptual aspects, and North West teachers teach a larger percentage of lessons in this category.

FIGURE 8.3 *North West Province and Botswana: Mathematical proficiency strands, 2009*

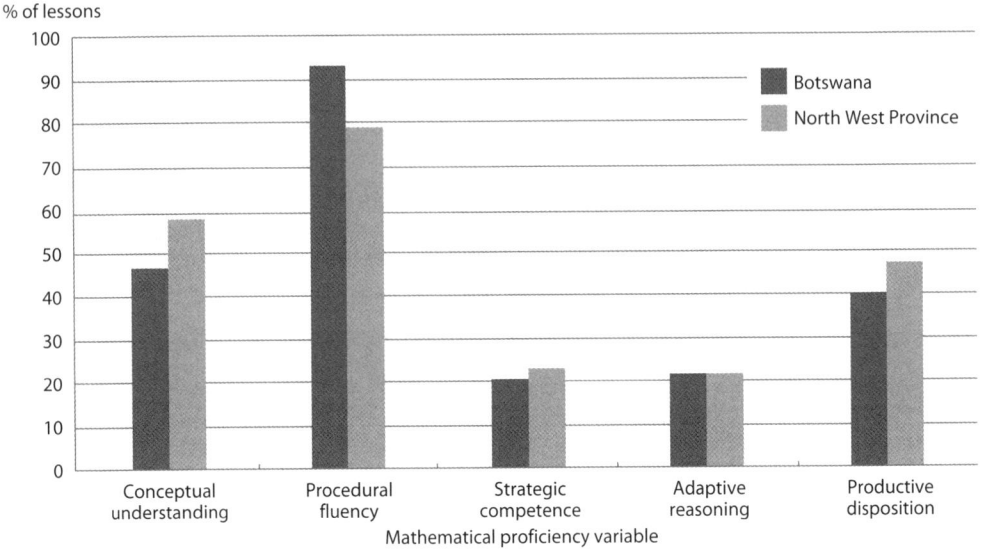

[Bar chart showing % of lessons for Botswana and North West Province across five mathematical proficiency variables: Conceptual understanding (~47% Botswana, ~59% North West Province), Procedural fluency (~93% Botswana, ~79% North West Province), Strategic competence (~21% Botswana, ~23% North West Province), Adaptive reasoning (~22% Botswana, ~22% North West Province), Productive disposition (~41% Botswana, ~48% North West Province).]

Source: North West Province and Botswana Schools Sample, 2009.

As we will see, this does not necessarily translate into a higher quality of teaching. The coding system for this aspect only takes into account the mathematics proficiency intended by the mathematical task (often guided by the textbook). We could observe that mathematical tasks and textbooks in North West Province had more conceptual aspects integrated with procedural aspects than mathematical tasks and textbooks in Botswana. It was clear from the observations that some teachers value conceptual understanding before learners move to the manipulation of symbols or computation. This is also consistent with the kinds of questions used by teachers in the classroom. However, not all teachers were able to teach conceptually in an efficient way. In both countries only about 20 per cent of the lessons' mathematical tasks included aspects of reasoning (comprehending why algorithms and rules work and justifying steps or final answers) and strategic competence (or problem solving).

The last category refers to learners seeing mathematics as sensible, useful, and worthwhile combined with a belief in their ability to do mathematics ('disposition'). This category was observed only during the lessons where learners were either involved in the application or reasoning of mathematics. This occurred in about half the lessons in North West Province and a smaller percentage in Botswana. However, in those lessons, learners seemed to enjoy and value the logical thinking and problem-solving activities.

Level of cognitive demand

As outlined in Chapter 3, the level(s) of cognitive demand learners engage in during the lesson are derived from a rubric in Stein et al.'s (2000) classification of higher and lower cognitive demand. As previously mentioned, these include Memorisation, Procedures without connections, Procedures with connections, and Doing mathematics.

The focus in this component is the thinking processes with which learners engage in the observed lessons. Beyond the topic covered in the lesson, lessons should involve the kind and level of thinking required of students on a particular topic or mathematical task, which enriches and relates to our previous measurement of mathematical proficiency. We refer to this aspect as the level of cognitive demand. Even though the level of cognitive demand is observed at the level of the learner, the teacher controls and directs the required level for his or her students. In a similar study using videotapes from a large group of TIMSS participants, researchers found that teachers implement lessons at a lower level than that intended by the lesson (Stigler et al. 1999). This was especially a characteristic of countries with lower overall student achievement.

Figure 8.4 shows that learners in both countries engage more in mathematical tasks at the lower levels of cognitive demand, such as recalling facts and procedures, than at the higher levels of cognitive demand, such as reasoning and thinking. Significant differences between countries were found at the lower levels. North West Province's learners engage more in tasks that involve just Memorisation and less in tasks that involve Procedures without connections in comparison with Botswana's learners. One explanation of these differences could be a North West Province emphasis on the area of number and operations, which has a heavy Memorisation component. Another explanation could be that North West Province's teachers tend to start each lesson with a review of facts before presenting new content, leaving less time to develop Procedures with or without connections. In contrast, Botswana's teachers expect learners to already know previous facts, hence less time is spent in recalling facts and more time is left for Procedures.

Almost no lessons we observed 'did mathematics' – that is, explained the underlying mathematics or engaged students in understanding the underlying mathematics of the concepts they were studying. For example, in a lesson on solving linear equations (appropriate for the Grade 6 level) the teacher mostly gave the students an algorithm to follow without any explanation why the algorithm works. She did not explain the use of inverse operations in the solution of equations. She talked about 'taking away', but failed to explain what she meant by it. (e.g. in $2a + 3 = 7$, she would say 'we take away the 3').

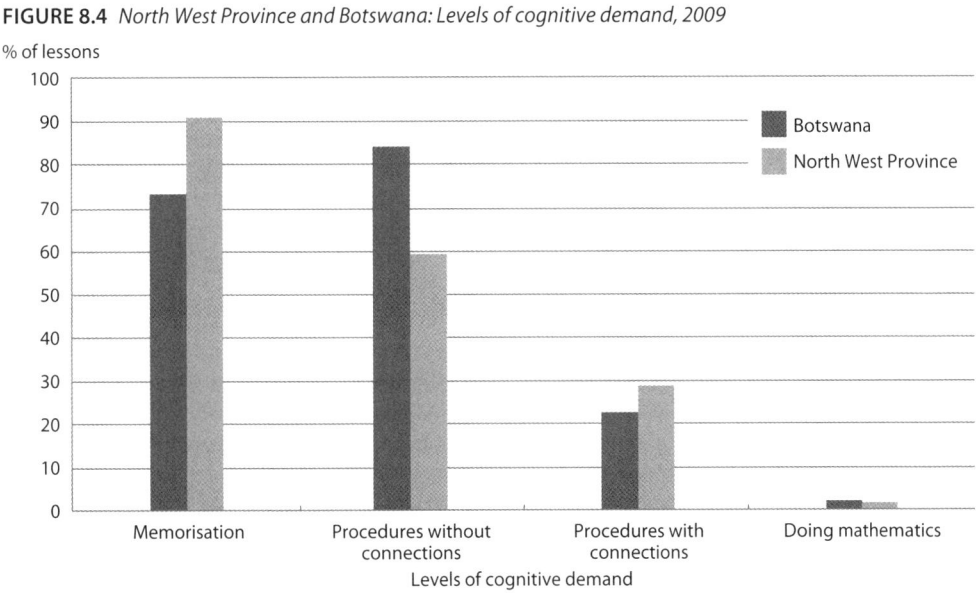

FIGURE 8.4 *North West Province and Botswana: Levels of cognitive demand, 2009*

Source: North West Province and Botswana Schools Sample, 2009.

The teacher seemed to be more concerned at 'showing all the steps' than for learners to be able to use a mental calculation and explain their answers. She gave many examples for learners to do (which was good, compared to lessons where only three examples are commonly given to learners to work on) but she did not allow for flexibility in the solutions or explanations given by learners.

Thus, learners are seldom engaged in difficult mathematical reasoning as represented in the Doing mathematics category. A very small percentage of lessons required students to understand the meaning of operations or underlying concepts behind the procedures, and a similarly small percentage required students to investigate or explore relationships between mathematical ideas. In neither country are the lessons long enough to engage learners in tasks of higher order thinking. The few lessons that do engage learners in high levels of cognitive demand are characterised by being longer, by teachers with deeper mathematical knowledge, and by tasks that are prepared well.

Observed teachers' knowledge

We characterise the observed teachers' knowledge in a lesson by focusing on three aspects that are derived from the notions of Pedagogical Content Knowledge (Shulman 1986) and Mathematical Knowledge for Teaching (Hill et al. 2005). The aspects are:
- Grade level mathematics knowledge – the presence of computational, linguistic, and representational accuracy for the mathematics at the grade level being taught. We take into account any mathematical errors during instruction.
- General pedagogical knowledge – the use of general instructional techniques beyond the lecture mode. Elements include how well the teacher has all the learners engaged, his/her use of proper classroom management techniques, and the quality of instructional materials.
- Mathematical knowledge in teaching (pedagogical content knowledge) – the degree to which the teacher can appropriately integrate the use of the instructional techniques with the mathematical concept being taught, and its effectiveness on learner learning. This includes the use of correct language to clearly convey mathematical ideas. In each aspect, the coder determined whether or not the teacher displayed the relevant knowledge.

Perhaps the biggest difference observed with respect to teaching between the two countries is the knowledge of Grade 6 mathematics observed (Figure 8.5).

Grade level mathematics knowledge

As shown in the graph, only about one-third of the teachers in the North West sample taught the content that corresponds to the grade level, in this case Grade 6. Most teachers in the lessons we observed in the North West taught the content at one, and sometimes at two grade levels below the 6th grade. They presented content as low as Grade 3 level in Grade 6 classes.

This was often the case when teachers gave a 'hands-on' lesson, an approach actively encouraged by the South African NCS, but, as we can see from our observations, not always appropriately implemented. In one lesson the activity set for the class was to make a clock using paper plates, coloured hands (pre-prepared) and pasting numbers onto the paper plates (from photocopied sheets of numbers). The teacher did interact with the learners. She checked and corrected the alignment and placing of numbers on the clock face but her explanations were confusing to learners. She used a ruler to check the number alignment across the face of the clocks, but none of the learners were able to correct their clock faces when she left them. She halted the activity to ask learners to show times they do things – wake up, go to school, and such like. Learners had to show the times on their clocks, but when they made mistakes, she

FIGURE 8.5 *North West Province and Botswana: Teachers' observed knowledge, 2009*

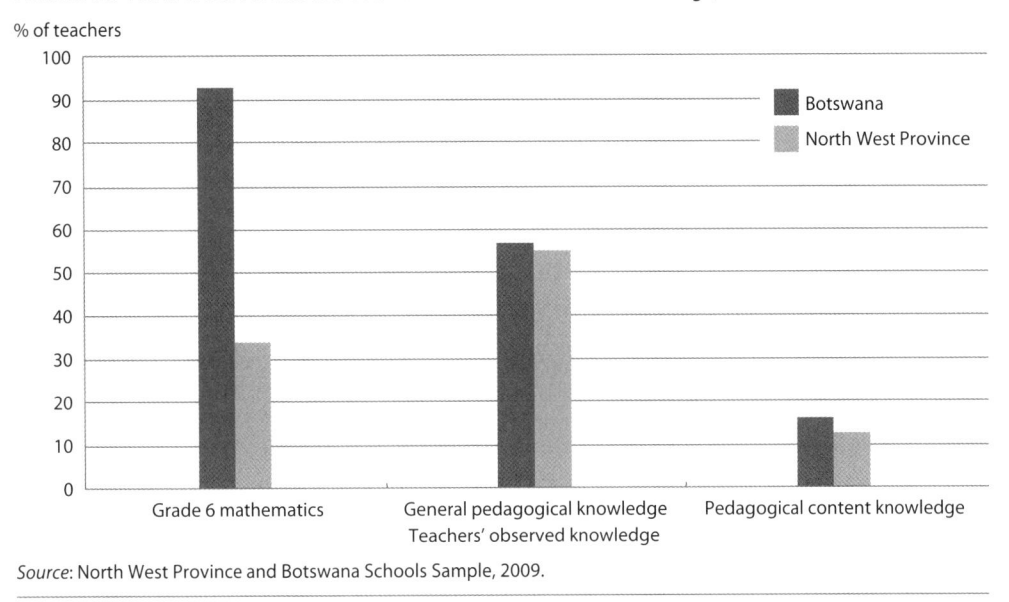

Source: North West Province and Botswana Schools Sample, 2009.

gave no conceptual explanations and simply moved the hands to the right position. She had a pleasant manner, her classroom was decorated with mathematical and other posters and learner work, but the content of the lesson was well below Grade 6 level for time (as per NCS).

This does not necessarily suggest that teachers in the North West do not know Grade 6 mathematics. Rather, this only means that they did not demonstrate their knowledge during the lessons. Teachers showed more knowledge of topics that align with Grade 5 level, and in some cases even lower than Grade 5. The reason for this could be that North West teachers feel that learners are not ready to learn Grade 6 topics and that they need to revisit topics from previous years before they present new material. This is a typical situation for teachers of mathematics around the world – teachers at a given grade level feel that learners are underprepared because previous instruction did not develop the necessary skills to be successful at the grade level they are teaching. However, a skillful teacher with knowledge about how concepts develop and how learners acquire them can focus on the new content while reinforcing previous knowledge.

With respect to Botswana's teachers, the great majority demonstrated knowledge of Grade 6 mathematics, and in particular knowledge of the topics (official syllabus) and expectations corresponding to Grade 6. This was evident as many teachers started the lesson by writing the title of the lesson on the board, which matched (almost word for word) the specific objective outlined in the official curriculum document. For example, one of the titles of the lessons was 'Areas of composite shapes' which matches specific objective 3.2.1.2 'Students should be able to calculate the area of composite shapes excluding semi-circles'. Although the coding system was not designed to measure the degree of fidelity of the implementation of the curriculum, we could observe that Botswana's teachers were more faithful to the Grade 6 level.

The problem with the implementation of the curriculum in Botswana is that teachers were only teaching the topics that relate to a low level of cognitive demand (calculate, identify, use the formula, etc.), leaving out expectations associated with a high level of cognitive demand (interpret, solve problems, discuss, etc.). This could be because there is not enough time during the school year to cover all the topics, because teachers do not have the capacity to teach at a high level, or because teachers teach fewer lessons than required by the academic year. In the next chapter we present evidence that the number of lessons taught in both Botswana and North West were far below the number planned in the academic calendar. Our measures of opportunity to learn and teachers' knowledge suggest that to some extent both factors contribute to this issue.

General pedagogical knowledge

In terms of the second aspect, pedagogical knowledge, the breakdown of the teachers in both countries was very similar. In both countries, teachers in about 50 per cent of the observed lessons demonstrated proper preparation for their lessons. They did this by using self-made posters to present definitions and by organising hands-on activities such as cutting, colouring and pasting.

Mathematical knowledge in teaching (pedagogical content knowledge)

The final element is the degree of effectiveness of the use of these techniques and how well they were connected with the mathematical concept being taught and is captured by the last category – pedagogical content knowledge. Note that very few teachers (17 per cent in Botswana and 13 per cent in North West) demonstrated an adequate level of pedagogical content knowledge. Of those that did, most showed a well-planned lesson with a rich task presented to learners and a good flow of the lesson. Others were effective because of powerful explanations and skillful levels of communication to bring the complex mathematical ideas to the level of the learner. Better teachers used questioning to elicit answers given independently by learners, from which an observer could say that the learner understood what he/she is talking about.

Overall quality of teaching

The various elements discussed in the previous paragraphs went into evaluating each teacher's teaching on a three-point scale (1 to 3), with 1 defined as a 'lower' level of teaching, 2 as a 'better' level of teaching, and 3 as a 'best' level of teaching. Of the 83 videotapes evaluated in Botswana, 33 were 'low', 35 'better', and 15 'best'. Of the 100 videotapes evaluated in North West, 33 were 'low', 56 were 'better', and only 11 were 'best'. In relative terms, the Botswana sample suggested that a higher fraction of teachers were teaching at a low overall level than in North West, but a higher fraction were teaching at the highest level. The Botswana lessons were rated the same, on average, as the North West videotapes (an average of 1.78 versus 1.78 in North West). When we averaged the ratings across teachers in each country, we got 1.86 for teaching quality in Botswana, and 1.63 in North West.[1] Figure 8.6 shows the percentages of videotapes with each rating.

In Chapter 9 we relate these overall ratings to other measures of teacher quality, namely teachers' score on the mathematics knowledge test we gave them (Chapter 6) and the degree of curriculum coverage they are able to achieve during the academic year – the opportunity to learn they provide to students. In Chapter 10, we use this overall teacher quality rating as our proxy for teaching quality in assessing the impact of teaching quality on learner learning gains.[2]

---

1   In those cases where we had two videotaped lessons for a teacher, we averaged the two. In cases with just one videotaped lesson, we took that lesson as the teacher's rating.
2   In Chapter 11, our measure of each teacher's quality rating in those cases where we have two videotape observations for a teacher is the higher of the two ratings.

FIGURE 8.6 *North West Province and Botswana: Overall teacher quality ratings, 2009*

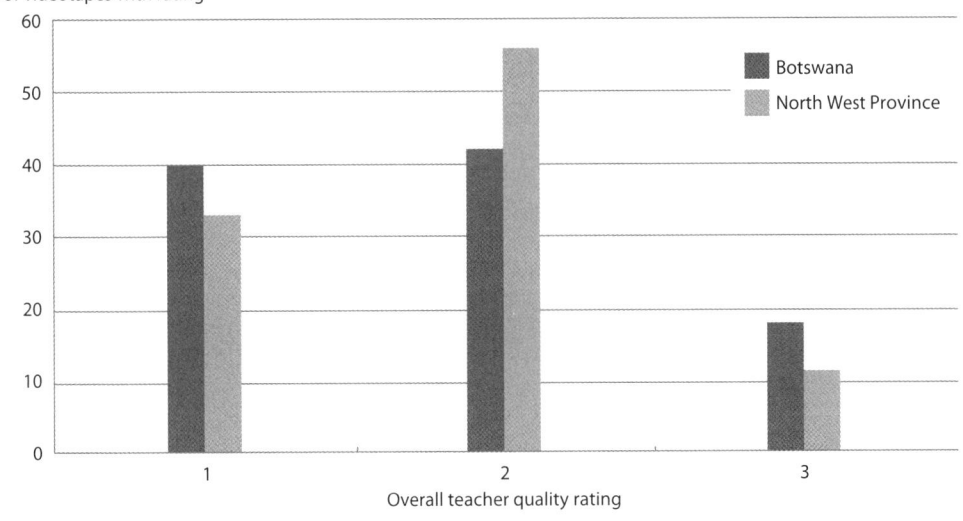

Source: North West Province and Botswana Schools Sample, 2009.

Summary

In both South East Botswana and the North West Province, classrooms where learners were engaged in high-level cognitive tasks, discourse, hands-on activities, collaborative work, and where teachers demonstrated skills and knowledge of mathematics and pedagogy, were the exception rather than the norm. Most teachers presented the knowledge to their learners with the intention of communicating that knowledge but not with the purpose of helping them to learn the material. Teachers have very few skills and tools to present the learners with a well-sequenced series of activities that help the learner acquire the underlying mathematical concept. Further, teachers did not demonstrate the ability to use models and multiple representations effectively to illustrate abstract concepts.

The major difference between the teaching we observed in Botswana and the North West Province is the coverage of mathematics topics. Teachers in Botswana implement the official curriculum more faithfully than North West teachers in terms of grade level topics, but, like teachers in North West, teachers in South East Botswana only emphasise low levels of cognitive demand. Botswana teachers, on average, have a somewhat higher rating than those in North West in the lessons we observed, primarily because a somewhat higher percentage in Botswana receive a '3' (best) rating. This could explain some of the difference we observed in the higher gains in our sample of Botswana's Grade 6 learners. The difference in curriculum coverage may well help to explain the difference in Grade 6 learner achievement gains in the two countries.

In the next chapter, we turn to a detailed assessment of curriculum coverage. In Chapter 10, we estimate the relationships between our key measures of teacher quality and consider how they differ between our two regions. Finally, in Chapter 10, we estimate the relationship between teacher quality and learner achievement gains.

CHAPTER 9

Opportunity to learn and teaching and learning mathematics in Grade 6 classes

Opportunity to learn is a crucial factor in understanding the degree of exposure to subject matter and, in some definitions, the quality of that exposure. In the previous chapter, we estimated one version of quality of exposure through an analysis of classroom videotapes. Since videotapes only give us one or two 'snapshots' of this aspect of OTL, we view those snapshots more as a measure of teachers' teaching quality. In this chapter, we focus on the degree and quality of exposure through the analysis of student notebooks in which the record the activities of each lesson.

This allows us to describe a broader version of OTL during the academic year in the sample of Grade 6 mathematics classes in North West Province and South East Botswana. First, we use various measures, which we defined in Chapter 3, to estimate the variation in OTL among Grade 6 classrooms. Second, we determine whether students from different socio-economic backgrounds have different opportunities to learn. Third, we estimate whether the degree of exposure (one of our measures of OTL) to the items on the student test is related to student achievement gains on those items.

What are the opportunities to learn in a sample of Grade 6 mathematics classes in North West Province and the South East Region of Botswana?

One of the objectives of the study was to establish the extent to which students in the sample schools had the time and opportunity, between the pre- and post-tests, to learn the mathematics topics associated with content in the test items. This chapter provides some of the descriptive findings on different dimensions of students' OTL. Every student in the same class received the same value on each of the measures employed to reflect OTL – 'content coverage by cognitive demand', 'content emphasis' and 'content exposure'.

Content coverage by cognitive demand

Content coverage in the study refers to the extent to which mathematics topics and sub-topics associated with the test items were covered or taught in the classes tested in 2009. The model used for the analysis of this variable was a simple count of the total number of topics or sub-topics on the content framework taught in 2009 prior to the post-test. Table 9.1 shows how many of the 110 mathematics topics related to the test items were covered by teachers in the two regions' sample of classes in the months between the pre- and post-test.

TABLE 9.1 *North West Province and Botswana: Number of mathematics topics related to test items covered between the pre- and post-test, 2009*

Statistic	Number of topics covered in North West Province	Number of topics covered in Botswana
Mean	40	39
SD	13.5	10.9
Minimum	16	11
Maximum	83	69

Source: North West Province and Botswana Schools Sample, 2009.

Abbreviation: SD, standard deviation.

On average, teachers in both samples of classes covered only about 35 per cent of the possible topics related to the test items between the pre- and post-test, with a minimum of 15 per cent in North West and 10 per cent in Botswana, and a maximum of 75 per cent in North West and 63 per cent in Botswana. Figure 9.1 shows that only 14 per cent of the sample of Grade 6 classes covered more than 50 per cent of the test topics in North West, and only three of the 64 classrooms, or less than 5 per cent of the sample of Grade 6 classes, covered more than 50 per cent of the test topics in Botswana.

On the topic framework in the OTL data collection instrument, there were:
- 48 mathematics topics/sub-topics clustered under the content area: numbers, operations and relationships,
- 21 topics/sub-topics clustered under the content area: measurement,
- 22 topics/sub-topics clustered under the content area: space and shape (geometry),
- 6 topics/sub-topics clustered under the content area: patterns, functions and algebra, and
- 13 topics/sub-topics clustered under the content area: data handling.

FIGURE 9.1 *North West Province and Botswana: Number of classrooms by percentage of test topics covered, 2009*

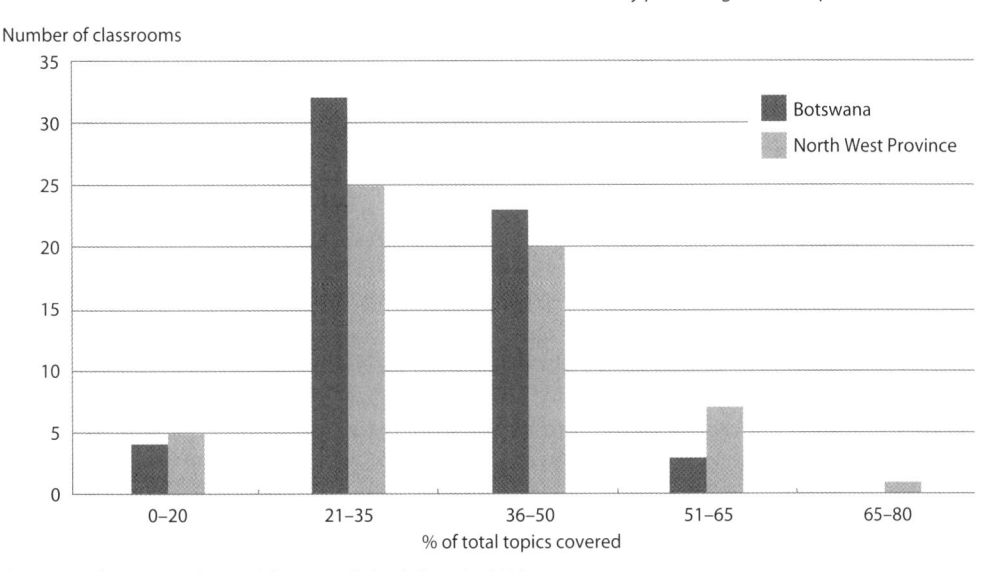

Source: North West Province and Botswana Schools Sample, 2009.

TABLE 9.2 North West Province and Botswana: Number of topics covered in each of the five content areas, 2009

	Numbers, operations and relationships n=48		Patterns, functions and algebra n=6		Space and shape (geometry) n=22		Measurement n=21		Data handling n=13	
	NW	BW	NW	BW	NW	BW	NW	BW	NW	BW
Mean	25	21	1	1	6	7	6	7	2	3
SD	8.4	7.9	1.3	0.9	5.4	4.2	3.3	4	2.3	2.2
Minimum	10	6	0	0	0	0	0	0	0	0
Maximum	45	34	5	4	20	14	12	14	11	8

Source: North West Province and Botswana Schools Sample, 2009.

Table 9.2 gives descriptive statistics on the number of test topics covered by Grade 6 classes in each of the five content areas. For example, we show that teachers in North West covered an average of 25 of the 48 possible topics in numbers, operations, and relationships (52 per cent) compared to 21 of 48 topics in Botswana, and so forth.

On average, the North West sample of classrooms covered:
- 52 per cent of the test topics relating to numbers, operations and relationships,
- 29 per cent of the test topics relating to space and shape (geometry),
- 28 per cent of the test topics relating to measurement,
- 18 per cent of the test topics relating to patterns, functions and algebra, and
- 14 per cent of the test topics relating to data handling.

On average, the Botswana sample of classrooms covered
- 44 per cent of the test topics relating to numbers, operations and relationships,
- 32 per cent of the test topics relating to space and shape (geometry),
- 33 per cent of the test topics relating to measurement,
- 16 per cent of the test topics relating to patterns, functions and algebra, and
- 21 per cent of the test topics relating to data handling.

A detailed breakdown of the percentage of classes that evidently covered each particular topic (based on work in the sample of student workbooks) shows that the number of topics covered varied greatly from class to class. Some classes covered many more topics than others.

The Assessment Statements in South Africa's and Botswana's National Curriculum Statements for Intermediate Phase Mathematics and Numeracy list minimum standards per grade and express expected levels of competence for Grade 4, 5 and 6. Data indicate that most Botswana and North West teachers covered topics at levels lower than Grade 6 standards. Grade 6 teachers most commonly focused on Grade 4 and 5 level expectations rather than Grade 6 level expectations.

One reason for this low standard could be that teachers find they need to address gaps in student knowledge that should have been mastered in earlier grades. Such gaps may be indicative of slow curricular and cognitive pacing in earlier grades. Certainly, testing has revealed that large numbers of Grade 6 students in South Africa and Botswana perform below their grade level. However, the data also indicate that the same content, concepts and skills may be being taught over and again in each grade, so that students are covering more of the same topics at the same level in each grade without much conceptual progression or increasing depth from grade to grade. This repetition could be because teachers believe that their students are not ready to move on to more advanced topics, but could also be because teachers themselves feel less competent and comfortable about teaching certain topics and content areas than others. To some extent, standards may be set by students' levels of development and by teacher competence rather than by curriculum grade level expectations. Our data also suggest that teachers may find it difficult to decide on the amount of time to devote to various topics.

The descriptive data on content coverage also show that the nine topics that were covered by 7 per cent or more of the classes in North West all relate to the content area of numbers, operations and relationships. However, other key test topics (i.e. covered in three or more items), such as investigating and extending numeric and geometric patterns represented in physical or diagrammatic form; investigating and extending numeric and geometric patterns not limited to sequences involving constant difference or ratio; and describing observed relationships or rules of numeric and geometric patterns – that all relate to the content area patterns, functions and algebra, were covered by very few classes. In North West, six of the ten 'least covered' topics (covered by less than 6 per cent of the classes) all relate to the content area data handling.

Tables 9.3a and 9.3b on the next page summarise details on the number and percentage of the test topics per main content area that were covered by various proportions of the classes we observed.

The data in the tables indicate the following:
- Fifty per cent in Botswana and 59 per cent in North West of the topics clustered under the content area numbers, operations and relationships in the OTL instrument were covered in 50 per cent or more of the Grade 6 classes.
- Thirty-eight per cent in Botswana and only 10 per cent in North West of topics clustered under the content area measurement in the OTL instrument were covered in 50 per cent or more of the Grade 6 classes.
- Thirty-two per cent in Botswana and only 14 per cent in North West of the topics clustered under the content area space and shape (geometry) in the OTL instrument were covered in 50 per cent or more of the Grade 6 classes.
- Seventeen per cent in Botswana and none in North West of topics clustered under the content area patterns, functions and algebra in the OTL instrument were covered in 50 per cent or more of the Grade 6 classes.
- Fifteen per cent in Botswana and none in North West of the topics clustered under the content area data handling in the OTL instrument were covered in 50 per cent or more of the Grade 6 classes.

Although an emphasis on number, operations and relationships is in line with guidelines for the Intermediate Phase, the data in Tables 9.3a and 9.3b on content covered signals that attention to content areas other than number, operations and relationships is much weaker in North West than in Botswana. In Botswana, even though the coverage of other areas is not as widespread as it should be, at least 50 per cent of classes cover some of the material (except in patterns, functions and algebra). Further evidence of this lack of attention to content area 'spread' in North West emerges from the analysis of data on content emphasis later in this section.

The second dimension of content coverage is cognitive demand. Figure 9.2 on page 119 shows descriptive findings on the overall level of cognitive demand evident in the sample of North West classrooms. The four cognitive demand levels provided by Stein et al. (2000) were used to analyse overall cognitive levels of engagement with mathematics content in each class.

TABLE 9.3a Coverage of topics in main content areas in North West classrooms, 2009

Topics covered by	Numbers, operations and relationships		Measurement		Space and shape (geometry)		Patterns, functions and algebra		Data handling	
	Frequency	%	Frequency	%	Frequency	%	Frequency	%	Frequency	Count
75% or more of the Grade 6 classes	9	19		0		0		0		0
50%–74% of the Grade 6 classes	19	40	2	10	3	14		0		0
Less than 50% of the Grade 6 classes but more than 25% of the classes	12	24	7	33	10	45	1	17	2	15
Less than 25% of the classes	8	17	12	57	9	41	5	83	11	85
Total number of possible topics	48		21		22		6		13	

Source: North West Province Schools Sample, 2009.

TABLE 9.3b Coverage of topics in main content areas in Botswana classrooms, 2009

Topics covered by	Numbers, operations and relationships		Measurement		Space and shape (geometry)		Patterns, functions and algebra		Data handling	
	Frequency	%	Frequency	%	Frequency	%	Frequency	%	Frequency	Count
75% or more of the Grade 6 classes	6	13		0		0		0		0
50% – 74% of the Grade 6 classes	18	37	8	38	7	32	1	17	2	15
Less than 50% of the Grade 6 classes but more than 25% of the classes	11	23	6	29	5	23		0	3	23
Less than 25% of the classes	13	27	7	33	10	45	5	83	8	62
Total number of possible topics	48		21		22		6		13	

Source: Botswana Schools Sample, 2009.

FIGURE 9.2 *North West Province and Botswana: Percentage of sample classes by overall level of cognitive demand, 2009*

% of classrooms observed

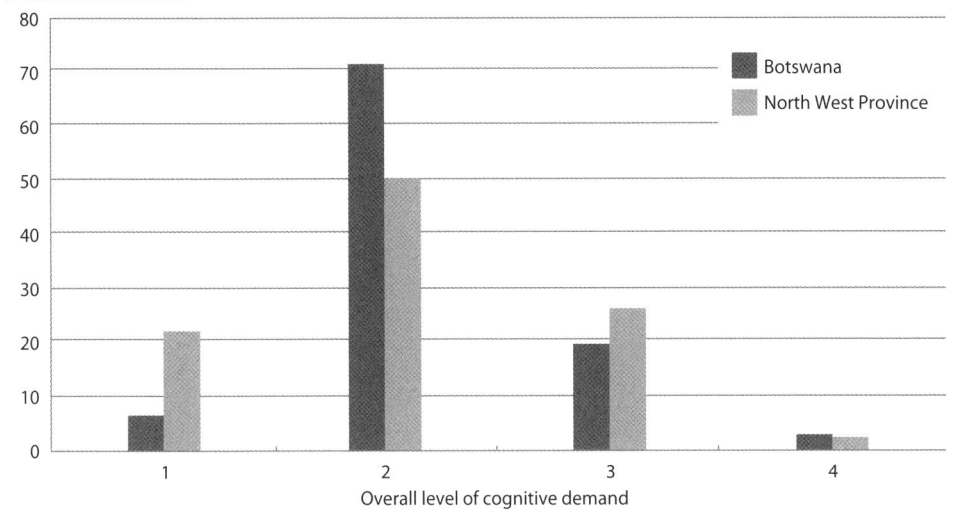

Source: North West Province and Botswana Schools Sample, 2009.

Frequencies for each of the following classifications are shown on Figure 9.2:
- Memorisation (1)
- Procedures without connections (2)
- Procedures with connections (3)
- Doing mathematics (4)

As the graph shows, in 22 per cent of the North West classes, students were mainly engaged in recalling rules and definitions. In 50 per cent of the classes, students were mainly engaged in routine mathematics procedures, which did not progress to engagement with underlying knowledge principles. This category was most prevalent. In 26 per cent of the classes, students were apparently engaged to a greater extent with the mathematics knowledge principles behind the procedures. Only 2 per cent of the classes were mainly engaged in 'difficult mathematical reasoning'.

In 6 per cent of the Botswana classes, students were mainly engaged in recalling rules and definitions. In 71 per cent of the classes, students were mainly engaged in routine mathematics procedures, which did not progress to engagement with underlying knowledge principles. This category was most prevalent. In 19 per cent of the classes, students were apparently engaged to a greater extent with the mathematics knowledge principles behind the procedures. Only 3 per cent of the classes were mainly engaged in 'difficult mathematical reasoning'.

Content emphasis

Content emphasis in the study refers to the relative amount of time each class spent on each of the various topics that related to the content of specific test items. Observation of students' workbooks was used to estimate the number of mathematics lessons actually spent on each of the topics listed in the framework. All the test items referred to more than one of topics on the framework. Table 9.4 on the next page provides descriptive statistics for the estimated number of lessons (between the pre- and post-test) that each class spent on topics in each of the five content areas.

TABLE 9.4 *North West Province and Botswana: Number of lessons that each class spent on topics per content area, 2009*

Measure	Numbers, operations and relationships		Measurement		Space and shape (geometry)		Data handling		Patterns, functions and algebra	
	NW	BW	NW	BW	NW	BW	NW	BW	NW	BW
Mean	42.7	27.2	6.18	9.8	5.81	6	1.9	5.8	1.39	2.7
SD	17.29	15.7	5.32	6.3	6.91	4.1	2.86	4.3	2.14	3
Minimum	10	10	0	0	0	0	0	0	0	0
Maximum	94	97	24	24.6	29	16.1	12.9	13	11	15

Source: North West Province and Botswana Schools Sample, 2009.

An analysis of the table shows that the amount of time (number of lessons) spent on content area topics associated with the items on the test given to students varied considerably from class to class. The data confirm that classes spent much more time on topics related to numbers, operations and relationships than on the other content areas. Indeed, the average of 42.7 lessons is 70 per cent of the estimated average time spent on test topics overall in North West classes.

Indications are that most of the North West and Botswana teachers over-emphasise topics related to the content area numbers, operations and relationships. They tend to spend more, or almost all, of their time on this content area with much less, or no time, spent on topics in other content areas, especially the areas of patterns, functions and algebra (in North West and Botswana) and data handling (in North West). This finding is corroborated by the percentage of lesson observations in which the various content areas were taught. The content areas least taught in observed lessons were patterns, functions and algebra, and data handling.

Content area 'spread' appears to an issue in most of the sample of Grade 6 mathematics classrooms in both countries, and especially in North West. Grade 6 teachers appear to put too much emphasis on a one content area to the exclusion of broader mathematical development. As Floden (2003: 255) points out, the danger is that OTL in mathematics 'is important for each topic area,' not just for mathematics as a whole: if mathematics learning was 'simply increasing mastery of a single skill, then it would not matter what topics were studied. Students who learnt more mathematics would do better on topics.' It should be remembered that this finding is based on student notebook content for almost the whole academic year.

Content exposure

Content exposure in the study refers to the overall amount of time spent engaged in learning relevant to mathematics in general, as opposed to time spent on the specific topics/sub-topics covered in the test items, or the amount of time allocated or timetabled for mathematics instruction. As students should write work in their notebooks each time they have a mathematics lesson, researchers used the dates in a sample of students' workbooks as evidence of students having had a mathematics lesson. The number of mathematics lessons for each class was estimated through a simple count of the total number of daily pieces of written work in workbooks by the end of October/ beginning of November 2009. By that stage of the school year, Grade 6 students should have had around 130–140 days of teaching recorded.

Table 9.5 provides descriptive statistics for the number of pieces of daily work in students' workbooks.

TABLE 9.5 *Number of mathematics pieces (recorded lessons) of daily work in Grade 6 workbooks by the end of October/ beginning of November 2009*

Statistic	Lessons recorded in North West	Lessons recorded in Botswana
Mean	52	77.5
SD	16.00	22.7
Minimum	21	33
Maximum	97	142

Source: North West Province and Botswana Schools Sample, 2009.

Data in Table 9.5 indicate that, on average, teachers in the North West sample of classrooms gave 52, and in the Botswana sample 78, mathematics lessons from the beginning of the year to the date of the post-test as opposed to the expected minimum of 130–140 lessons. This is little more than a third of that expected in North West, and somewhat more than a half of that expected in Botswana.

Figure 9.3 shows frequencies for the number of mathematics lessons observed in the sample of student workbooks in each class.

As the graph shows, 22 of the 64 (34 per cent) Grade 6 classes in Botswana and 50 of the 62 (81 per cent) Grade 6 classes in North West had fewer than 66 lessons recorded in the student workbooks. 27 (42 per cent) in Botswana but only two (3 per cent) in North West of the classes' workbooks showed evidence of 81 or more lessons taught in that classroom from the beginning of the school year to the last observation of notebooks at the end of October/early November. These findings signal that the average number of mathematics lessons given by teachers in the sample of North West schools is considerably less than the number of lessons taught in Botswana's classrooms, yet in both countries considerably fewer lessons were given than officially programmed under official guidelines. About one-fifth of the Botswana teachers taught over 100 lessons between the beginning of the year and the

FIGURE 9.3 *North West Province and Botswana: Frequency of observed mathematics lessons, 2009*

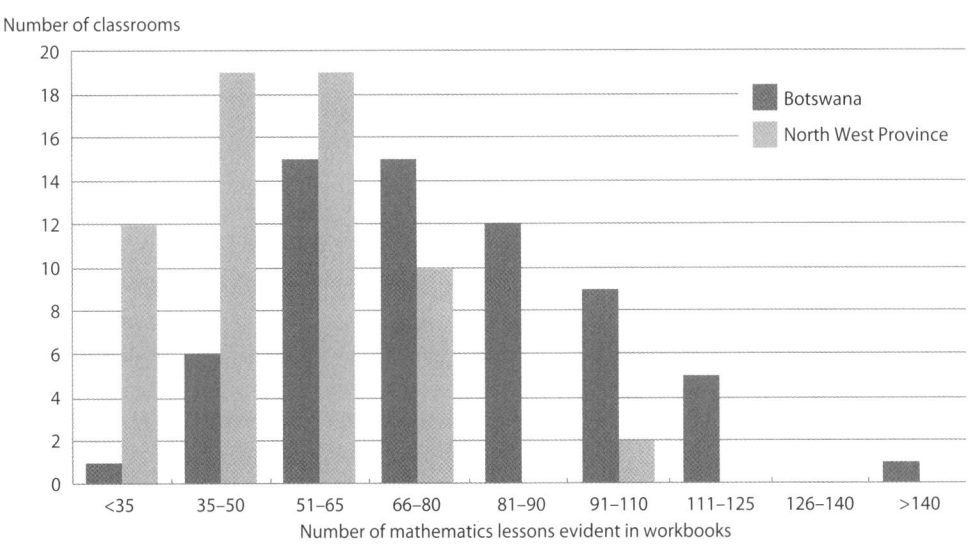

Source: North West Province and Botswana Schools Sample, 2009.

end of October/early November – many more than in our North West sample. That said, more than half the teachers, even in Botswana, seriously short-changed their students in mathematics.

Qualitative data from students' workbooks also revealed evidence of a slow pace of work within lessons, as reflected in the number and type of written mathematical tasks that learners completed in a lesson on average per day. We can provide examples scanned from Grade 6 students' workbooks at the same point in the school year (24/25 August 2009) in classes at two different schools in North West Province. These clearly reflect differences in pacing within lessons. Students in one class were expected to do fewer tasks in a lesson than in another class. Data suggest that teachers may have problems deciding on the amount of time students should have for completing exercises, or their students may be taking a very long time to complete exercises. It is unclear whether teachers simply have low expectations of their students, and are deliberately setting a slow pace, or whether the slow pace of work is controlled by students' level of development.

Do students of different socio-economic background in the North West Province have different opportunity to learn?

This section investigates whether there is an association between average classroom OTL, measured by the number of test topics covered (content coverage), and the number of mathematics lessons overall (content exposure) and the classroom SES variable, which is the average aggregated individual learner SES based on articles in the home for each classroom. Table 9.6 shows the correlation of classroom

TABLE 9.6 *North West Province and Botswana: Correlations of various measures of opportunity to learn with classroom SES, 2009*

Variable	North West correlation with SES	Botswana correlation with SES
Content coverage – total number test topics covered between pre- and post-test	0.02	−0.27**
Content emphasis – total estimated number of lesson spent on each of the test topics	0.20	−0.16
Exposure – total number of mathematics lessons given between pre- and post-test	0.06	−0.04
Total topics covered – numbers	0.06	−0.14
Total topics covered – patterns	0.20	−0.34***
Total topics covered – shapes	−0.03	−0.02
Total topics covered – measurement	0.12	−0.18
Total topics covered – data handling	−0.03	−0.09
Number of lesson spent on numbers	0.14	−0.16
Number of lessons spent on patterns	0.18	−0.21*
Number of lessons spent on shapes	−0.14	−0.03
Number of lessons spent on measurement	0.19	0.06
Number of lessons spent on data handling	−0.02	0.03

Source: North West Province and Botswana Schools Sample, 2009.

* $p<0.10$, ** $p<0.05$, *** $p<0.01$.

SES with various measures of OTL, including the total number of test topics covered in each of the five content areas, and the total estimated number of lessons spent on each of the test topics.

From these correlations, it appears that content coverage, content emphasis, and exposure are positively but not significantly related to average classroom student socio-economic background in North West and negatively and, in the case of content coverage, significantly negatively, related to SES in Botswana. That is, classrooms in the sample with lower student SES do not appear to have had significantly less OTL. Bearing in mind that topics associated with the test items also relate to Grade 4, 5 and 6 level expectations, it is possible that in classes with students from relatively higher socio-economic backgrounds, teachers focus more on Grade 6 level expectations (as opposed to those topics associated with the test items).

Relationship between the number of lessons per test topic (content emphasis) and learning gains

We developed an innovative way to conduct a preliminary analysis of the relationship between OTL and the gains that students made in the tests. Since the student notebooks recorded the number of lessons that each teacher gave on topics relating to each test item, we estimated that number for each test item and related it to the gain that the teacher's class made on that test item between the pre- and the post-test. For each class, we combined the total number of lessons reported for each of the OTL topics/sub-topics that related to each of the items on the test. We used 38 of the test items (two items were badly printed on the Botswana version of the test, so we left them out of this analysis, even for North West Province), and based our results on observations for 63 classrooms each in South Africa and Botswana with OTL and student test data. This generated a matrix of 2 394 OTL observations, 2 394 classroom average test score gains and 2 394 initial test scores. We then estimated the relationship between the three matrices (OTL and the gains that students made in the tests, controlling and not controlling for the initial test score).[1]

The North West teachers taught an average of 2.5 lessons, and the Botswana teachers 2.2, related to each test item from the beginning of the school year to the last observation in the student notebooks at the end October/early November. There is considerable variation in the number of lessons taught on topics relating to each test item – the standard deviation is 2.1 lessons across the 38 test items in North West and a much lower 1.4 lessons in Botswana. This suggests that Botswana teachers varied the amount of teaching on items much less than North West teachers. This is consistent with our results analysing content coverage.

We estimated student gains on each test item in each classroom as a function of the number of lessons on topics relating to each test item taught by each teacher, controlling and not controlling for the initial/pre-test student score on each item for all classrooms. We also estimated the same model(s) for the following sub-groups:
- Classrooms in which students initially scored less than 20 on the pre-test.
- Classrooms in which students initially scored 20–39.9 on pre-test.
- Classrooms in which students initially scored greater than 39.9 on pre-test.

This allowed us to test whether the OTL influenced gains differentially across sub-groups. Tables 9.7a and 9.7b show the regression results using the matrix of classroom times test item (about 2 400 possible observations).

---

1 The forms of the equation we test in Table 9.7 with the item gains are (in Models 1 and 3), the same as in equation (2a) in Chapter 3, and (in Models 2 and 4) another version of equation (2b) : $A_{post} - A_{pre} = bA_{pre} + cOTL + d\ OTL^2$. This specification, $A_{T2} - A_{T1} = \alpha A_{T1} + \Sigma \beta_j T_j + \delta C + \varepsilon$ is equivalent statistically to the regression $A_{T2} = \gamma A_{T1} + \Sigma \beta_j T_j + \delta C + \varepsilon$, where $\alpha = \gamma - 1$. The coefficients β_j and δ are equal in both specifications.

TABLE 9.7a *North West Province: Estimated gains on test items per classroom related to opportunity to learn and average pre-test score, 2009*

Variable	Model 1	Model 2	Model 3	Model 4
All classrooms				
OTL	0.0002	0.0014	0.0043*	0.0078***
	(0.0009)	(0.0009)	(0.0019)	(0.0018)
OTL squared			−0.0003*	−0.0005***
			(0.0001)	(0.0001)
Average pre-test score		−0.2517***		−0.2567***
		(0.0155)		(0.0155)
Intercept	0.0348***	0.1035***	0.0301***	0.0977***
Adjusted R^2	−0.000	0.098	0.002	0.104
No. of observations	2 394	2 394	2 394	2 394
Classrooms scoring <20 on pre-test				
OTL	−0.0008	−0.0009	0.0037	0.0032
	(0.0012)	(0.0012)	(0.0025)	(0.0024)
OTL squared			−0.0003*	−0.0003
			(0.0002)	(0.0002)
Average pre-test score		−0.3844***		−0.3780***
		(0.0814)		(0.0813)
Intercept	0.0819***	0.1277***	0.0766***	0.1222***
Adjusted R^2	−0.001	0.022	0.003	0.025
No. of observations	934	934	934	934
Classrooms scoring 20–39.9 on pre-test				
OTL	0.0021	0.0021	0.0122***	0.0123***
	(0.0014)	(0.0014)	(0.0032)	(0.0032)
OTL squared			−0.0008***	−0.0008***
			(0.0002)	(0.0002)
Average pre-test score		−0.0402		−0.0488
		(0.0849)		(0.0844)
Intercept	0.0269***	0.0381	0.0169**	0.0305
Adjusted R^2	0.001	0.000	0.01	0.01
No. of observations	901	901	901	901
Classrooms scoring >39.9 on pre-test				
OTL	0.0040	0.0035	0.0060	0.0068
	(0.0022)	(0.0021)	(0.0054)	(0.0053)
OTL squared			−0.0002	−0.0003
			(0.0004)	(0.0004)
Average pre-test score		−0.2756***		−0.2775***
		(0.0533)		(0.0534)
Intercept	−0.0471***	0.1125***	−0.0496***	0.1095***
Adjusted R^2	0.004	0.048	0.003	0.047
No. of observations	559	559	559	559

Source: North West Province Schools Sample, 2009.

* $p<0.10$, ** $p<0.05$, *** $p<0.01$.

TABLE 9.7b *Botswana: estimated gains on test items per classroom related to opportunity to learn and average pre-test score, 2009*

Variable	Model 1	Model 2	Model 3	Model 4
All classrooms				
OTL	−0.0029*	−0.0021	−0.0069***	−0.0050*
	(0.0012)	(0.0020)	(0.0020)	
OTL squared			0.0003*	0.0002
			(0.0001)	(0.0001)
Average pre-test score		−0.1675***		−0.1659***
		(0.0147)		(0.0147)
Intercept	0.0539***	0.1099***	0.0586***	0.1128***
Adjusted R²	0.003	0.053	0.005	0.055
No. of observations	2 394	2 394	2 394	2 394
Classrooms scoring <20 on pre-test				
OTL	−0.0067***	−0.0067***	−0.0133***	−0.0132***
	(0.0017)	(0.0017)	(0.0029)	(0.0029)
OTL squared			0.0004*	0.0004*
			(0.0002)	(0.0002)
Average pre-test score		0.1214		−0.1102
		(0.1033)		(0.1028)
Intercept	0.1038***	0.1186***	0.1131***	0.1264***
Adjusted R²	0.021	0.025	0.031	0.032
No. of observations	678	678	678	678
Classrooms scoring 20–39.9 on pre-test				
OTL	−0.0054***	−0.060**	−0.0171***	−0.0182***
	(0.0022)	(0.0022)	(0.0043)	(0.0042)
OTL squared			0.0013*	0.0014***
			(0.0004)	(0.0004)
Average pre-test score		−0.4152***		−0.4229***
		(0.0907)		(0.0903))
Intercept	0.0665***	0.1878***	0.762***	0.2000***
Adjusted R²	0.007	0.030	0.018	0.038
No. of observations	897	897	897	897
Classrooms scoring >39.9 on pre-test				
OTL	0.0039	0.0054**	0.0084	0.0113*
	(0.0020)	(0.0021)	(0.0045)	(0.0046)
OTL squared			−0.0004	−0.0006
			(0.0004)	(0.0004)
Average pre-test score		−0.1316***		−0.1373***
		(0.0394)		(0.0395)
Intercept	−0.0047	0.0694**	−0.0100	0.0657**
Adjusted R²	0.003	0.002	0.004	0.017
No. of observations	819	819	819	819

Source: Botswana Schools Sample, 2009.

* $p<0.10$, ** $p<0.05$, *** $p<0.01$.

The different specifications of independent variables used in the item gain regressions are: Model 1 – OTL (lessons per test item); Model 2 – OTL and pre-test score; Model 3 – OTL and OTL squared; Model 4 – OTL, OTL squared and pre-test score.

The results in Tables 9.7a and 9.7b show that the relation between test score gain on items and the number of lessons given by teachers on each test item differs considerably between North West and Botswana.

In North West classrooms, gain is generally positively related to the number of lessons when the squared term is included. This result seems driven by what happens in the mid-range of test scores (20–39.9), although, of course, these pre-test scores are still very low (but not the lowest). The average inflection point[2] on the 'parabola' in the quadratic OTL (lessons on topics related to test items) specification is 6.7 lessons per item. In other words, both absolute gains and relative gains (controlling for initial test score) increase as average lessons taught on item test topics increase up to a rather high number of lessons. This is the case whether initial test score is included or not. However, at about 6 or 7 lessons per item, the gains begin to decrease according to this estimate.[3]

While there are a few items in which the average is above or near the inflection point, the average lessons per item is 2.5, indicating that the inflection point is generally at a much greater number of lessons than this average. As we discuss later, regression estimates using the classroom averages as observations also show that the total number of lessons on topics related to the test is positive and significantly related to classroom gain scores, even when controlling for other variables, such as average classroom SES, teacher test score and teacher teaching ratings.

The test score gain on items in Botswana classrooms is generally negatively related to the number of lessons given by teachers on each test item, even when the squared term is included. This result seems driven by what happens in the lower (< 20) and especially mid-range of test scores (20–39.9). The average inflection point on the 'parabola' in the quadratic OTL (lessons on topics related to test items) specification is 16 lessons per item for the lowest-scoring classrooms and 6.5–6.6 lessons per topic for the middle scoring classrooms. The relationship of lessons on topics to test score gains becomes positive and statistically significant for the highest scoring classrooms (40 per cent or higher on the initial test) when initial test score is controlled for. In other words, both absolute gains and relative gains (controlling for initial test score) are generally negatively related to test score gains up to a high number of lessons per topic (about 11). However, the number of lessons up to which the relationship is negative becomes progressively smaller in classrooms with higher initial test scores and is positive in classrooms with higher average initial test scores. This suggests that the process of teaching in Botswana is such that classrooms with higher-scoring students are benefiting more from more lessons than are classrooms with lower-scoring students.

In Chapter 11, we test whether content coverage, content emphasis, and exposure are related to test score gains. We find that content emphasis, as measured by total lessons on test topics – a more approximate measure of the number of lessons per test item used here – and content coverage are, indeed, also positively and significantly related (linearly) to learner achievement gains in North West and negatively, but not significantly, related to learner gains in Botswana. This corroborates our results

---

2   The inflection point of a parabola is the coefficient of the X term divided by twice the coefficient of the squared term.

3   One problem that often occurs in these types of regressions is serial correlation in the independent variables – in this case, between item gains on the test across classrooms. We tested for this and found no significant problems of serial correlation between gains.

in Tables 9.7a and 9.7b: that OTL is an important factor in understanding how much students learn in North West classrooms but is not a positive factor in Botswana classrooms. These differences between North West and Botswana require further explanation, but it is clear from the results here and in Chapter 10 that in North West the amount of attention teachers pay to various components of the mathematics curriculum does make a difference to how much students learn.

We cannot argue that lessons per item cause higher test score gains in North West, since the number of lessons given seems to correlate with at least one measure of teacher test score across classrooms (see the previous discussion of teacher test scores), however, our finding from Table 9.7a estimates is a powerful result. It suggests that OTL does have a positive impact on gains, both absolute and relative, in North West schools, and suggests that teachers in North West Province could increase student learning by touching more on the topics in the curriculum. The finding in Botswana that more lessons on items generally has a negative effect on gains could be related to the way Botswana teachers in lower-scoring classrooms approach the teaching of mathematics. It is clear that teachers give more lessons on topics in classrooms where students score higher on the initial test, and these classrooms have much smaller gains. Even though we controlled for initial test score, there may be variables we do not observe in these higher scoring classrooms that are correlated with the greater number of lessons and contribute to the smaller gains. Again, assigning causality to OTL should be treated with caution, but these estimates do suggest that there are differences in the processes we observe in the two regions' classrooms.

CHAPTER 10

Are more knowledgeable teachers better teachers and do they provide more opportunity to learn?

It is difficult to imagine that a Grade 6 mathematics teacher can be good at her or his craft without having a reasonable understanding of mathematics concepts and a good grasp of how to teach the mathematics curriculum. Based on how well the teachers in our North West sample answered the mathematics questions we posed to them, it seems that only a minority have the level of knowledge that would make them good mathematics teachers. The Botswana teachers did significantly better in answering the questions that we gave them, but they too cannot be considered as really being well prepared to teach Grade 6 mathematics.

In this chapter, we assess whether there are positive relationships between two principal measures of teaching 'quality' – teacher experience and teacher mathematics knowledge – and two other measures we use for teaching quality – the exposure to the subject matter offered by the teacher to students in her or his class and the quality of teaching that subject matter in the classroom.

Referring back to the structural model we describe in Chapter 3, in this chapter we estimate equations (1a) and (1b).

Are teachers with more mathematics knowledge likely to teach mathematics better?

One way to test the proposition that those teachers who have more content and pedagogical content knowledge are better at teaching is to observe these same teachers in their classrooms teaching mathematics lessons. As shown in Chapter 7, we were able to assess teachers' mathematics lessons from many perspectives including the depth at which the teachers explained the mathematics, and the clarity of the explanations. One result of this teaching assessment is an overall 'grade' for each teacher's teaching, with 1 given for a lower quality of mathematics teaching, 2 for a mid-level quality, and 3 for a high level of mathematics teaching quality. The analysts evaluating the teaching video did not have access to the teacher mathematics test score so had no information about the teacher's mathematical knowledge beyond what they viewed on the video.

Did those teachers in our two samples who scored higher on the mathematics knowledge test also teach at a higher level of quality? For those teachers who were filmed only once, we use the overall rating based on that one video. In North West Province, for those who were filmed twice, and if there is a difference in the two ratings, we use the higher of the two. We use the average of the two teaching quality scores when we had two observations for a teacher in Botswana rather than the higher score because far fewer teachers had two lessons videotaped than in North West.

Table 10.1 shows teacher mathematics teaching quality related to teacher mathematics knowledge, by type of teacher test grading.

The table shows that whether we use the teacher test grading based on equal weighting of the 24 questions (Grading B), or give more weight to the multi-part questions (Grading A), teachers' mathematical knowledge is positively and statistically significantly related to the rating they received on their mathematics teaching in North West Province. This is particularly evident at the higher levels of mathematics scores. Those teachers with high scores on the mathematics test generally received the highest evaluation for their teaching, and this is robust when we control for teacher experience.

In our Botswana sample, the estimated relation shows that teachers' mathematical knowledge is positively and statistically significantly related to the rating they received on their mathematics teaching when we use the teacher test grading that weighs every answer equally (Grading A), but not when we

TABLE 10.1 *North West Province and Botswana: Teacher mathematics teaching quality as related to teacher mathematics knowledge, by type of teacher test grading, 2009*

Region/variable	Teaching rating, Model 1	Teaching rating, Model 2	Teaching rating, Model 3	Teaching rating, Model 4
North West Province				
Teacher test score, Grading A	0.028***	0.032***		
	(0.007)	(0.007)		
Teacher test score, Grading B			0.024***	0.027***
			(0.006)	(0.006)
Teacher experience		-0.050		-0.039
		(.036)		(0.037)
Teacher experience squared		0.001*		0.001
		(0.001)		(0.001)
Intercept	0.708**	0.804	1.055***	1.089*
Observations	62	62	62	62
Adjusted R²	0.216	0.298	0.198	0.272
Botswana				
Teacher test score, Grading A	0.011*	0.012*		
	(0.007)	(0.006)		
Teacher test score, Grading B			0.005	0.005
			(0.008)	(0.008)
Teacher experience		-0.005		-0.010
		(0.034)		(0.034)
Teacher experience squared		0.000		0.000
		(0.001)		(0.001)
Intercept	1.172***	1.227***	1.525***	1.631***
Observations	64	64	64	64
Adjusted R²	0.033	0.006	-0.009	-0.034

Source: North West Province and Botswana Schools Sample, 2009.

* p<0.10, ** p<0.05, *** p<0.01.

grade giving equal weight to each of the 24 questions (Grading B). It is also evident that the teacher quality rating is more weakly related to teachers' mathematics knowledge than in North West (Table 10.1 and Figure 10.1b). As in North West, teacher experience is not a factor in teacher quality ratings.

When we estimate the effect on student achievement gain of teaching quality and teachers' mathematics knowledge in the next chapter, we find that in Botswana both variables are significantly

FIGURE 10.1a *North West Province: Teacher mathematics teaching overall rating (higher of the two ratings when two videotaped lessons) and teacher mathematics knowledge, 2009*

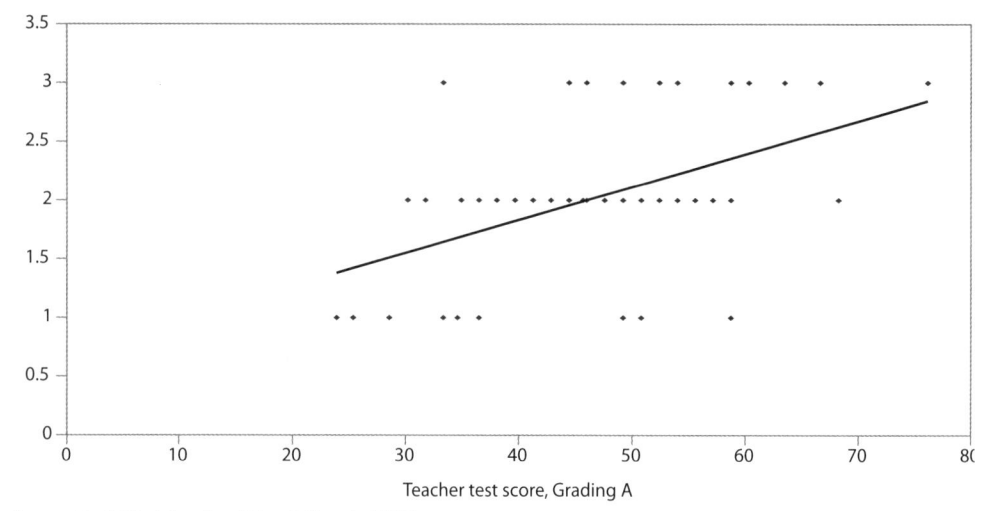

Source: North West Province Schools Sample, 2009.

FIGURE 10.1b *Botswana: Teacher mathematics teaching overall rating (average of the two ratings when two videotaped lessons) and teacher mathematics knowledge, 2009*

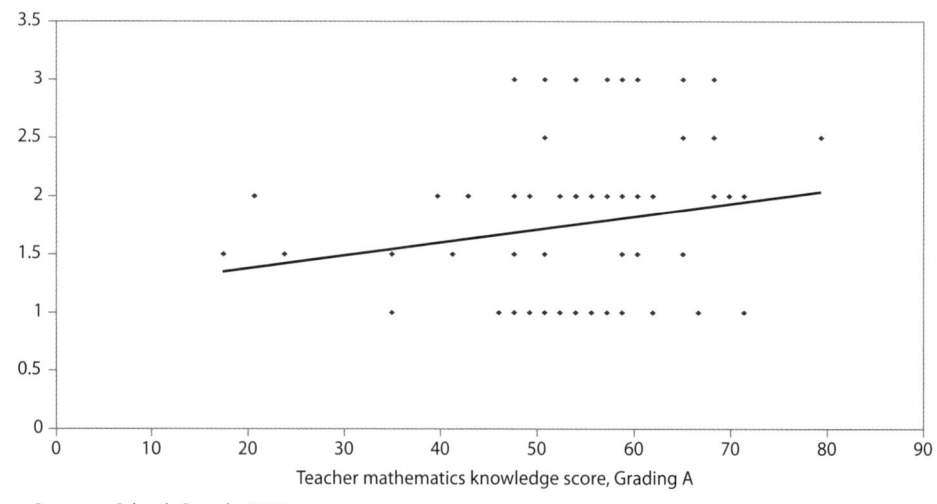

Source: Botswana Schools Sample, 2009.

FIGURE 10.2 *North West Province and Botswana: Teacher mathematics teaching highest overall rating and teacher mathematics knowledge by level of teacher test score, 2009*

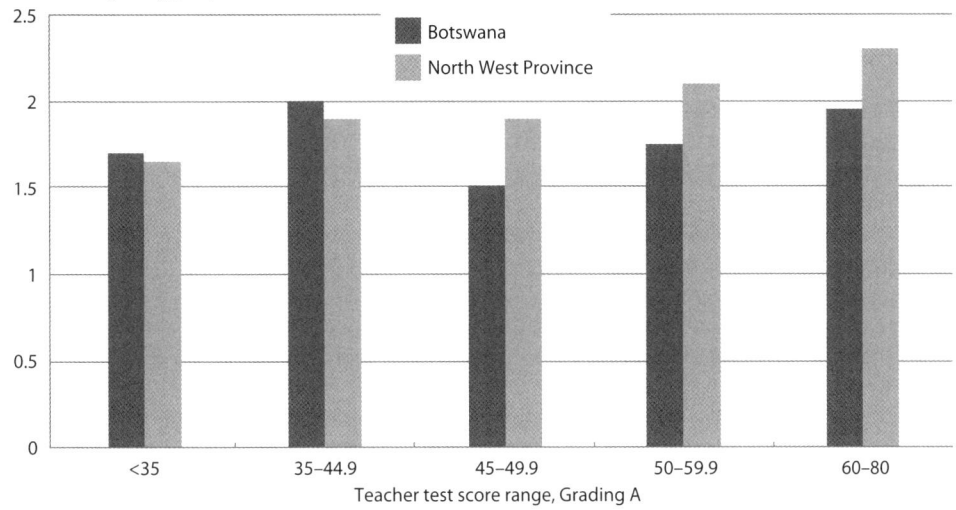

Teacher teaching rating (1–3)

[Bar chart comparing Botswana and North West Province across teacher test score ranges: <35, 35–44.9, 45–49.9, 50–59.9, 60–80]

Teacher test score range, Grading A

Source: North West Province and Botswana Schools Sample, 2009.

related to student gains, whereas in North West only teaching quality is positively related to student gains. This may be because teaching quality and teacher mathematics knowledge are more strongly correlated in North West, which would tend to make teacher mathematics knowledge influence student gains through teacher quality.

Figure 10.2 shows that, on average, the mathematics teaching experts rating teaching quality gave higher grades to teachers in North West Province than in Botswana, except for teachers with low mathematics scores. Nevertheless, on average, teachers in Botswana scored higher on the mathematics knowledge test. For example, there were many more Botswana teachers in the 60–80 test score range than in North West. Also, the average teaching rating for teachers in the sample was slightly higher in Botswana than in the North West sample. The figure also corroborates that the relation between teacher mathematics knowledge and teaching quality rating is stronger in North West than in Botswana, although we observe a positive relation in both samples from the middle to the higher range of mathematics scores. More than two-thirds of Botswana teachers are in the upper three categories of mathematics test scores, whereas about one-half of North West teachers are in those three categories.

One reason we observe this positive relationship could be that 'better' teachers (those who receive overall ratings of 2 or 3) tend to teach in classrooms with higher socio-economic background students who are more receptive to somewhat deeper, more conceptual mathematics, hence teachers perform better mathematically in such settings. Although this is not a highly likely relationship, we tested it by controlling for students' average socio-economic background in the regression estimates in Table 10.1. This control had essentially no effect on the coefficient of teacher test score, using either form of grading the teacher test, and, in addition, average student socio-economic background is not itself related to teacher teaching rating in the North West sample and only weakly related in the Botswana sample.

Are teachers with higher mathematics knowledge likely to teach more topics and more lessons on topics?

In many countries, the implementation of the required or recommended curriculum is loosely regulated at the classroom level. Strong supervision by inspectors and even school principals is not the norm in South Africa, while the inspection system is more regularised in Botswana. Nevertheless, in both countries, what takes place in classrooms is largely governed by classroom teachers. In both Botswana and North West we found that the average number of lessons given by teachers in a subject such as mathematics is considerably smaller than the number of lessons officially planned, although the number of lessons recorded in students' notebooks in Botswana from the beginning of the school year to the beginning of November is much greater than those recorded in student notebooks in North West Province just across the border (77 versus 52). In addition, the number of topics covered (topics were confined to those associated with the items on the test we gave students) and the number of lessons given per topic vary greatly from teacher to teacher. Some teachers cover a lot more material than others. We showed this in detail in the previous chapter on opportunity to learn.

As discussed in Chapter 8, we reviewed student notebooks twice during the academic year (once in late June and once at the end of October) in each of the classes in our sample. Since students are generally asked to write in their notebooks each time that they have a mathematics lesson, we were able to record the number of daily lessons during almost the entire academic year (all but the month of November and early December, a period of relatively less teaching). We were also able to record the number of topics pertaining to the items on the mathematics test we gave the students, and the total number of lessons on those topics. We realise that teachers sometimes do not have students write in their notebooks (sheet work is put on classroom walls, for example), but non-notebook recorded work is much less prevalent in both countries.

Teachers with more mathematics knowledge may feel more comfortable with the subject matter in the curriculum, hence may be more likely to spend time teaching the curriculum material. They may also cover more topics because they may be more familiar with a greater range of topics. As far as giving more lessons on the topics related to the test items, the relationship is less clear. Teachers with more mathematics knowledge may like teaching mathematics more, so may be more likely to give a larger number of lessons on the topics, but they may also be more efficient, so could spend less time on each topic. They could also choose to devote more time to topics not covered by our student test – topics more challenging for students in their classes.

When we use Grading A to evaluate the teacher test, we find a positive and significant relationship between teacher mathematics knowledge and both the number of topics and total number of lessons on the topic in North West Province (Table 10.2). Using Grading B, the relationship between the teachers' test score and the amount of coverage provided on the test items is still positive, but not statistically significant. Adding teacher experience to our estimates increases the coefficient of teacher test score for total lessons, and, in addition, teacher experience and experience squared are also positively and significantly related to the total lessons on topics. This suggests that more experienced teachers with more mathematics knowledge tend to teach significantly more lessons on topics in North West Province, although not necessarily more topics.

In Botswana, when we relate the number of our student test topics covered and the total lessons given on the test topics to teacher mathematical knowledge, the number of topics is not statistically significantly related to teacher test score, regardless of how we graded the test. When we related the total number of lessons on the topic to the teacher's mathematics knowledge score, regardless of the way the test was graded, the number of total lessons on the topics is positively and significantly related to teacher mathematics knowledge. However, when we include teacher experience in our estimates, not only are more experienced teachers likely to teach significantly fewer lessons on our test topics, but teacher experience and mathematics knowledge are strongly enough correlated to reduce the significance of the mathematics knowledge variable on lessons taught on topics. It is apparent that younger teachers in Botswana score higher on the mathematics test and tend to teach more lessons on the test topics.

TABLE 10.2 *North West Province and Botswana: Opportunity to learn related to teacher test score, by type of opportunity to learn and teacher test grading, 2009*

Region/variable	Total lessons on topics		Total topics		Total lessons on topics		Total topics	
	Model 1	Model 2	Model 1	Model 2	Model 1	Model 2	Model 1	Model 2
North West Province								
Teacher test Grading A	0.676*** (0.249)	0.740** (0.257)	0.251* (0.151)	0.231 (0.155)				
Teacher test Grading B					0.355 (0.229)	0.422* (0.249)	0.110 (0.136)	0.0891 (0.146)
Teacher experience		2.797** (1.276)		0.802 (0.765)		2.650* (1.362)		0.686 (0.795)
Teacher experience squared		−0.062** (0.026)		−0.025 (0.016)		−0.060** (0.028)		−0.023 (0.016)
SES index		0.872 (0.791)		0.502 (0.474)		0.936 (0.843)		0.562 (0.492)
Intercept	29.29**	−9.676	28.32***	20.43	46.47***	9.30	35.60***	28.37**
Observations	62	62	62	62	62	62	62	62
Adjusted R^2	0.094	0.143	0.028	0.094	0.022	0.067	−0.006	0.065
Botswana								
Teacher test Grading A	0.378* (0.192)	0.0.240 (0.202)	0.072 (0.100)	0.095 (0.109)				
Teacher test Grading B					0.369* (0.213)	0.227 (0.226)	0.058 (0.110)	0.090 (0.122)
Teacher experience		−3.280*** (1.023)		−0.525 (0.551)		−3.287*** (1.031)		−0.527 (0.554)
Teacher experience squared		0.101*** (0.034)		0.016 (0.018)		0.100*** (0.348)		0.016 (0.018)
SES index		−0.721 (0.778)		−0.861** (0.419)		−0.770 (0.787)		−0.880** (0.423)
Intercept	30.72***	65.07***	34.72***	45.15***	33.29***	67.92***	35.82***	46.26***
Observations	64	64	64	64	64	64	64	64
Adjusted R^2	0.044	0.153	−0.007	0.043	0.031	0.148	−0.011	0.040

Source: North West Province and Botswana Schools Samples, 2009.

* $p<0.10$, ** $p<0.05$, *** $p<0.01$.

An argument could be made that the relation between teacher mathematics knowledge, teacher experience and the number of lessons on test topics is mediated through the socio-economic background of the students – the higher the average socio-economic background of students in the class, the higher teacher mathematics knowledge (and experience) and perhaps the more likely that the teacher will offer more lessons on the topics. Yet, when we control for the average social class of students in the North West classes, teacher mathematics knowledge remains statistically significantly related to total lessons on the topics and does not change the coefficients of teacher knowledge or experience in either country. This means that for students of all socio-economic backgrounds in our sample, higher teacher mathematics knowledge is related to more coverage of mathematics curriculum. One stark contrast between the findings in the two regions is that in Botswana, higher socio-economic background classrooms receive significantly fewer lessons per topic and are taught fewer of the topics on the test we gave students, and this relationship is statistically significant in the case of topics taught in Botswana.

The average estimated number of lessons on the test topics in our North West sample is only 61, and in Botswana, 51. The number of topics is 40 in North West and 38 in Botswana (out of more than 100 possible topics). The average teacher test score in North West is 46.7 per cent using Grading A and 40.4 per cent using Grading B, and in Botswana 53.1 per cent using Grading A and 47.3 per cent using Grading B. These figures show that there is a great deal of room for improvement, in both countries.

If increasing teacher mathematics knowledge is one way to increase the number of lessons given and the number of topics covered, only a 10 point increase in teacher score using the Grading A (about one standard deviation increase) in North West is associated with an increase of 6.3 lessons on the test topics (about a 0.3 increase in standard deviation). In Botswana a 10 point increase in teacher score using Grading A (less than one standard deviation increase) is associated with an increase of about 4.5 lessons on the test topics (about a 0.2 increase in standard deviation) when we control for average student socio-economic background in the class. In Botswana, the effect size is about the same in reference to Grading B of teacher test score. Nevertheless, in Botswana, the relation of some of the teacher knowledge-lessons taught is mediated by teacher experience.

Summary

Teachers with greater mathematics knowledge, as measured by the teacher test administered, are on average better teachers, as measured by the detailed evaluations we did of their teaching videotapes (Chapter 8). Teachers with more mathematics knowledge also tend to give more lessons to their students on the topics covered by the items on the test we gave the students. Both their better teaching and the greater number of lessons given should contribute to greater student learning. If teachers' knowledge of mathematics is associated with better teaching and more effort to present students with opportunities to learn, then how well teachers are able to handle mathematical content and mathematical pedagogy questions may be important for improving student learning. Indeed, it is possible that the impact of teacher mathematics knowledge is mainly expressed through their better teaching and through more lessons given on topics prescribed by the curriculum, especially the 'harder' topics that tend to receive considerably less coverage, according to what we found in our OTL research (Chapter 9).

Both the relation between teacher test score and the quality of teaching, and the relation between teacher test score and the number of lessons given per topic and the number of topics taught are stronger in North West than in Botswana. This is a key result, since it suggests that improvement in teacher mathematics knowledge in North West Province could have a bigger impact on teaching quality and the number of lessons taught on relevant mathematics topics than in Botswana, where teachers score higher on the teacher test. The only caveat in our results is that in Botswana, the results on lessons taught are more consistent across the way the test is graded, but then are highly complicated by the relationship between teacher experience, teacher mathematics knowledge and the number of lessons taught.

This chapter shows that that these important classroom factors are linked. Teacher mathematics knowledge is linked to better teaching and to more coverage of the curriculum. Teacher experience is also linked to more coverage of the curriculum, but in opposite ways in the two countries. As the analysis in the previous chapter suggested, and as we will show in the next chapter, more attention to topics related to test items results in higher student achievement on those items in North West Province. This leads to the conclusion that there are ways to improve student learning on the South African side of the border through better coverage of the curriculum, and on both sides of the border through better teaching of the curriculum.

In the next chapter, we pull these threads together to assess the overall impact of teacher skills on student learning gains in the Grade 6 year.

CHAPTER 11

Testing the overall model of student achievement

Now that we have analysed our key variables, namely, student achievement, individual learner characteristics (socio-economic index, reading material in the home, language spoken at home), teacher characteristics (such as experience and education), teacher mathematics knowledge, teacher classroom teaching quality, opportunity to learn and the level of violence in the school, we can estimate the relationship between learner achievement gains and learner characteristics, teacher inputs, opportunity to learn, school average student socio-economic background and school violence. We consider these last two variables as indicators of peer effects and school context.

As explained in the introduction to this study and in Chapter 2 on methodology, the main objective of our analysis is to explain how skilled teachers in the classroom may influence student learning. To accomplish this objective, we attempt to isolate the learner gains associated with a particular teacher during one year of being exposed to that teacher in that school. This is not an easy task, as in a few classrooms teachers change during the school year, and not all learners stay in the same classroom throughout the year. However, controlling for the learner's initial conditions at the beginning of the year and carefully measuring the quality of teaching and the opportunity to learn, as well as other classroom conditions (class size, peer characteristics, classroom/school violence) during the year, the achievement results the learner attains at the end of the year should logically be attributed to his or her exposure to that classroom during that year.

We will present this analysis in three progressive steps:
- The estimate of learner mathematics achievement gains as a function of individual learner characteristics.
- The estimate of learner mathematics post-test mathematics achievement as a function of learner characteristics and a variable representing each classroom in the sample. This allows us to estimate the part of the variation in learner achievement gains explained by variation in learner characteristics and the part explained by variation in classroom conditions, normally defined as the 'teacher effect' plus 'peer effect'.
- The estimate of learner mathematics post-test mathematics achievement as a function of learner characteristics and measures of teacher characteristics, opportunity to learn and peer effects.

This analysis suggests that teacher (classroom) effects on learner achievement are large in North West Province and not as large in Botswana, but still important. We can explain at least part of the variation in learner achievement gains in two further steps:
- By our measure of teacher teaching quality and teacher mathematics knowledge.
- By opportunity to learn.

Our estimates suggest that educational policies in North West that improve teaching quality and the amount of time teachers spend teaching the mathematics curriculum would improve student learning, and in Botswana, educational policies that improve teaching quality and teacher mathematics knowledge would improve student learning. Thus, in both countries, focusing on the improvement of teacher quality, whether through better teaching, higher levels of teacher mathematics knowledge, or better coverage of the curriculum, can yield positive results for students in school systems that differ but still suffer from relatively low student achievement.

Learner characteristics and mathematics achievement

We have seen that higher SES learners scored significantly higher on the pre-test they took in March 2009 (Figures 6.5a and 6.5b on page 81). In traditional cross-section analyses, such as the TIMSS and SACMEQ, this relationship suggests that higher SES learners learn more than lower SES learners while they are in school. However, this is not necessarily the case. Considerable research has been done showing that higher SES learners begin kindergarten (or 1st grade) with higher test scores than lower SES learners and that subsequent gains during the primary grades of learners from differing SES backgrounds do not differ greatly, if at all (for example, Jencks & Phillips 1998).

Our data allow us to test whether learners with differing characteristics make greater or smaller achievement gains during their Grade 6 year. We test two models of gains (Table 11.1 on page 138). In the first model, we use the post-test as the dependent variable, testing whether the post-test is related to learner characteristics, controlling for the initial test score. This corresponds to equation (2a) in Chapter 3. In the second model, the dependent variable is the difference between the learner's post-test and pre-test scores, which corresponds to equation (2b) in Chapter 3.

The advantage of the second model is that it avoids the problem of correlation between the initial test and learner characteristics. This correlation could bias the estimates of the relation between those characteristics and learner achievement gain, although the correlation between individual characteristics and initial test score is not great either in our North West sample ($r = 0.41$) or in the Botswana sample ($r = 0.35$) – in large part because our samples of schools are located in only part of the range of socio-economic backgrounds in each society. The disadvantage of the second model is that, unlike Model I, the difference in test scores (Model II) assumes that there is no decay in learning over the year, so may underestimate the effects of learner characteristics on learning gain.

Bearing this in mind, the results in Table 11.1, Model I, show that in North West and Botswana, older learners, higher SES learners, and learners who have spent less time in school all make larger gains, estimating gains as the post-test score controlling for pre-test score. In North West, learners who speak English or Afrikaans as their home language, and those students who have no books, magazines or newspapers in the home have lower gains. In Botswana, those students who have about 50 books in the home also have significantly lower gains, which is difficult to explain. Male and female students do not differ significantly in their gain scores. It is important to note that these variables explain hardly any of the variation in gains, whereas our learner characteristics explain 17 per cent of the individual learner pre-test mathematics score in North West Province and 13 per cent in Botswana. Thus, individual learner characteristics have a moderate influence on the level of their test scores but almost no influence on the individual gains in a given year of primary school, at least not in Grade 6 as measured by the gain scores on our test.

We can conclude from these and earlier results that higher social class students begin the year with a higher achievement level, but in North West Province do not make larger gains; therefore, there is some equalisation of achievement across learners of lower and higher SES, although the equalisation is small. This result in North West is interesting because it suggests that although higher socio-economic background students make smaller absolute gains (Model II), those students with at least some social

TABLE 11.1 North West Province and Botswana: Estimates of individual student achievement gains as a function of student characteristics, 2009

	North West Province		Botswana	
	Model I Dependent variable post-test score	Model II Dependent variable post-test minus pre-test score	Model I Dependent variable post-test score	Model II Dependent variable post-test minus pre-test score
Variable				
Initial test score	0.539***		0.760***	
Male	−0.001	0.002	−0.006	−0.005
Number of years in school	−0.003***	−0.001	−0.005***	−0.004***
Age	−0.008***	−0.004*	−0.009***	−0.004*
SES index	0.001*	−0.001**	0.002***	0.001***
Dominant language[a]	0.010	−0.023**	0.007	0.008
Minor language[b]	−0.001	0.001	−0.002	−0.012
Homework never	−0.031*	−0.018	−0.003	−0.002
Homework once/week	−0.016**	−0.007	−0.008	−0.004
Homework every day	0.007	−0.007	−0.001	0.000
No books, etc. in home	−0.024***	−0.020*	−0.012*	−0.008
About 20 books, etc. in home	0.009*	0.007	−0.006	−0.002
About 50 books, etc. in home	0.005	0.004	−0.015**	−0.015**
About 100 books, etc. in home	0.024***	0.015*	−0.008	−0.014
> 100 books, etc. in home	0.012*	0.009	−0.005	−0.002
Read to when younger	0.008	0.008	0.005	0.005
Don't know if read to	0.013*	0.011	0.006	0.007
Never reads at home	0.016*	0.021*	0.008	0.011
Reads three times/week	0.003	0.007	−0.000	0.002
Reads more than three times/week	0.012*	0.012*	0.008	0.004
Constant	0.261***	0.091***	0.234***	0.101***
Observations	3 530	3 530	1 666	1 666
Adjusted R^2	0.278	0.007	0.553	0.017

Source: North West Province and Botswana Schools Sample, 2009.

Note: Reference language is Setswana. Reference homework is 'two to three times per week'. Reference books, magazines and newspapers in the home is 'about ten'. Reference read to when younger is 'no'. Reference for reading at home is 'once a week'.

[a] Main language spoken at home is English or Afrikaans.
[b] Main language spoken at home is non–Setswana African language

* $p<0.10$, ** $p<0.05$, *** $p<0.01$.

capital (reading material in the home) make larger absolute gains. In Botswana, higher social class students begin the year with a higher achievement level and also make larger gains.

The fact that in our sample of Botswana schools achievement seems to become more unequal over the course of the year supports what we learnt from the item analysis: learners in higher scoring classrooms make larger achievement gains when they get more lessons, whereas the opposite happens in lower scoring classrooms. There appears to be something about the teaching/learning process in Botswana schools that favours higher SES students.

Earlier, in Chapter 6, we showed that there is a much stronger relation in North West Province than in Botswana between average learner socio-economic background in a classroom and the average pre-test mathematics score in that same classroom. Average school SES explains about one-half the variance in the average pre-test score across classrooms in North West Province and about one-fifth of the variation in average pre-test score in Botswana. When we compare this result with the result discussed above of only a moderate relationship between individual learner SES and initial test score (also lower in Botswana), this suggests that higher scoring students tend to be grouped into classrooms with other higher scoring students, and, on average, these higher scoring students are of higher SES. This clustering appears to be much less evident in Botswana than in North West.

In both countries, there is still a great deal of variance in SES among individual learners within classrooms. As we have argued, the clustering of better and worse performing students in a non-random fashion across schools poses a threat to estimating the effect of teacher and other classroom conditions on student achievement when achievement is measured by just one test given at one point in the academic year. If teachers with more mathematics knowledge tend to teach in these higher scoring schools, we could incorrectly identify this higher teacher mathematics knowledge as causing the higher average student test scores. This is why we went to such pains to get gain scores by testing students twice during the academic year.

What is the contribution of classroom (teacher and peer) variation to learner achievement gains?

In this second stage of the analysis, we estimate the overall contribution of classroom variation, largely identified with teacher differences and perhaps peer differences, to learner achievement gains. We do this by first estimating the relationship between the learners' post-test and pre-test scores. We then add classroom 'fixed effects' – a dummy variable for every classroom (omitting one). By adding classroom fixed effects, we are able to estimate the additional variation in the learner post-test that is associated with classroom differences. This indicates the size of the 'classroom effect' (and by implication, the potential 'teacher effect') on the post-test, controlling for the pre-test. We then add student characteristics to the regression estimate of post-test score. This estimate tells us how much more of the variation in post-test score is attributable to individual learner differences that we have not picked up with the initial test score.

Table 11.2 reports these results. The adjusted R^2s suggest a major difference between the contribution of variables associated with classroom differences to learning gain differences among students in the two border regions. On the North West side, the R^2s indicate that the initial test score only explains 26 per cent of the variance in the post-test score and that adding the classroom dummies – the classroom fixed effect – explains an additional 28.5 per cent of that variation. Adding individual learner characteristics, such as those in Table 11.1, only increases the R^2 by 0.013 to 0.558. Thus, we can explain about 56 per cent of the variance in the post-test by the learners' pre-test score, plus student

TABLE 11.2 *North West Province and Botswana: Estimates of learner post-test mathematics achievement as a function of learner initial (pre-test) achievement, classroom 'fixed effects' and learner socio-economic background, 2009*

Independent variable	North West Province			Botswana		
	Initial test score only	Initial test + classroom fixed effects	Initial test + classroom fixed effects + learner SES	Initial test score only	Initial test + classroom fixed effects	Initial test + classroom fixed effects + learner SES
Initial test score	0.601***	0.478***	0.461***	0.833***	0.765***	0.721***
	(0.081)	(0.065)	(0.063)	(0.019)	(0.020)	(0.023)
Male			−0.002			−0.004
			(0.004)			(0.005)
Number of years in school			−0.001			−0.005***
			(0.001)			(0.001)
Age			−0.006***			−0.009***
			(0.001)			(0.002)
SES index			0.000			0.002***
			(0.000)			(0.000)
Dominant language[a]			−0.006			−0.001
			(0.007)			(0.009)
Minor language[b]			−0.012**			0.000
			(0.005)			(0.018)
Homework never			−0.018			−0.005
			(0.016)			(0.011)
Homework once/week			−0.003			−0.005
			(0.005)			(0.008)
Homework every day			−0.009			−0.012*
			(0.008)			(0.006)
No books, newspapers, magazines			−0.016			−0.010
			(0.010)			(0.006)
About 20 books, etc. in home			0.005			−0.004
			(0.004)			(0.006)
About 50 books, etc. in home			0.003			−0.014**
			(0.004)			(0.006)
About 100 books, etc. in home			0.013**			−0.009
			(0.006)			(0.011)
More than 100 books, etc. in home			0.002			−0.011
			(0.006)			(0.010)
Read to when younger			0.004			0.004
			(0.005)			(0.008)
Don't know if read to			0.016**			0.005
			(0.006)			(0.011)
Never reads at home			0.008			0.005
			(0.009)			(0.014)

Independent variable	North West Province			Botswana		
	Initial test score only	Initial test + classroom fixed effects	Initial test + classroom fixed effects + learner SES	Initial test score only	Initial test + classroom fixed effects	Initial test + classroom fixed effects + learner SES
Read three times/week			0.014*** (0.005)			0.002 (0.008)
Read more than three times/week			0.023*** (0.005)			0.010 (0.009)
Classroom 'fixed effects'	No	Yes	Yes	No	Yes	Yes
Constant	0.156***	0.189***	0.254**	0.097***	0.101***	0.240**
Observations	3 530	3 530	3 530	1 666	1 666	1 666
Adjusted R^2	0.260	0.545	0.558	0.530	0.562	0.577

Source: North West Province and Botswana School Samples, 2009. Standard errors of coefficients in parentheses - in regression estimates where classroom fixed effects are included,, standard errors are adjusted using a cluster correction.

Notes: Reference language is Setswana. Reference homework is 'two to three times per week'. Reference books, magazines and newspapers in the home is 'about ten'. Reference read to when younger is 'no'. Reference for reading at home is 'once a week'. In regression estimates where classroom fixed effects are included, standard errors are adjusted using a cluster correction.

[a] Main language spoken at home is English or Afrikaans.
[b] Main language spoken at home is non–Setswana African language.

* $p<0.10$, ** $p<0.05$, *** $p<0.01$.

characteristics highly related to family human and social capital, plus the (unspecified) variation among classrooms. About one-half of this variation is related to variation in classroom characteristics – mostly associated with teacher variation but also perhaps peer effects.

In Botswana, the adjusted R^2s indicate that the initial test score explains 53 per cent of the variance in the post-test score and that adding the classroom dummies – the classroom fixed effect – only explains an additional 3.2 per cent of the variation in the post-test score. Adding individual learner characteristics, such as those in Table 11.1, only increases the R^2 by 0.015 to 0.577. Thus, we can explain about 58 per cent of the variance in the post-test by the learners' pre-test score, their family human and social capital, and the (unspecified) variation among classrooms. Unlike in North West, little of this variation in the post-test score in Botswana is related to variation in classroom characteristics.

One way to check the logic of these findings is to measure the standard deviation of student test scores among the individual students in each country sample and among classroom averages. In both cases, the individual student variation on the initial and final tests is the same on the initial test (12.2 and 12.5 points in North West and Botswana, respectively), and is somewhat higher in Botswana on the second test (14.5 in Botswana versus 12.5 in North West). However, the variation in average student test score across classrooms is much lower in Botswana than in North West – 5.0 versus 8.5 on the initial test and 6.8 versus 8.5 on the second test.

A second way to check the logic is to estimate the relationship between the final test and the classroom dummies without controlling for the initial student test score. For North West, the percentage of final test score variance (R^2) explained by the classroom dummies alone is 0.424, and in Botswana, it is 0.161. Thus, in South Africa, the 'overlap' between classroom effects and student initial test score is about 0.14, and in Botswana, it is about 0.13. This verifies that classroom variation in North West is much larger than in Botswana, and that none of the difference is due to differential correlation of classroom covariates with the variation in student initial test score.

From a policy standpoint, the important finding of the estimates in Table 11.2 is the very high percentage of the variance in the learner post-test achievement scores in North West and the very small percentage in Botswana that are related to inter-classroom differences.[1] The finding is important because it suggests that in North West there is something about the differences in classrooms that had a significant effect on learner mathematics performance in Grade 6, whereas in Botswana schools, inter-classroom differences do not help to explain much of the higher post-test scores. In the next section, we will attempt to identify what that something was in North West – particularly whether it was related to teacher mathematics knowledge, teacher teaching quality, whether learners had sufficient opportunity to learn the curriculum on which the test items were based, and whether similar variables explain the much smaller portion of the total variation related the variation in classroom conditions in Botswana.

The impact of teacher skills and other classroom conditions on learner mathematics achievement gains

We have determined that in North West a major part of the variation in the post-test learners took at the end of their Grade 6 academic year is related to variation in classroom conditions, but in Botswana the role of classroom variation is much smaller. Now we need to try to identify what it is about those classrooms in both countries that might explain such variation.

To identify these classroom characteristics, we generate two different estimates of teacher (plus peer) effects on learner mathematics achievement gains (value added) and compare these to the typical estimates of teacher and peer effects using the post-test score with no control for the pre-test score. The first of the test score gain models assumes that the learners' mathematics post-test score is a function of previous mathematics knowledge, as measured by the pre-test score and teacher and other classroom inputs during the Grade 6 school year. This first model also assumes that over the course of the year the learners lose some of their previous knowledge (knowledge decay), and so part of the value added by teachers or other classroom conditions during the year is the recuperation of previous knowledge lost. To the degree that our teacher variables are correlated with the initial test score, this model biases the teacher effect upward.

The second model measures the gain, or value added, as the difference in the post-test and the pre-test scores. This assumes that no knowledge is lost over the course of the year. Teacher effects would therefore tend to be biased downward.

---

1   In our sample, almost all these inter-classroom differences are also inter-school differences, since in only four schools in North West and five schools in Botswana did we obtain data on two different teachers in the same school. This is not sufficient to give us a statistically significant estimate of how much inter-classroom differences within the same school explain compared to how much inter-school differences explain.

We saw in the first column of Table 11.2 that this knowledge 'decay' is much smaller in Botswana than in North West. In Botswana the coefficient of the initial test is 0.833, suggesting that only 17 per cent of the knowledge of the initial test decays when we do not include other variables, whereas in North West, it is 0.601, suggesting that 40 per cent of the learner mathematics knowledge of the initial test decays. This is related to our finding that more of the variation in the learner post-test in North West is explained by classroom variation than in Botswana.

These are two-level OLS regressions, in which learners are nested in classrooms, and we must account for within classroom variation as well as across classroom variation. The coefficients of classroom level variables in such two-level OLS estimates are unbiased, but unless we account for the within classroom variation, the standard errors of the estimated coefficients for the classroom variables are biased downward. We use a cluster correction to adjust the standard errors upward. The reported significance levels of our estimated coefficients in Table 11.3 on the next page are based on adjusted standard errors.

The results in Table 11.3 suggest that in both our North West and Botswana samples, better classroom teaching, as evaluated from the videotapes, has a positive impact on both the level of the learner post-test (Model I) and on the gain (Models II and III). In North West, more lessons taught on topics also have a significant positive effect on learner post-test (Model I) and on the gain in achievement (Models II and III). Teacher mathematics knowledge and teacher experience are not significantly related to achievement gains in North West, nor are average learner SES, class size or the violence index.

In Botswana, learner performance on the post-test is positively related, in addition to better teaching, to teacher knowledge score using Grading B and to average classroom student SES, but not to lessons on topics or to topics taught (Model I). Student learning gains, depending on the model (II or III), are also negatively related to average class size. They are also positively related to average classroom SES, but not quite statistically significantly.

It is important to note that all the teaching- and peer-related coefficients in the Botswana estimates decline as expected from the post-test (cross-section) model to the value-added (gain) model assuming knowledge decay, to the value-added (gain) model using only achievement gains. This is consistent with the notion that estimates using a single learner test score overestimate teacher and peer effects on learner achievement, and that the two value-added models 'bracket' the true size of the estimated teacher and peer effects.

The same is true in North West for the coefficients of best teaching quality, total lessons on topics, total topics taught and average classroom SES. However, this is not the case in North West for 'better teaching quality'. That coefficient tends to get larger (or at least does not decrease) instead of the expected decline in size as we move from model specifications that should upwardly bias the coefficients of teacher effects to specifications that should downwardly bias the coefficients. One reason for this possible opposite movement could be that the correlation of the 'better teaching quality' variable with other included teacher characteristics and classroom conditions influences the size of its coefficient so that it rises instead of falls. However, even when these other variables are not included in the estimate, the better teaching quality coefficient tends to get larger (or at least does not decline) in each succeeding specification. 'Better quality' teachers are, on average, just as likely as 'lower quality' teachers (the reference category) to teach students with lower or higher initial test scores (the better quality variable is not significantly correlated with initial learner test score), whereas 'best quality' teachers are significantly more likely to teach students with higher initial test scores.

TABLE 11.3 North West Province and Botswana: Cross-section and value-added estimates of teacher and other classroom variables on learner mathematics achievement, 2009

Variable	North West Province			Botswana		
	Value-added models			Value-added models		
	Model I	Model II	Model III	Model I	Model II	Model III
	Post-test only	Post-test controlling for initial test score	Test score gain (post-test minus pre-test score)	Post-test only	Post-test controlling for initial test score	Test score gain (post-test minus pre-test score)
Initial test score		0.5181***			0.7602***	
Teacher experience (years)	−0.0045	−0.0040	−0.0036	−0.0004	0.0016	0.0022
Teacher experience squared	0.0001	0.0001	0.0000	0.0000	−0.0001	−0.0001
Teacher test score B	−0.0007	−0.0009	−0.0010	0.0010*	0.0005*	0.0004*
Better teaching quality [a]	0.0425*	0.0468**	0.0508**	0.0332**	0.0197**	0.0154**
Best teaching quality [a]	0.0240	0.0237	0.0234	0.0334	0.0177	0.0128
Total lessons on topics	0.0013*	0.0013*	0.0012*	0.0001	0.0000	0.0000
Observed class size	−0.0005	−0.0005	−0.0005	−0.0004	−0.0009	−0.0010*
Average class SES	0.0103***	0.0048*	−0.0004	0.0043*	0.0023	0.0016
Class violence index	−0.0010	0.0003	0.0002	0.0008	0.0006	0.0005
Learner characteristics included?	YES	YES	YES	YES	YES	YES
Constant	0.3464***	0.2129***	0.0888	0.5740***	0.1875***	0.065
Adjusted R^2	0.197	0.346	0.084	0.193	0.568	0.044
observations	3 530	3 530	3 530	1 666	1 666	1 666
Total topics taught [b]	0.0025**	0.0023*	0.0021*	0.0007	0.0003	0.0002

Source: North West Province and Botswana Schools Sample, 2009.

[a] Reference variable: 'lower teacher quality'.
[b] We ran an alternative set of regressions with total test topics taught in lieu of total lessons on test topics. All other variables were the same as reported here. These are the estimated coefficients for total topics taught with all other variables included. We did not run total topics taught and total lessons on topics in the same estimate because they are sufficiently correlated to bias the estimated relation with learner post-test score.

* $p<0.10$, ** $p<0.05$, *** $p<0.01$.

We conclude that on both sides of the border, the difference between better and lower quality teaching has a robust impact on the post-test score, whether a cross-sectional (Model I) or a value-added (gain) model (Models II and III) is used. Best quality teaching has a positive but not significant impact. This is perhaps because there are relatively few 'best quality' teachers in our sample as a result of the sample focusing on low-income, mostly no-fee schools.[2] There are somewhat more 'best quality' teachers in the Botswana sample, and this seems to show up in a smaller difference in the coefficient of 'best' and 'better quality' teachers on that side of the border.[3]

As we showed in Chapter 10, teacher characteristics associated with better mathematics teaching are – not surprisingly – correlated with each other. Some of our variables are more strongly correlated with each other in one country than in the other, and this may influence the estimates of particular coefficients. For example, we showed that 'better' and 'best quality' teachers are more likely to have higher mathematics knowledge scores in both countries, but the relationship is much stronger in North West. This could mean that by including both variables in the regression estimates for learner gains, the effect of teacher test score is picked up by teaching quality. We also showed that in both countries, teachers' mathematics knowledge, at least as measured by Grading A, are positively correlated with total lessons taught (Table 10.2). It is therefore possible that more knowledgeable teachers are more likely to provide students with more OTL. In sum, when teachers have more mathematics knowledge they are likely to teach more effectively and teach more often, and both more effective teaching and more OTL contribute to greater student learning.

The effect size of the teacher quality impact on learner gains

How do the estimated coefficients of better teaching and lessons per topic translate into the amount of impact they have on learner achievement gains? Analysts call this the 'effect size' of a particular policy variable on student outcomes, and it is measured by the relationship of the policy variable. In this case, that variable is improving the quality of teaching from 'lower quality' to 'better quality', or increasing the number of lessons taught on test topics – to the gain in student achievement on the post-test, or on achievement gain in terms of standard deviations of the post-test or the standard deviations of the gain. In the North West sample, the standard deviation of the post-test is 0.12 and of the absolute gain, 0.11. In the Botswana sample, the standard deviation of the post-test is 0.14 and of the absolute gain, 0.10.

In North West Province, improving teaching from 'lower' to 'better' teaching, as measured by the rating system used by our mathematics educator evaluators, would increase learner test scores by $\frac{0.042}{0.12} = 0.35$ standard deviations if we use the relation of teaching quality to variation in post-test score, and would increase the gain by $\frac{0.051}{0.11} = 0.46$ standard deviations if we use the relationship of teaching quality to the variation in absolute gain. The effect size of improving teaching quality is therefore large: 0.35 to 0.46 standard deviations depending on whether we use the variation of post-test achievement or achievement gain as the denominator.

In the case of total lessons on topics, the mean total lessons taught on test topics in our sample is 61 and the standard deviation is 22. If we could increase the number of lessons taught on these test topics

---

2 In our pilot study in Gauteng, where we included in our sample a number of schools serving higher income students and former Model C schools, highest performing teachers (rating equal to 3) had a highly significant positive coefficient in the achievement gain equation.

3 Indeed, the coefficient for best quality teaching in the cross-sectional estimate in Botswana is close to significant statistically at the 10 per cent level.

by one standard deviation, or 22 lessons, the increase in learner post-test score (Model II), according to our estimate (0.0013 × 22 = 0.0286) would represent an effect size of $\frac{0.0286}{0.12} = 0.24$ standard deviations. Similarly, in terms of the absolute achievement gain (Model III), the effect size would be 0.0012 × 22 = 0.0264, and $\frac{0.0264}{0.11} = 0.24$. Therefore, the effect size is 0.24 standard deviations in both cases.

In the case of total topics taught, the mean in our sample is 40 topics taught and the standard deviation is 13. If we could increase the number of topics taught by one standard deviation, or 13 topics, the increase in learner post-test score, according to our estimate, 0.030, would represent an effect size of $\frac{0.030}{0.12} = 0.25$ standard deviations. In terms of the absolute achievement gain, the effect size would be $\frac{0.027}{0.11} = 0.25$. The effect size is the same in both cases, and is about one-fourth of a standard deviation.

Improving teaching in Botswana from 'lower' to 'better' teaching, as measured by the rating system used by our mathematics educator evaluators, would increase learner test scores by $\frac{0.033}{0.14} = 0.24$ standard deviations if we use the relation of teaching quality to variation in post-test score, and would increase the gain by 0.12 (underestimated) to 0.14 (overestimated) standard deviations if we use the two measures of value added – underestimated absolute gain or overestimated post-test as a function of pre-test. The effect size of improving teaching quality is therefore fairly large, but not nearly as large as in North West Province.

In the case of teacher mathematics knowledge score, the mean of the teacher test using Grading B is 47.4 with a standard deviation of 11. If we could increase the teacher test score by one standard deviation, or 11 percentage points, the increase in learner post-test score, according to our estimate, 0.0055, would be an effect size of $\frac{0.005}{0.10} = 0.055$ standard deviations. Similarly, in terms of the absolute achievement gain, the effect size would be $\frac{0.0044}{0.10} = 0.04$ standard deviations. In this case, the effect sizes are small.

The observed class size (observed from the classroom lesson videotapes) in Botswana is also significantly related to absolute achievement gains. The mean class size in the Botswana sample is 28 students, and the standard deviation is 5.5, so a decrease in class size of one standard deviation (5.5 students) would be associated with an increase in test score gain of (.001 × 5.5) = $\frac{0.0055}{0.10}$, or 0.055 standard deviations. Again, the effect size is small.

In terms of effect sizes connected with improved teacher quality, these are considered large and the effect size is particularly large in North West. In terms of the effect size connected with additional lessons on topics and additional topics in North West, the effect size is considered quite large. In other words, improving teacher quality in both countries and the number of lessons devoted to mathematics topics or the number of topics in the curriculum in North West can have a sizable effect on learner achievement gains over the period of an academic year. However, in terms of increasing teachers' mathematics knowledge in Botswana, the effect size is small. Nonetheless, increasing teachers' mathematics knowledge may be an effective way of improving teachers' teaching quality in both countries, as we showed in Chapter 8. It also may have some impact on the number of lessons taught, particularly in parts of the curriculum that are not currently well covered.

The results in both countries have important implications for educational policy. In the North West Province of South Africa, they suggest that teaching quality and the amount of effort put into covering the curriculum can have a significant impact on learner mathematics achievement gains in each year of schooling. In Botswana, improving teaching can also have an important impact on how much mathematics students learn during the year. The inputs we have identified are quite specific and quite subject to intervention. They also make sense in terms of what we expect to make a difference in student learning.

TABLE 11.4a *North West Province: Estimates of teacher quality on average classroom learner achievement gains by curriculum category of items, 2009*

Specification I – Absolute learner achievement gain controlling for initial test score					
Variable	Numbers	Patterns	Shapes	Measurement	Data
Initial test score	−0.1764	−0.3260**	−0.5413***	−0.1780	−0.4527***
Better teaching	0.0040	0.0181	−0.0017	−0.0103	−0.0166
Best teaching	0.0206	0.0248	−0.0180	−0.0430	−0.0042
Lessons on topics	0.0003	0.0032	0.0028**	0.0017	0.0003
Teacher test score B	−0.0009	−0.0007	−0.0009	0.0006	0.0006
Average class SES	0.0015	0.0074***	0.0069**	0.0025	0.0040
Intercept	0.0893***	0.1049***	0.1776***	0.0353	0.0084
Adjusted R^2	0.018	0.069	0.438	0.009	0.111
Observations	62	62	62	62	62
Specification II – Absolute learner achievement gain					
Variable	Numbers	Patterns	Shapes	Measurement	Data
Better teaching	0.0012	0.0151	−0.0110	−0.0079	−0.0126
Best teaching	0.0150	0.0228	−0.0284	−0.0460*	−0.0076
Lessons on topics	0.0003	0.0020	0.0030**	0.0018	0.0003
Teacher test score B	−0.0010	−0.0008	−0.0016*	0.0005	0.0004
Average class SES	−0.0018	0.0037	−0.0053**	−0.0003	0.0015
Intercept	0.0811**	0.0491	0.1542***	0.0228	−0.0405
Adjusted R^2	−0.008	−0.004	0.210	−0.005	−0.042
Observations	62	62	62	62	62

Source: North West Province Schools Sample, 2009.

* $p<0.10$, ** $p<0.05$, *** $p<0.01$.

The impact of teacher skills and other classroom conditions on learner mathematics achievement gains in the curriculum content areas

It is possible that various aspects of teacher quality, including opportunity to learn, as well as classroom conditions, affect different components of the mathematics curriculum differently. We described these various components (numbers, patterns, shapes, measurement, and data) in Chapter 4. In this section, we estimate the relationship between our teacher quality/classroom conditions variables and the value added on each learning objective component of the learner test. As done previously, we estimate two models for each of the content areas – one in which the post-test is a function of the gain controlling

TABLE 11.4b *Botswana: Estimates of teacher quality on average classroom learner achievement gains by curriculum category of items, 2009*

Specification I – Absolute learner achievement gain controlling for initial test score					
Variable	Numbers	Patterns	Shapes	Measurement	Data
Initial test score	−0.0210	−0.2544*	−0.4130**	−0.1698	−0.5104**
Better teaching	0.0068	0.0408***	0.0171	0.0116	0.0033
Best teaching	−0.0005	0.0271	0.0139	0.0148	0.0070
Lessons on topics	−0.0006*	0.0017	−0.0006	0.0011	0.0008
Teacher test score B	−0.0003	0.0008	0.0004	0.0008	0.0016**
Average class SES	0.0046***	0.0017	0.0069**	0.0073***	0.0048**
Observed class size	−0.0005	0.0006	0.0008	−0.0022	−0.0009
Intercept	0.0387	0.0887	0.1018	0.0353	0.0084
Adjusted R^2	0.135	0.119	0.009	0.090	0.136
Observations	64	64	62	64	64
Specification II – Absolute learner achievement gain					
Variable	Numbers	Patterns	Shapes	Measurement	Data
Better teaching	0.0060	0.0396***	0.0093	0.0098	−0.0018
Best teaching	−0.0014	0.0290	0.0108	0.0140	0.0024
Lessons on topics	−0.0006*	0.0008	−0.0025	0.0009	0.0011
Teacher test score B	−0.0003	0.0008	0.0002	0.0007	0.0017**
Average class SES	0.0044***	0.0001	−0.0004	0.0065***	0.0027
Observed class size	−0.0005	0.0004	−0.0000	−0.0023	−0.0004
Intercept	0.0345	0.0221	0.0414	0.0153	−0.0809
Adjusted R^2	0.149	0.082	−0.078	0.080	0.060
Observations	64	64	64	64	64

Source: North West Province Schools Sample, 2009.

* $p<0.10$, ** $p<0.05$, *** $p<0.01$.

for the pre-test, teacher quality and other variables,[4] and the second in which the dependent variable is the absolute gain between the pre- and post-tests.

In this case, we estimate the regressions only across classrooms – in other words, we make a single-level estimate, omitting learner variance within classrooms. This gives us a close approximation to the results had we run the more complete two-level regressions. We do not show the results of the regressions with teacher experience, class size and the violence index since these three variables were not significant in any of the regressions. We also do not show the results for topics taught, since it was not significant in any of the regressions.

---

4 This specification, $A_{T2} - A_{T1} = \alpha A_{T1} + \Sigma \beta_j T_j + \delta C + \varepsilon$ is equivalent statistically to the regression $A_{T2} = \gamma A_{T1} + \Sigma \beta_j T_j + \delta C + \varepsilon$, where $\alpha = \gamma - 1$. The coefficients β_j and δ are equal in both specifications.

Results by curriculum category in North West

The results by curriculum category in North West suggest that although the impact of lessons on topics is consistently positive across all categories, much of the impact of that variable is on the average classroom learner gain in the shapes section of the curriculum. This makes some sense because the South African government has put a lot of emphasis recently on teaching geometric shapes. On the other hand, the overall positive and significant effect of 'better teaching' on learner gain shown in Table 11.4a appears to come from gains in the heavily weighted (in terms of time spent by teachers) numbers and patterns. Surprisingly, 'best teaching' has a negative effect on gains in the measurement category, although teachers in our sample spent relatively little time on either measurement or data. When we control for initial test score, classrooms with higher average SES learners tend to make larger gains. Of course, these same higher SES classrooms score higher initially, so when we use absolute gain, the relation between average classroom SES and average classroom learner gains tends to be negative.

Results by curriculum category in Botswana

In Botswana's classrooms (Table 11.4b), this breakdown of curriculum categories suggests that the impact of lessons on topics is not significantly different from zero except in the teaching of numbers – the negative relation is one we picked up earlier in the item analysis and probably comes from over-teaching or poor teaching of numbers in lower scoring classrooms. Even in this case, the effect size is very small.

CHAPTER 12

Conclusions

An in-depth study of thousands of Grade 6 students in 126 classrooms in 116 schools in the neighbouring regions of two countries is likely to produce important results for understanding the reasons that lower-income South African students are learning less than their counterparts in Botswana. We think that the study tells us a lot. Most of it may be obvious, but the relative inefficiency of South African (and to a lesser extent, of Botswana) schools and the corresponding potential for improvement is evident in our analyses in every chapter.

We asked: Why do Botswana students perform better than South African students in international tests? Is it a question of better classroom and school resources? Or do Botswana schools use similar resources more effectively?

Our large samples of Grade 6 classrooms on either side of the Botswana-South Africa border in South East Botswana and North West Province, South Africa helped us begin to resolve these puzzles. The two regions have similar cultures, language, and some overlapping history, but because of the vagaries of European colonialism, have undergone different educational development processes over the past 40 years. Botswana has higher income per capita but is more unequal than South Africa and yet enjoys higher rankings on human development indices. There has been higher overall educational spending in Botswana because of greater resources available, but spending on primary schooling in the two countries is not vastly different. In this context, differential achievement on international and regional tests required closer examination of what goes on inside classrooms.

Our study focused mainly on no-fee public schools in both urban and rural areas. We measured learner achievement gains over a seven-month period, as well as learner characteristics, the quality of teaching in those classrooms, the opportunity given students to learn the mathematical knowledge we included on the learner test, and other classroom conditions that might have influenced how much students improved their achievement during their Grade 6 year.

The great advantage of our analysis is that we can clearly identify the gains made by learners in our sample with specific teachers, specific classroom conditions and specific classroom processes. Even though one can question whether our test truly measured how much mathematics learners knew near the beginning and toward the end of the school year, we based the test on what they were supposed to have learnt before entering Grade 6 and how much they should have learnt during that academic year. We also carefully measured their exposure to the curriculum and the quality of teacher knowledge and teacher teaching along multiple dimensions. We interviewed a subset of teachers in depth and gathered considerable information on teachers and principals.

Key findings

The study has two major sets of findings.

Finding 1: Teacher quality and opportunity to learn contribute to student achievement gains

Our most important results relate to explaining the gain (the value added) in achievement by learners during the seven months of the academic year between the pre-test and post-test.

Before we discuss those results, we need to note that, on average, students in our sample did not do well on the tests we gave them at the beginning and end of the year. Many learners in both countries had better knowledge of parts of the mathematics curriculum, mainly numbers and patterns, but had very poor knowledge of much of the 6th grade curriculum, especially measurement and data handling. Overall, initial and post-test learner scores in both countries were driven down by learners' inability to answer mathematics questions on major portions of the Grade 6 curriculum, although students in our sample of Botswana schools did better than those in our North West schools.

We also found that learners and teachers in the two countries did well, and poorly, on the same items on their respective tests and that mathematics lessons did not differ greatly. In other words, there were many similarities in the teaching and learning skills observed in the two sets of classrooms. Nevertheless, Botswana students did better on the initial and final tests and had larger achievement gains.

The study determined that learners' performance (test score gains) in Grade 6 mathematics is directly related to three elements of teaching quality, namely:
- teachers' knowledge of the mathematics they are supposed to be teaching,
- the quality of their mathematics teaching, which includes the level at which they teach the subject matter, and
- their coverage of the curriculum on which our learner (and teacher) tests were based.

Botswana teachers did better than their South African counterparts on the mathematics knowledge test, were somewhat better at teaching the mathematics curriculum, and covered more of it. Botswana teachers were also more disciplined in following the official curriculum and using the materials to guide their teaching.

Thus, on all three measures of teacher quality, teachers we observed and tested in Botswana did better than those in North West, yet even the teachers in Botswana were, on average, not nearly as well versed in mathematics as they should have been, were teaching their students at fairly low levels, and covered the required curriculum far from adequately.

It is difficult to say whether low teacher performance in mathematics is the result of poor initial preparation in mathematics or whether the high proportion of relatively older teachers in our sample have simply forgotten the mathematics they knew at one time. It is probably a combination of both, but teachers with low levels of mathematics knowledge, no matter the reason, are likely to avoid teaching subjects they know poorly. This seems to be the case in classrooms in both countries, but especially in North West Province.

We also found that the amount of time during the year that teachers actually teach learners mathematics is disturbingly low, particularly in the classrooms we surveyed in North West Province. Descriptive data reveal that the average number of mathematics lessons given by most teachers is considerably less than the number of lessons officially intended, indicating that 'time on task' is a problem in many of the sample schools and classrooms. In North West Province, rather than teaching the 130–140 lessons that were programmed in the period for which students recorded lessons in their notebooks (beginning of the academic year up to the beginning of November), we counted an average of 52 daily lessons during that period. In Botswana, the figure was much higher (78 lessons), but still far from the number of lessons required by the school calendar.

There was considerable variation in the number of lessons from classroom to classroom, but these low average figures imply that students were not getting much exposure to mathematics during their 6th grade year, particularly in North West classrooms. Teachers and principals we interviewed did not consider teacher absenteeism a major issue, although they seemed to be more willing to recognise it in Botswana than in South Africa. Principals reported that the biggest reason for absenteeism was ill health followed by domestic responsibilities. However, we learnt through our interviews that teachers are often also pulled away from school in North West by teacher in-service training and union meetings, and in Botswana by school meetings and other activities. Even if learners were involved in mathematics activities during the year that were not recorded in their notebooks, the outcomes-based education that formed the basis for accountability in both Botswana and South African schools makes it doubtful that there would be many such unrecorded class activities. The low exposure to the curriculum is therefore an obvious problem that needs to be corrected if learners are expected to improve their knowledge of mathematics.

Although the responses on our teacher and principal questionnaires suggested that teachers are unwilling to confront this issue, in the Mafeking meeting in July 2011 with teachers who participated in our study, they were quite open in admitting that they often did not teach because they lacked mathematics confidence and could not handle many elements of the Grade 6 curriculum.

This is further supported by evidence from the notebooks of a slow pace of work within lessons as reflected in the number and type of written mathematical tasks that learners completed daily. This slow micro-pacing suggests that teachers may find it difficult to determine the amount of time students should have for completing exercises, or that students are taking a long time to complete exercises, or that teachers are having difficulties explaining mathematical topics clearly to learners. Descriptive data on OTL also confirm that our sample of Grade 6 teachers most commonly focus on topics related to the content area number, operations and relationships, and on Grade 4 and 5 level topics rather than Grade 6 level topics. Teachers regularly engage students in routine mathematics procedures, not with underlying knowledge principles. According to our later discussions with teachers, this situation exists both because they (the teachers) find they need to address gaps in students' knowledge from earlier grades and because they lack confidence or are not competent enough to teach certain content areas or topics at higher levels.

When we relate all these classroom inputs to student achievement, we find that there is a significant relation between students' learning gains and the quality of their teachers' teaching pedagogy in both countries. In North West classrooms there is also a significant relation between students' learning gains and the number of lessons their teachers taught on the test topics (and the number of test topics taught). In Botswana classrooms, OTL for students is not a significant predictor of student learning gains, but the teachers' mathematics knowledge, average class size and average classroom SES are. The effect sizes of better teacher quality and more lessons taught (and more topics taught) on learners' mathematics achievement gains in North West Province schools are large. The effect size of better teacher quality on mathematics achievement gains is significant in Botswana, but much smaller than in our North West results. Increases in teacher mathematics knowledge and decreases in class size result in even smaller effect sizes.

The positive (although not statistically significant) relation in our sample of Botswana schools between average classroom student socio-economic background and test score gain, even when the absolute gain score is the dependent variable (Table 11.3 on page 144, 'Test score gain'),[1] is also important, in part because we do not find similar results for North West Province. This may simply represent a positive peer effect in Botswana's classrooms but not in those in North West. But there may be more to this finding. If gains are greater for higher social class classrooms, this could mean that production of mathematics achievement may be more effective in such classrooms and that the Botswana school system may be increasing inequality in mathematics learning. Note that higher average gain scores in higher social class classrooms mean that pupils in such classrooms are learning more than lower social class pupils each year they are in school. Most of us accept that lower higher social class students start out at an advantage in school, but it runs counter to most notions of fairness that students who already start out ahead should increase their advantage in a public institution. Strictly speaking, this is a peer effect, since we are controlling for teacher characteristics in the value-added equation. Teachers teaching mathematics to higher social class groups of students could be teaching at a more rapid pace, which would constitute an unobserved teacher effect.

Finding 2: Potential efficiency gains in South Africa are larger than in Botswana and larger than gains from increasing resources per student

The second key set of findings addresses whether our sample of low-income students in Botswana perform better in mathematics than in South Africa because Botswana schools have more resources than North West schools or are more efficient in working with the resources available to them. We know that the initial test score is higher in Botswana and so is the gain score of the post-test minus the pre-test. What can our research say about resources devoted to schooling in the two countries and the efficiency with which those resources are being used?

We know that Botswana spends somewhat more per primary student than South Africa does (see Table 1.2 on page 10), that primary school teacher salaries are somewhat higher compared to competing professional salaries in Botswana than in South Africa, and that teachers' mathematics test scores are higher in our sample of Botswana teachers than in our sample of North West teachers. Furthermore, Botswana spends a higher proportion of its gross domestic product on education (public spending only) than does South Africa (8.9 per cent versus 5.7 per cent). So there is considerable evidence that somewhat more resources are being devoted to schooling in Botswana, and, assuming that there is a positive relation between resources and school output, these additional resources should produce higher achievement gains in Botswana than in North West.

However, we also have evidence that Botswana uses these resources more efficiently than does South Africa. In Table 11.2 on page 140, we showed that there is much more variation between classrooms in North West than in Botswana, which suggests that, overall, Botswana classrooms deliver education in a more homogeneous (and systematically similar) way than those in South Africa. From our teacher lesson videotapes, we observed that in the Botswana sample, teachers' lessons are much more aligned with specific sections of the prescribed curriculum than is the case in North West. This supports the notion that teaching in Botswana is more 'regularised' across classrooms than in North West and helps explain why student test score gains vary less across classrooms in Botswana and why it is possible to have less variance and yet a higher overall average gain in these classrooms.

---

1   Even though the coefficient is not significant at a 0.10 level, the p-level is 0.12, which suggests that with a larger number of observations, the relation might be statistically significant.

This also helps us understand why the coefficient of teacher teaching quality can be higher in North West (Table 11.3 on page 144), yet fails to indicate that this higher coefficient means greater 'effectiveness' of teacher resources in North West. Rather, this higher coefficient suggests to us that there is more variation in teacher effectiveness in North West, hence more scope for producing more output with the same resources, hence more room for greater efficiency.

Without our comparison with Botswana, it would be difficult to see this point. Botswana is able to produce higher achievement gains even though the effect sizes of improved teacher classroom teaching on student achievement gains are smaller than in North West. Thus, we have to assume that Botswana uses resources more effectively than North West Province. The smaller coefficient in Botswana schools for 'better teachers' suggests that there is less potential for improving student achievement gains in Botswana by improving teacher mathematics teaching, not because mathematics teachers are less effective, but rather because the Botswana school system is closer to its maximum effectiveness with its current level of resources than is the case in South Africa.

One way that economists describe these relationships is in terms of a production possibilities curve, which describes the trade-off in the production of different outputs for a given level of technology and production efficiency. In Figure 12.1, we present a set of such production possibilities curves, one for North West Province, one for Botswana, and one that we call the 'production possibilities frontier'(PPF). The PPF we show here is the locus of outputs possible if these two school systems were using their resources as effectively as possible given the resources and technology (including management technology) available to them. We have assumed, for the sake of presentation, that Botswana and North West Province could produce the same amount of all output – all the products and services produced in the country – and the same amount of school achievement gain if they were equally efficient.

Figure 12.1 shows three production possibilities curves for student achievement gain versus all other economic output: one for North West Province (PP_S), one for Botswana (PP_B), and the third, the production possibilities frontier for the two countries (PP_F). The three curves are drawn to reflect our claim of higher efficiency of production of student achievement in Botswana schools than in North West schools, and, in turn, our claim that Botswana is not producing school achievement at the PPF.

FIGURE 12.1 *Botswana and North West Province: Production possibilities curves and school achievement*

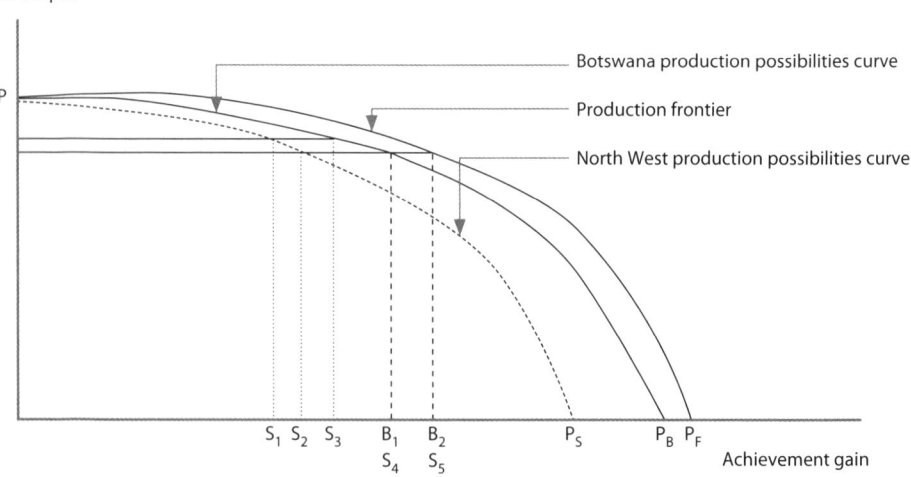

Source: Compiled by author

We also posit in Figure 12.1 that Botswana spends more resources than North West to produce achievement gains – the lower resource line shows that more resources are devoted to producing achievement gains rather than other goods and services. Thus, as we observed in our study, North West classrooms produce S_1 student achievement gains, and Botswana classrooms, using more resources per student and using their resources more efficiently than North West Province schools (as reflected in Botswana's higher production possibilities curve), produce B_1 student achievement gains. This is consistent with the results in our study.

Our argument is that classrooms in North West could increase student achievement gains in two ways:
- By increasing resources devoted to achievement gain production up to the same level as Botswana, but not increasing efficiency (a movement along the North West production possibilities curve, increasing achievement gain from S_1 to S_2), or
- By increasing efficiency of using existing resources – a movement from S_1 to S_3.

Figure 12.1 shows that North West can reach the currently higher achievement gains produced in Botswana's classrooms (a movement from S_1 to S_2 plus a movement from S_2 to S_4) by both increasing resources up to the Botswana level and by increasing the effective use of those resources by moving up to the Botswana production possibilities curve. If Botswana schools want to reach higher levels of achievement gains with existing resources, they can increase efficiency up to the production frontier (B_1 to B_2).

In effect, North West (and by implication South African) schools need to increase the level of their resources (for example, teachers with greater knowledge of mathematics). Even more importantly, these schools need to increase the effectiveness of the use of those resources – more lessons on test subjects (greater OTL) and better classroom teaching of mathematics – in order to reach Botswana levels of achievement gains in every year of the primary grades. We imagine that the same would be true at all the primary grade levels.

Botswana classrooms can also increase their achievement gains using available resources, mainly by improving mathematics teaching, but according to our results, there is less room for Botswana classrooms to make such increases than is possible in North West Province.

Nevertheless, given the total amount of resources available in Botswana and South Africa, the relatively low test scores in schools in both countries (see the SACMEQ II results shown in Figure 1.1 on page 11) suggest that the PPFs in the two countries with regard to producing student achievement gains for lower SES students are not very far out compared to what they could be. This raises a question that goes somewhat beyond the current study: what would be needed to shift the PPFs of these countries outward for achievement gains?

We would speculate that the education systems of both countries are marked by very low expectations for teachers and students, beginning with teacher training, the knowledge and skill considered sufficient to teach subjects, expectations concerning teacher responsibility for student learning, and expectations of how thoroughly teachers are expected to know and cover all elements of the national curriculum. Possibly more emphasis in teacher training on mathematics content knowledge and pedagogical mathematics content knowledge, as well as how to teach the required national curriculum, would shift the production frontier.

Unfortunately, improving the overall quality of teachers already in the system has proven to be extremely challenging. South Africa and Botswana have many teachers who are inadequately trained, and who are likely to remain in the system for many years. In spite of numerous attempts at improving existing teacher quality through upgrading programmes for un- and under-qualified teachers, most programmes appear to have had almost no effect on the quality of learning outcomes in schools. Clearly, new approaches have to be taken to in-service training, in which teachers may be required to spend large parts of their vacation period learning how to teach mathematics more effectively by focusing on improved content knowledge, increased pedagogical content knowledge, and increasing the content demand in their teaching. The matric learner catch-up holiday programmes in South Africa could be institutionalised for mathematics teachers and in-depth training could be provided to teachers on a systematic, grade-by-grade and year-by-year basis. Instead of trying to do all subjects and grades at once, and thus failing by doing too much at the same time, the effort could be focused and gradual.

More effective in the short term might well be a concerted focus on ensuring that those teachers already in employment and about to enter teaching are employed and expected to teach what they are qualified to teach. Teachers teaching out-of-phase is a recognised problem in South Africa, but there are as yet no convincing strategies to address it.

Part of our meeting with participating teachers in July 2010 in Mafeking was a short workshop going over three of the learner test items that were particularly problematic for learners in both countries. The teachers were asked to analyse why learners might have picked wrong answers to the multiple choice questions (error analysis), and how they could teach learners the mathematical concepts underlying each of the three test items. The teachers found this an interesting and illuminating exercise, in sharp contrast, they reported, to the 'usual' in-service training they received, which focuses on procedural or administrative issues rather than improving their capacity to teach subject matter. All in-service training should be devoted to improving teacher knowledge, for, as we have shown, a key factor in better teaching is greater teacher knowledge, including improved techniques for teaching specific subject matter. This is already on the South African agenda through the teacher development framework, but it requires effective follow-up and follow-through.

In addition, findings from our study suggest that emphasising the extent to which opportunity to learn is absent or present – through time spent on mathematics work, content coverage, the spread of topics across each grade year, and cognitive and curricular pacing within and across grades – could be an effective strategy. This is especially pertinent in schools that are performing poorly, such as most of those in our sample.

Were the provision and efficient use of a well-structured and carefully designed textbook and workbook series (including a well-designed teacher guide to the series) accompanied by equally well-designed in-service courses for using the workbooks effectively, it could shift the existing production possibilities curve to the right (especially in North West Province), and perhaps also move the PPF, provided that teachers actually implement the use of the books purposefully. Once again, the South African government has introduced workbooks; but their quality, distribution and use should be improved as intended. In this sense, creating greater capacity and teacher confidence could result in a different set of expectations among teachers and students. This, in turn, would be analogous to a technological innovation increasing output per unit of input.

We began our study by pointing out that the differences in learner achievement between Grade 6 learners in Botswana and South African classrooms are significant but not terribly large. We not only confirmed this, but also showed that the reasons for those differences are rooted in a combination of differences in the quality of teacher inputs – teachers' mathematical knowledge and the quality of classroom teaching – and the amount of coverage of the required curriculum, which is certainly greater in Botswana than in North West classrooms. These 'little things' apparently add up to produce the

FIGURE 12.2 *The combination diamond of learner performance improvement*

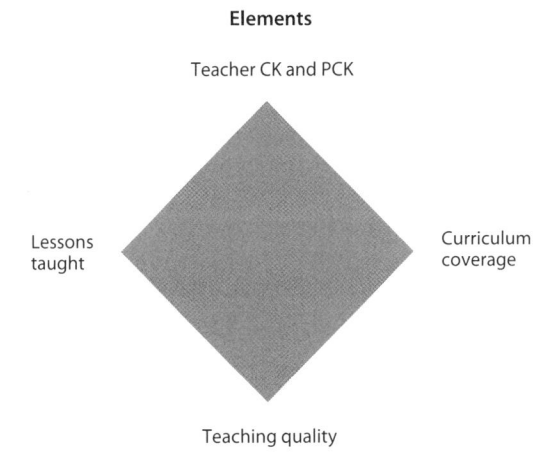

Elements

- Teacher CK and PCK
- Lessons taught
- Curriculum coverage
- Teaching quality

---

greater achievement gains in Botswana classrooms. Over the years, these greater achievement gains accumulate, so that the culturally and socio-economically similar students in North West schools find themselves one-half a standard deviation behind Botswana students by the end of Grade 6.

We can conceptualise our combination of related effects as a diamond of greater teacher content and pedagogical content knowledge, more effective teaching, more lessons taught, and greater curriculum coverage (Figure 12.2). The first two of these factors can be improved with high quality teacher pre-service and in-service training, and the latter two elements, through improved accountability, either through more effective principal instructional supervision, or through school-based student performance monitoring, or both.

This is not rocket science, and much of it is obvious to a careful observer of classrooms in the two regions we studied. Our results merely provide an empirical picture of the process of mathematics learning in a large sample of schools on two sides of the border – largely filling in important details for readily observable differences in two systems. The picture may not be terribly flattering, but the relationships we measure do point to specific ways to make that picture better.

In both countries, but especially on the South African side of the border, more knowledgeable teachers teaching what they were trained to teach, teaching more effectively in classrooms, and covering more material, unsurprisingly results in students learning more. Were North West provincial authorities to implement a serious in-service teacher training programme, assess and take steps to correct the nature of teacher shortages in subjects such as mathematics, and make sure that teachers taught mathematics lessons every day as they were supposed to, there is no doubt that mathematics learning in North West schools would improve and probably reach current levels of achievement gains in Botswana. Of course, Botswana should be taking exactly the same steps to improve their students' achievement, but, as we argue, there is less room in Botswana to make as large gains with existing resources. In effect, to increase learner gains substantially, Botswana would have to bring teacher capacity and implementation to yet higher levels, which would require even more knowledgeable teacher trainers and more sophisticated accountability systems (including higher levels of capacity building for school principals and other supervisors). The cost of such improvements would probably be substantially greater than similar size improvements (from lower levels) in South Africa.

What can policy-makers do to get education out of the low achievement trap?

The name of the education game in southern Africa, as we have shown rather exhaustively in these pages, is to get out of the low achievement trap. Botswana has a more effective education system than South Africa and has somewhat better resources going into education, but, given how much it has to spend, nonetheless produces rather low levels of learner knowledge. Policy-makers in Botswana need to reassess their benchmarks for educational quality and raise expectations across the board if they hope to reach levels of student achievement commensurate with their GDP per capita.

In some sense, South African policy-makers have an easier task, in that South African education production is so inefficient and under resourced in terms of teacher quality that the steps needed to reach Botswana levels of student achievement gains are more apparent. We have shown what those steps, as well as the high payoff taking them, would have for the vast majority of South African students. However, while the steps may be evident, taking them in the South African political and social context may be exceedingly difficult, since they will require changing a now deeply ingrained culture of inefficiency in producing learner achievement. Most schools in the South African educational system have, plainly and simply, organised themselves to produce something that is not student achievement. That suggests that our recommendations, evident as they may be to most reformers, represent more than just showing teachers and principals how to improve their effectiveness – it may require changing the underlying production mix of the system away from serving teachers to making students academically competent.

References

Addy N (2012) Comparing teachers' roles in curriculum reforms: Cases from Botswana and South Africa. Unpublished PhD dissertation, Stanford University

Adler J & Pillay V (2007) An investigation into mathematics for teaching: Insights for a case. *African Journal of Research in Mathematics, Science and Technology Education* 11: 87–108

Alexander N (2005) Language, class and power in post-apartheid South Africa. Address at the Harold Wolpe Memorial Trust open dialogue event at the TH Barry Lecture Theatre, Iziko Museum, Cape Town (27 October, 2005)

Andrews P (2009) Mathematics teachers' didactic strategies: Examining the comparative potential of low inference generic descriptors. *Comparative Education Review* 53(4): 559–581

Arends F (2007) *The employment status of teachers*. Teacher Education Project Number 4 Draft Report. Pretoria: HSRC

Ball DL & Bass H (2000) Interweaving content and pedagogy in teaching and learning to teach: knowing and using mathematics. In J Boaler J (Ed.) *Multiples perspectives on the teaching and learning of mathematics*. Westport: Ablex Publishing

Ball DL, Hill HC & Bass H (2005) Knowing mathematics for teaching: Who knows mathematics well enough to teach third grade, and how can we decide? *American Educator*, Fall 2005: 14–22

Barbarin O & Richter L (2001) *Mandela's children. Growing up in post-apartheid South Africa*. New York: Routledge

Bartlett S (2000) The development of the teaching appraisal: A recent history. *British Journal of Educational Studies* 48: 24–37

Baumert J (2006) Teacher knowledge and student progress: What do we mean by 'teachers' professional competence? Lecture presented at Stanford University (11 January, 2006)

Bertram C, Appleton S, Muthukrishna N & Wedekind V (2006) The career plans of newly qualified South African teachers. *South African Journal of Education* 26(1): 1–13

Blum J, Krishnan N & Legovini A (2010) *Doing the math on a math and science programme: South Africa's Dinaledi*. Washington, DC: World Bank. Draft (March, 2010)

Botswana Central Statistics Bureau (2006) *Education Statistics*. Gaborone: Central Statistics Office Accessed 16 February 2012, http://www.cso.gov.bw

Botswana Central Statistics Bureau (2011) *Education Statistics*. Gaborone: Central Statistics Office Accessed 16 February 2012, http://www.cso.gov.bw

Boyd DJ, Grossman PL, Lankford H, Loeb S & Wyckoff J (2009). Teacher preparation and student achievement. *Education Evaluation and Policy Analysis* 3(4): 416–440

Brophy JE & Good TL (1986) Teacher behavior and student achievement. In MC Wittrock (Ed.) *Handbook for research on teaching*. New York: Macmillan

Carnoy M, Marshall J & Socias M (2004) *How do school inputs influence math scores: A comparative approach*. Stanford: Stanford University School of Education

Carnoy M & Marshall J (2005) Cuba's academic performance in comparative perspective. *Comparative Education Review* 49(2): 230–261

Carnoy M, with Gove A & Marshall JH (2007) *Cuba's academic advantage: Why students in Cuba do better in school*. Stanford: Stanford University Press

Carnoy M, with Luschei T, Marshall JH, Naranjo B, & Sorto A (2007). *Improving Panama and Costa Rica's education systems for the 21st century economy: A comparative study*. Stanford: Stanford University School of Education

Carnoy M, Chisholm L et al. (2008) *Towards understanding student academic performance in South Africa: A pilot Study of Grade 6 mathematics lessons in South Africa*. Report prepared for the Spencer Foundation. Pretoria: HSRC

Carroll J (1963) A model of school learning. *Teachers College Record* 64(8): 723–33

Chetty D, Chisholm L, Gardiner M, Magau N & Vinjevold P (1993) Rethinking teacher appraisal in South Africa: Policy options and strategies. Johannesburg: University of the Witwatersrand

Chilisa B (1990) Botswana's experiences with criterion-referenced-testing. Paper presented at the German Foundation for International Development seminar on Testing for Science and Agriculture. Berlin: April 22–28.

Chilisa B (1998) Botswana experiences with criterion referenced testing. Paper presented at the German Foundation for International Development Seminar on Testing for Science and Agriculture, Berlin: April 22–28

Chilisa B (1999) New developments in the national examination system in Botswana. *Educational Measurement: Issues and Practice* 18(4): 28–29

Chisholm L (1999) The democratisation of schools and politics of teachers work in South Africa. *Compare* 29(2): 111–126

Chisholm L (2009) *An overview of research, policy and practice in teacher supply and demand, 1994–2008*. Cape Town: HSRC Press

Chisholm L (2012 forthcoming) Education policy borrowing across African borders: Histories of learner-centred education in Botswana and South Africa. In G Steiner-Khamsi and F Waldow (Eds) *World yearbook of education 2012: Policy borrowing and lending in education*. London & New York: Routledge

Chisholm L, Hoadley U, wa Kivilu M et al. (2005) *Educator workload in South Africa*. Report funded and prepared for the Education Labour Relations Council. Cape Town: HSRC Press

Chisholm L, Volmink J, Ndhlovu T, Potenza E, Mohamed H et al. (2000) A South African curriculum for the twenty-first century: Report of the Review Committee on Curriculum 2005. Presented to the Minister of Education, Professor Kadar Asmal, Pretoria (31 May)

Clotfelter C, Ladd H & Vigdor J (2007) *How and why do teacher credentials matter for student achievement*. NBER Working Paper No. 12828. Cambridge, MA: National Bureau of Economic Research

Comaroff JL & Comaroff J (1991) *Of revelation and revolution: Christianity, colonialism and consciousness in South Africa* (Vol. 2). Chicago: University of Chicago Press

Crouch L & Fasih T (2004) *Educational development: Implications for further efficiency analysis*. Washington, DC: World Bank

DBE (Department of Basic Education) (2011) *Curriculum news*. Accessed 20 June 2011, http://www.education.gov.za/LinkClick.aspx?fileticket=RlQ3WgihTOA%3d&tabid=348&mid=1018

DBE/DHET (Departments of Basic and Higher Education) (2011) *Integrated strategic planning framework for teacher education and development in South Africa 2011-2025*. Pretoria

DHET (Department of Higher Education and Training) (2010). Draft policy on the minimum requirements for teacher education qualifications selected from the higher education qualifications framework. Published for comment, 19 November

DoE (Department of Education) (2002) *The revised national curriculum statement for Grades R-9 (schools). Overview*. Pretoria: DoE. Accessed 20 June 2011, http://www.education.gov.za/LinkClick.aspx?fileticket=RlQ3WgihTOA%3d&tabid=348&mid=1018

DoE (2006a) *Monitoring and evaluation report on the impact and outcomes of the education system on South Africa's population: Evidence from household surveys*. Pretoria: DoE

DoE (2006b) *National policy framework for teacher education and development in South Africa*. Pretoria: DoE. Accessed 13 November 2009, www.info.gov.za/view/DownloadFileAction?id=70084

DoE (2008) Expanded mathematics, science and technology strategy. Presentation at the SAMS Workshop (31 July–1 August, 2008)

DoE (2008a) *Portfolio Committee on Education: DoE briefing on teacher education* (27 May 2008). Accessed 10 March 2010, http://www.pmg.org.za/report/20080527.briefingdepartment-education-teacher-supply

DoE (2008b) *Internal question paper 11/2008 – Written answer to Parliamentary Question No. 584* (28 March 2008). Accessed 10 March 2010, http://www.education.gov.za/dynamic/dynamic.aspx?pageid=329&catid=14&category=Parliamentary%20Questions&legtype=null

DoE (2008c) *Vacancy rates and filling of vacancies in education*. Presentation to the education portfolio committee

(27 May 2008). Accessed 9 November 2009, www.pmg.org.za/files/docs/080527vacancy.ppt

DoE (2009) *Annual report 2008/09*. Accessed 9 November 2009, http://www.education.gov.za/dynamic/dynamic.aspx?pageid=329&catid=10&category=Reports&legtype=null

Drummond J & Manson A (1993) The rise and demise of African agricultural production in Dinokana village, Bophuthatswana. *Canadian Journal of African Studies* 27(3): 462–479

Filmer D & Pritchett L (1999) The effect of household wealth on educational attainment: Evidence from 35 Countries. *Population and Development Review* 25(1): 85–120

Fleisch B (1999) School management and teacher accountability. In *Education Africa forum* (3rd edition). Johannesburg: Education Africa

Fleisch B (2008) *Primary education in crisis: Why South African schoolchildren underachieve in reading and mathematics*. Cape Town & Johannesburg: Juta

Fleisch B & Perry H (2006) Access, survival and achievement: A study of the impact of participation on levels of academic performance in SACMEQ II. Seminar paper, School of Education, University of the Witwatersrand

Floden R (2003) The measurement of opportunity to learn. In AC Porter & and A Gamoran (Eds) *Methodological advances in cross-national surveys of educational achievement*. Washington, DC: National Academy of Sciences. Accessed 14 May 2004, http://books.nap.edu/catalog/10322.html

Fuller B, Hua H & Snyder C (1994) When girls learn more than boys: The influence of time in school and pedagogy in Botswana. *Comparative Education Review* 38(3): 347–376

Gearhart M, Saxe G B, Seltzer M, Schlackman J, Ching C et al. (1999) Opportunity to learn fractions in elementary mathematics classrooms. *Journal for Research in Mathematics Education* 30(3): 286–315

Good K (2009) *Diamonds, dispossession and democracy in Botswana*. Johannesburg: Jacana

Govender L (2004) Teacher unions, policy struggles and educational change, 1994 to 2004. In L Chisholm (Ed.) *Changing class: Education and social change in post-apartheid South Africa*. Cape Town: HSRC Press

Gustafsson M & Patel E (2008) *Managing the teacher pay system. What the local and international data are telling us*. Mimeo. Pretoria

Habagaan MMR (1998) A study of secondary school teachers' perceptions of the Annual Teacher Performance Appraisal (ATPA) currently in use in Botswana secondary schools: A case study in two secondary schools in Gaborone City. Unpublished MA dissertation, University of Bath

Hanushek EA (1986) The economics of schooling: Production and efficiency in public schools. *Journal of Economic Literature* 24: 1141–1177

Hanushek E & Kimko D (2000) Schooling, labour force quality, and the growth of nations. *American Economic Review* 90(5): 1184–1208

Hanushek E & Woessman L (2008) The role of cognitive skills in economic development. *Journal of Economic Literature* (46)3: 607–668

Harley K & Wedekind V (2004) Political change, curriculum change and social formation, 1990-2002. In L Chisholm (Ed.) *Changing class: Education and social change in post-apartheid South Africa*. Cape Town: HSRC Press

Heckman J (1979) Sample selection bias as a specification error. *Econometrica* 47(1): 153–61

Henningsen M & Stein MK (1997) Mathematical tasks and student cognition: Classroom-based factors that support and inhibit high-level mathematical thinking and reasoning. *Journal for Research in Mathematics Education* 28:524–549

Heugh K (2007) Language and literacy Issues in South Africa. In N Rassool (Ed.) *Global issues in language, education, and development: Perspectives from postcolonial countries*. Series: Linguistic Diversity and Language Rights. Clevedon, UK: Multilingual Matters

Hill HC, Blunk ML, Charalambous CY, Lewis JM, Phelps GC et al. (2008) Mathematical knowledge for teaching and the mathematical quality of instruction: An exploratory study. *Cognition and Instruction* 26: 430–511

Hill HC, Rowan B & Ball DL (2005) effects of teachers' mathematical knowledge for teaching on learner achievement. *American Educational Research Journal* 42: 371–406

Hill HC, Schilling SG & Ball DL (2004) Developing measures of teachers' mathematics knowledge for teaching. *Elementary School Journal* 105: 11–30

Hoadley U (2007) The reproduction of social class inequalities through mathematics pedagogies in South African primary schools. *Journal of Curriculum Studies* 39(6): 679–706

Hoadley U (2008) Social class and pedagogy: A model for the investigation of pedagogic variation. *British Journal of Sociology of Education* 29(1): 63–78

Hoadley U & Muller J (2009) Codes, pedagogy and knowledge. Advances in Bernsteinian sociology of education. In M Apple, S Ball & L Gandin (Eds) *The Routledge international handbook of the sociology of education*. London: Routledge

Horgan G, Moss M, Kesupile A, Maphoris J & Haseley L (1991) Towards a child-centred classroom. In M Evans & J Yoder (Eds) *Patterns of reform in primary education: The case of Botswana*. Gaborone: Macmillan Botswana

Howie S (1997) *Mathematics and science performance in the middle school years in South Africa: A summary report on the performance of South African students in the Third International Mathematics and Science Study (TIMSS)*. Pretoria: HSRC

Howie SJ & Plomp T (2002) Mathematics literacy of school leaving pupils in South Africa. *International Journal of Educational Development* 22(4): 603–615

Hunt Davis Jr. R (1984a) Charles T Loram and the American model for African education in South Africa. In P Kallaway (Ed.) *Apartheid and education: The education of black South Africans*. Ravan Press. Johannesburg.

Hunt Davis Jr. R (1984b) The administration and financing of African education in South Africa 1910–1953. In P Kallaway (Ed.) *Apartheid and education: The education of black South Africans*. Ravan Press. Johannesburg

Hyslop J (1988a) School student movements and state education policy 1972–1987. In W Cobbett and R Cohen (Eds) *Popular struggles in South Africa*. London: James Currey

Hyslop J (1988b) *State education policy and the social reproduction of the urban african working class: the case of the Southern Transvaal 1955–1976*. Journal of Southern African Studies 14(3): 446–476

Hyslop J (1989) School boards, school committees and educational politics: aspects of the failure of Bantu education as a hegemonic strategy, 1955–1976. In P Bonner, I Hofmeyr, D James & T Lodge (Eds) *Holding their ground: Class, locality and culture in 19th and 20th century South Africa*. Johannesburg: Ravan Press

Hyslop J (1990a) Teacher resistance in African education from the 1940s to the 1980s. In M Nkomo (Ed.), *Pedagogy of domination:Toward a democratic education in South Africa*. Trenton, Africa World Press

Hyslop J (1990b) Schools, unemployment and youth: Origins and significance of student and youth movements 1976–1987. In B Nasson and J Samuel (Eds) *Education: From poverty to liberty*. Cape Town: David Philip

Hyslop J (1991a) Social conflicts over African education in South Africa from the 1940s to 1976. PhD dissertation, University of the Witwatersrand, 1991

Hyslop J (1991b) Food, authority and politics: Student riots in South African schools 1945–1976. In S Clingman (Ed.) *Regions and repertoires: Topics in South African politics and culture*. Johannesburg: Ravan Press

Hyslop J (1993) A destruction coming in: Bantu education as response to social crisis. In P Bonner, P Delius & D Posel (Eds.) *Apartheid's genesis 1935–1972*. Johannesburg: Ravan Press/Witwatersrand University Press

IEA (International Association for the Evaluation of Educational Achievement) (2008) *Teacher education study in mathematics (TEDS-M)*. Amsterdam, Netherlands: IEA

IIEP (Institute of Educational Planning) (2010). *IIEP Newsletter* 28(3): 4

Irvine M (1966) The story of the revival of one of South Africa's greatest schools. *Optima* (42) 1, 19–26

Irving M (2010) The best and brightest: Wage dynamics and teacher shortages in South Africa. Unpublished research paper, Stanford University, Stanford

Jaff R, Rice M, Hofmeyr J & Hall G (1995) *The national teacher education audit: The colleges of education*. Auckland Park: EDUPOL

Jansen J (2004) Autonomy and accountability in the regulation of the teaching profession: A South African case study. *Research Papers in Education* 19(1): 57–66

Jansen J & Christie P (1999) (Eds) *Changing curriculum: Studies on outcomes-based education in South Africa*. Cape Town: Juta

Jansen J, Lubiski R, Lolwana P, De Clercq F, Sanger A et al (2009). *Final report: Ministerial Committee on a National Education and Evaluation Development Unit (NEEDU)*. Pretoria. Government Gazette No. 32133, 17 April. Accessed 20 June 2011, http://www.pmg.org.za/files/docs/090417education-%20needu.pdf

Jencks C & Phillips M (Eds) (1998) *The black-white test score gap*. Washington, DC: Brookings Institution Press

Kallaway P (Ed) (2002) *The History of apartheid education 1948–1994*. New York: Peter Lang

Kazima M, Pillay V & Adler J (2008) Mathematics for teaching: observations of two case studies. *South Africa Journal of Education* 28: 283–299

Knight J & Sabot R (1990) *Education, productivity, and inequality: The East African natural experiment.* Washington, DC: Oxford University Press, for the World Bank

Kremer M, Muralidharan K, Chaudhury N, Hammer J & Rogers H (2004) *Teacher absence in India.* Washington, DC: World Bank

Kruss G (2008) *Teacher education and institutional change in South Africa.* Cape Town: HSRC Press

Kruss G (2009) *Opportunities and challenges for teacher education curriculum in South Africa.* Cape Town: HSRC Press

Ladd H (2008) Teacher effects: What do we know? In G Duncan & J Spillane *Quality: Broadening and deepening the debate.* Evanston, Ill: Northwestern University

Lankford H, Loeb S & Wyckoff J (2002) Teacher sorting and the plight of urban schools: A descriptive analysis. *Educational Evaluation and Policy Analysis* 24: 37–62

Lawrence M & Manson A (1994) 'Dog of the Boers': The rise and fall of Mangope in Bophuthatswana. *Journal of Southern African Studies, Special Issue: Ethnicity and Identity in Southern Africa* 20(3): 447–461

Lee D (1982) Exploring the construct of 'opportunity-to-learn'. *Integrated Education* 20(1–2): 62–63

Levin HM (1980) Educational production theory and teacher inputs. In C Bidwell & D Windham (Eds) *The analysis of educational productivity, Vol. 2: Issues in macro analysis.* Cambridge, MA: Ballinger

Luschei T (2006) In search of good teachers: patterns of teacher quality in two Mexican states. Unpublished PhD dissertation, Stanford University School of Education, Stanford

Macdonald CA (1990) *Crossing the threshold into Standard Three in black education : The consolidated main report of the Threshold Project.* Pretoria : Human Sciences Research Council

Magubane B (n.d.) Resistance and repression in the Bantustans. In South African Democracy Education Trust (Ed.) *The road to democracy in South Africa, Volume 2, (1970–1980).* Pretoria: UNISA Press

Malherbe EG (1922) *Education in South Africa* (Vol. 1*).* Cape Town: Juta

Manatsha BT & Maharjan K L (2009) Fancy figures and ugly facts in Botswana's rapid economic growth. *Journal of International Development and Cooperation* 15(1–2): 19–46

Marshall JH (2003) If you build it will they come? The effects of school quality on primary school attendance in rural Guatemala. PhD dissertation, Stanford University School of Education, Stanford

Marshall, JH and Sorto MA (2012). Teaching What You Know or Knowing How to Teach? The Effects of Different Forms of Teacher Mathematics Knowledge on Student Achievement in Rural Guatemala. *International Review of Education* (forthcoming). Published on-line 22 February 2012

Marshall JH & White KA (2001) Academic achievement, school attendance and teacher quality in Honduras: An empirical analysis. Tegucigalpa, Honduras: UMCE.

McDonnell L (1995) Opportunity-to-learn as a research concept and policy instrument. *Educational Evaluation and Policy Analysis* 17(3): 305–322

McLean L (1985) Drawing implications from item, topic and classroom-level scores in large-scale science assessment. Paper presented at the annual meeting of the American Educational Research Association, Chicago (April 1985)

Mda T & Erasmus J (2008) Department of Labour scarce and critical skills. Educators. Research report commissioned by the Department Of Labour, South Africa

Mohlala T (2009) Guess who's coming to class. Thought leader: *Mail and Guardian* (9 April, 2009). Accessed 8 October 2009, http://m.thoughtleader.co.za/post.php?ID=4206)

Monyatsi PP (2003) Teacher appraisal: An evaluation of practice in Botswana secondary schools. Unpublished DEd thesis, University of South Africa, Pretoria

Motala S (2006) Education resourcing in post-apartheid South Africa: The impact of finance equity reforms in public schooling. *Perspectives in Education*, 24(2), 79–93

Motswakae RJ (1990) A study of strategies for the introduction of staff development and appraisal scheme in secondary schools in Scotland and comparisons with comparable developments in Botswana. Unpublished MEd dissertation, Moray House College, Scotland Centre for Education Overseas

National Centre for Education Statistics (2003) *Teaching mathematics in seven countries: Results from the TIMSS video study*. Washington, DC: U.S. Department of Education

National Planning Commission (2011) *Diagnostic Overview. Report of the National Planning Commission*. Presidency. Republic of South Africa

National Research Council (2001) *Adding It Up: Helping children learn mathematics*. Washington, DC: National Academy Press

Nitko AJ (1989) *Steps in the development of criterion-referenced tests and the knowledge and skills required for each step*. Gaborone: Botswana Ministry of Education

Nitko AJ (1990) *Implementing Criterion-referenced Examinations in Botswana*. Junior Secondary Education Education Improvement Project (JSEIP): Gaborone, Botswana

Organisation for Economic Cooperation and Development (OECD) (2003) *Literacy skills for the world of tomorrow: Further results from PISA 2000*. Paris: OECD

Paterson A (2004) Agricultural and industrial curricula for South African rural schools: Colonial origins and contemporary continuities. In S McGrath, A Badroodien, A Kraak & L Unwin (Eds) *Shifting understandings of skills in South Africa: Overcoming the impact of a low skills regime*. Cape Town: HSRC Press

Paterson A & Arends F (2008) *Who are we missing? Teacher graduate production in South Africa, 1995–2006*. Cape Town: HSRC Press

Paterson A & Arends F (2009) *Teacher graduate production in South Africa*. Cape Town: HSRC Press

Pelgrum WJ (1989) *Educational assessment: Monitoring, evaluation and the curriculum*. De Lier: Academisch Boeken Centrum

Peltzer K, Shisana O, Udjo E, Wilson D, Rehle T et al. (2005) *Educator supply and demand in the South African public education system: Integrated report*. Cape Town: HSRC Press

Porter A & Smithson J (2001) Are content standards being implemented in the classroom? A methodology and some tentative answers. In S Fuhrman (Ed.) *From the Capitol to the classroom: Standards-based reform in the States*. Chicago: University of Chicago Press

Raab E (2009) *School fees in South Africa: Increasing quality or decreasing equality?* Washington: Academy for Educational Development

Reddy V (2006) *Mathematics and science achievement in South Africa in TIMMS 2003*. Cape Town: HSRC

Reddy V, Prinsloo C, Netshitangani T, Moletsane R, Juan A & Van Rensburg J (2010) An investigation into educator leave in the South African ordinary public schooling system. Research commissioned by UNICEF. Study undertaken for the Department of Education. Pretoria: HSRC; UNICEF: Basic Education

Reeves C (2001) Do schools spend enough time teaching and learning? *Education Africa Forum* (4th edition). Johannesburg: Education Africa

Reeves C (2005) The effect of 'opportunity-to-learn' and classroom pedagogy on mathematics achievement in schools serving low socio-economic status communities in the Cape Peninsula. PhD dissertation, School of Education Faculty of Humanities, University of Cape Town, Cape Town

Reeves C (2006) Can schools reverse social disadvantage by pedagogy or opportunity to learn? Paper presented to the Consortium for Research on Schooling (April, 2006)

Reeves C & Muller J (2005) Picking up the pace: variation in the structure and organization of learning school mathematics. *Journal of Education* 23: 103–130

Republic of Bophutatswana (1978) *Report of the national education commission. Education for Popagano*. Mafikeng: National Education Commission

Republic of Botswana National Archives: F.H. Dutton Inspector's Reports for the years 1910, 1911 and 1927

Republic of Botswana (1977) *National commission on education*. Gaborone: Government Printer

Republic of Botswana (1991) *Teacher performance appraisal*. Gaborone: Government Printer

Republic of Botswana (1993) *National commission on education*. Gaborone: Government Printer

Republic of Botswana (1994) *The Revised National Policy on Education*. Government Paper No. 2 of 1994. Government Printer

Rivkin S, Hanushek E & Kain J (2005) Teachers, schools, and academic achievement. *Econometrica* 73(2): 417:458

Robinson J A, Acemoglu D & Johnson S (2003) An African success story: Botswana. In D Rodrik (Ed.) *In search of prosperity: Analytic narratives on economic growth*. Princeton: Princeton University Press

Rosenshine B & Berliner D (1978) Academic engaged time. *British Journal of Teacher Education* 4 (1): 3–26

Rosenshine B & Furst N (1973) The use of direct observation to study teaching. In TM Travers (Ed.) *Second handbook of research on teaching*. Chicago: Rand McNally

Rothstein R (2005) *Class and schools*. New York: Teachers College Press

Rowan B (2002) *Conceptual Paper – What large-scale survey research tells us about teacher effects on student achievement: Insights from the Prospects study of elementary schools*. Accessed November 2002, http://www.cpre.org/Publications/

SACMEQ (Southern African Consortium for Monitoring Education Quality) (2010) What are the levels and trends in reading and mathematics achievement? *SACMEQ Policy Issue* No. 2 (September).

Sanders W (1998) Value-added assessment. *The School Administrator* 55(11): 24

Santibañez LM (2002) Why we should care if teachers get A's: Impact on student achievement in Mexico. Unpublished Ph.D, Stanford University School of Education, Stanford

Schmidt W, Jorde D, Cogan L, Barrier E, Gonzalo I et al. (1996). *Characterizing pedagogical flow: An Investigation of mathematics and science teaching in six countries*. Dordrecht, The Netherlands: Kluwer Academic Publishers

Schmidt W, McKnight C, Houang R, Wang H, Wiley D et al. (2001) *Why Schools matter: A cross-national comparison of curriculum and learning*. San Fransisco: Jossey-Bass

Schmidt W, Tatto MT, Bankov K, Blömeke S, Cedillo T et al. (2008). *The preparation gap: Teacher education for middle school mathematics in six countries*. East Lansing, MI: Centre for Research in Mathematics and Science Education, Michigan State University

Schneider B, Carnoy M, Kilpatrick J, Schmidt W & Shavelson R (2007) *Estimating causal effects using experimental and observational design*. Washington, DC: AERA

Seekings J (2004) Trade unions, social policy and class compromise in post-apartheid South Africa. *Review of African Political Economy* 31(100): 299–312

Segundo Estudio Regional Comparativo y Explicativo (2008) *Primer reporte: Los aprendizajes de los estudiantes de America Latina y el Caribe*. Santiago de Chile: UNESCO

Setati M (2005) Mathematics education and language: Policy, research and practice in multilingual South Africa. In R Vital & J Volmink (Eds) *Researching mathematics education in South Africa*. Cape Town: HSRC Press

Setati M & Adler J (2001) Between languages and discourses : Language practices in primary multilingual mathematics classrooms in South Africa. *Educational Studies in Mathematics* 43: 243–69

Shavelson RJ, Webb NM & Burstein L (1986) The measurement of teaching. In MC Wittrock (Ed.) *Handbook for research on teaching*. New York: Macmillan

Shulman LS (1986) Those who understand: Knowledge growth in teaching. *Educational Researcher* 15: 4–14

Simkins C & Paterson A (2005) *Learner performance in South Africa. Social and economic determinants of success in language and mathematics*. Cape Town: HSRC Press

Simkins C, Rule S & Bernstein A (2007) *Doubling for growth: Addressing the maths and science challenge in South Africa's schools*. Executive summary, CDE Research No. 15. Johannesburg, South Africa

Simkins C, Rule S & Bernstein A (2007) *Doubling for growth: Addressing the maths and science challenge in South Africa's schools*. Full report, CDE Research No. 15. Johannesburg, South Africa.

Sorto A, Marshall JH, Carnoy M & Luschei T (2009) Teacher knowledge and teaching in Panama and Costa Rica: A comparative study in primary and secondary education. *Revista Latinoamericana de Investigaction en Matematica Educativa* 12(2): 251–290

Stein M, Smith M, Henningsen M & Silver E (2000) *Implementing standards-based mathematics instruction : A casebook for professional development* . New York: Teachers College Press

Stigler J, Gonzales P, Kawanaka T, Knoll S & Serrano A (1999) *The TIMSS videotape classroom study: Methods and findings from an exploratory research project on eighth grade mathematics instruction in Germany, Japan, and the United States*. Washington, DC: National Center for Education Studies

Tabulawa R (2003) International aid agencies, Learner-centred pedagogy and political democratisation: A critique. *Comparative Education* 39(1): 7–26

Tabulawa R (2009). Education reform in Botswana. Reflections on policy contradictions and paradoxes. *Comparative Education* 41: 87–107

Taylor N (2001) Outcomes, effort and values in schooling. Paper presented to the New Millennium Business conference, Wits University, Business School (15 May, 2001)

Taylor N & Pereira C (2010) *Western Cape Education Department literacy and numeracy intervention: Baseline study*. Johannesburg and Cape Town: Jet Education Services and WCED

Taylor N & Vinjevold P (Eds) (1999) *Getting learning right: Report of the President's Education Initiative*. Johannesburg: Joint Education Trust

Thema BC (1947) The development of native education in Bechuanaland Protectorate: A historical survey 1840–1946. In partial fulfillment of the MEd degree at the University of South Africa, Pretoria

Thompson D & Senk S (2001) The effects of curriculum on achievement in second-year algebra. *Journal for Research in Mathematics Education* 32(1): 58–84

Tyack D (1993) School governance in the United States. Historical puzzles and anomalies. In J Hannaway and M Carnoy (Eds). *Decentralization and school improvement: Can we fulfil the promise?* San Francisco: Jossey-Bass

UNDP (United Nations Development Program) (2010*) Human development report 2010*. Houndmills, Basingstoke, Hampshire and New York: Palgrave Macmillan

UNESCO, Education for All (2005) *Global monitoring report*. Paris: UNESCO

Van der Berg S (2005). *How efficient are poor schools? Poverty and educational outcomes in South Africa*. SACMEQ, IIEP Paris

Van den Berg S & Louw M (2008) South African student performance in regional context. In G Bloch, L Chisholm, B Fleisch & M Mabizela (Eds) *Investment choices for South African education*. Johannesburg: Wits University Press

Van der Berg S, Burger C, Burger M, Du Rand G, Gustofson et al. (2011) *Low quality education as a poverty trap*. Stellenbosch: Stellenbosch University

Wang J (1998) Opportunity to learn: the impacts and policy implications educational evaluation and policy analysis. *American Educational Research Association* 20(3): 137–156

Wildeman R (2010) *Resources and outcomes in public schools: The case of South Africa*. Cape Town: Idasa

Willms JD & Somers MA (2001). Family, classroom, and school effects on children's educational outcomes in Latin America. *International Journal of School Effectiveness and Improvement* 12(4): 409–445

Yoder J & Evans M (1991) Introduction. In M Evans & J Yoder (Eds) *Patterns of reform in primary education: The case of Botswana*. Gaborone: MacMillan Botswana

Yoder J & Mautle G (1991) The context of reform. In M Evans & J Yoder (Eds) *Patterns of reform in primary education: The case of Botswana*. Gaborone: Macmillan Botswana

Contributors

Nii Addy, Visiting research fellow, Institute for the Study of International Development (ISID), McGill University
email: naddy@stanford.edu / nii.addy@mail.mcgill

Fabian Arends, Senior Research Manager, Education and Skills Development Research Programme, Human Sciences Research Council, Pretoria
email: farends@hsrc.ac.za

Hlengani Baloyi, Researcher, Select Committee on Education and Recreation, Parliament of RSA. At the time of the project, a PhD candidate at the University of the Witwatersrand.
email: hbaloyi@parliament.gov.za

Martin Carnoy, Vida Jacks Professor of Education, Stanford School of Education
email: carnoy@stanford.edu

Bagele Chilisa, Professor of Education, University of Botswana
email: chilisab@mopipi.ub.bw

Linda Chisholm, Advisor, Ministry of Basic Education, Pretoria, South Africa, seconded from the Education and Skills Development Research Programme at the Human Sciences Research Council, Pretoria
email: Chisholm.L@dbe.gov.za

Jesse Foster, doctoral candidate, International and Comparative Education at Stanford University
email: jessefoste@gmail.com

Margaret Irving, doctoral candidate, Education, Stanford University
email: mlirving@stanford.edu

Thenjiwe Major, lecturer in Education, University of Botswana
email: majorte@mopipi.ub.bw

Lillian Mokgosi, Education Advisor, UNICEF South Sudan, Republic of South Sudan
email: lzmokgosi@unicef.org

Kolentino Mpeta, doctoral candidate, Statistics, University of Botswana
email: knmpeta@gmail.com

Paul Nleya, University of Botswana, Department of Educational Technology
email: nleyapt@mopipi.ub.bw

Erin Raab, doctoral candidate, International and Comparative Education, Stanford University
email: erin.raab@gmail.com

Cheryl Reeves, postdoctoral fellow, Cape Peninsula University of Technology, Cape Town
email: cheryl.reeves@intekom.co.za

Ingrid Sapire, Faculty of Education Curriculum Division, University of the Witwatersrand
email: Ingrid.sapire@wits.ac.za

M. Alejandra Sorto, Associate Professor of mathematics, Texas State University, San Marcos
email: sorto@txstate.edu

Gaelebale Tsheko, University of Botswana, Department of Educational Foundations, Research and Evaluation
email: tshekogn@mopipi.ub.bw

Index

A
absenteeism 3, 47, 64
    teacher 33, 35–36, 64, 70–72&*figs*, 152
accountability, teacher 8–9, 21, 32–33, 45, 152, 155
African National Congress (ANC) 32
Afrikaner nationalism 16
apartheid legacy 1n1, 3, 13–14, 16–18, 22, 30, 33–34, 92
Argentina 2
Asia 6
Assessment Policy Act, South Africa 19
Australia 40
authoritarianism 16, 18

B
Bantu education 1, 13, 16, 19, 33
Bantu Education Act 16
Bantustans 1, 13, 16–17, 33, 58–60
Bechuanaland Protectorate 13–15
Bophuthatswana 1, 16–17, 28, 58
    Popagano Report 17
    Primary Education Upgrade Programme (PEUP) 17–18
Botswana Curriculum Guide 42&n2

C
Canada 6
child labour 9
class size 3, 8, 12, 29, 70, 105, 136, 143–144*tab*, 146, 148&*tab*, 152
    see also pupil-teacher ratios
classroom observation 3–4, 9, 22, 35, 37, 39–41, 43, 47–48, 63
    see also observation/analysis of lessons in this study
classroom pedagogy see teacher pedagogical practice
colonialism 33, 150
    mission education 14–16
Congress of South African Trade Unions (COSATU) 32
Constitution of South Africa 18
curriculum, Botswana/South Africa 3–4, 8–9, 12–15, 18–19, 21, 33–36, 40, 42, 45–47, 117, 155
    assessment 14, 19
    Curriculum and Assessment Policy Statements, Botswana 19, 116
    diversity 44
    outcomes-based (OBE) 18–21, 152
    review 19
    see also National Curriculum Statements, South Africa; observation/analysis of lessons in this study: curriculum/content coverage
curriculum development 22, 40
    Curriculum-Driven-Test-Development Model (CDTDM) 19

D
data collection for study 46–50&*tab*
    problems with process of 51
democracy, liberal 17–18, 33
democracy, transition to 6, 14, 18, 34
Department of Higher Education and Training (DHET), South Africa 28
Department of Teaching Service Management (TSM), Botswana 25
Draft Policy on Requirements for Teacher Education (South Africa) 28

E
eastern Africa 9
economic growth, Botswana/South Africa 12, 33, 52–53
    GDP/income per capita 2, 11, 52–53*tab*, 54–56, 60, 150, 153, 158
    income inequality 53&*tab*–54, 60, 150
education colleges/higher education sites 22, 25–27, 31&*tab*, 34, 91
    barriers to access 30
    institutional mergers/rationalisation 28, 91–92
education policy 6–7, 13–14, 32, 158
    Botswana 6, 12–14, 17, 19, 21, 33, 137
    South Africa 6, 12–14, 19, 28, 34, 70, 137
education spending, Botswana/South Africa 2, 11–12, 14, 53–55&*tab*, n7, 56&*tab*, 150, 153, 155
    teacher assignment 7, 155
    see also resources, classroom/school
educational development 13–14, 16–19, 22–23, 25–26, 28, 33–34, 150, 156
empirical questions used in study 7
ethnic nationalism 17
expectations of students 36, 45, 122, 155, 158

F
family/home characteristics 8, 37, 139, 141
    language 136–138, 140*tab*
    parental involvement 70
    parents' education levels 47, 100
    reading material 138–140&*tabs*

Fort Hare College 24
Finland 1, 6

G
Gaborone 14, 24, 26, 46, 56, 60
Gauteng pilot study 7, 9, 38, 41, 47–48, 74, 145n2
Germany 8
Government White Paper on Job Evaluation for Higher Education Quality Council (HEQC) review 28

H
Hebron 28
HIV/AIDS 53, 64, 70–71&*fig*
homelands *see* Bantustans
human capital 3, 141

I
International Association for the Evaluation of Educational Achievement (IEA) studies 44
    Trends in International Mathematics and Science Study (TIMSS) 1, 9, 40, 45, 48, 109, 137
International Labour Organization 26
international student performance studies 1, 44–45

J
Junion Secondary Education Improvement Project (JSEIP), Botswana 17

K
Kagisano 17
Kenya 11*tab*
key findings of this study 151–157
Khama, Seretse 16–17
Korea 1

L
labour market, teacher 23, 26, 29
labour migration 16, 60
Land Acts 16
language of instruction/language policy 8–9, 13–14, 18, 20&n1–21, 33, 47, 63, 82–84&*figs*, 87–88, 136
    code switching 20, 82, 88
Latin America 1, 6, 36, 39
    Brazil 2, 40
    Chile 2, 40
    Costa Rica 1–2, 41
    Cuba 1, 40
    Guatemala 41
    Panama 41
learning levels 35
learning outcomes 20, 33, 36, 38–42, 46
Lebanon 2
Lesotho 11*tab*
Lobatse 24, 46, 56, 60

M
Mahikeng (Mafikeng) 28, 46, 58–60&*tab*, 92, 152
Malawi 10–11&*tabs*
Mangope, Lucas 16, 18
Mankwe Teacher Education College 28
mass removals 16
mathematical teaching quality 3, 5–7, 18, 21, 28, 33, 35, 39–41, 47, 70, 104, 113, 126, 128–129&*tab*, 130&*figs*–131, 134–137, 143–144*tab*, 145&n2&3–146, 147–148&*tabs*, 150–152, 154
    improvement of 4–5, 13, 26, 137, 146, 155–157&*fig*, 158
    mathematical quality of instruction (MQI) instrument 41
    see also observation/analysis of lessons
mathematics knowledge, students
    five strands of proficiency 42, 107–108*fig*
    and knowledge decay 37, 137, 142–143
    order of operation rule (BODMAS) 77*tab*, 87, 96
    review of notebooks/workbooks 5, 35, 47–50&*tab*, 71, 80, 106*fig*, 114, 116, 119–121&*tab*/*fig*, 122–123, 132, 152
    see also opportunity to learn; teacher mathematics knowledge/skills/capacity; student tests/test scores
mathematics knowledge, teachers 2–5, 7–9, 19, 33–39, 43–44, 47, 88–89, 92&n1, 103, 110–111&*fig*, 128–131&*figs*, 132–134, 136, 145–146, 150–152, 156
    mathematical knowledge for teaching (MKT) 41, 155
    pedagogical content knowledge 38–39, 43, 88, 97, 104–105, 110, 112, 128, 155–157
    see also teacher experience; teacher test scores
Mauritius 10–11&*tabs*
Mexico 8
Mozambique 10–11&*tabs*

N
Namibia 10–11&*tabs*
nation building 17
National Commissions on Education (NCEs), Botswana 17, 19, 21
National Curriculum Statement, South Africa (NCS) 42, 46, 116
    Revised National Curriculum Statement 19
National Planning Commission, South Africa 20, 54
non-racialism 1, 16
Norms and Standards for Educators (NSE), South Africa 28

O
observation/analysis of lessons in this study 5, 40, 43, 47, 105–107&*figs*, 109–112&n1&2, 113&*fig*, 114–115, 123–125&*tabs*, 127–128, 143–144*tab*

cognitive demand, level of 42, 45, 49–50*tab*, 108–109*&fig*, 110–111, 113–114, 117, 119*&fig*
content emphasis/focus 19, 49–50*tab*, 114, 117, 119–120*&tab*, 122tab–123, 126, 152
content exposure /time spent teaching 45, 49–50tab, 114, 120–121*&tab/fig*, 122*tab*–123, 126, 132, 134–135, 137, 143–144*tab*, 146, 150–152
curriculum/content coverage 3, 45, 49–50*tab*, 63, 71, 106–107*&fig*, 107, 110–116*&tabs/fig*, 117–118*tabs*, 122*tab*–123, 126, 132, 134–135, 137, 146, 151, 153, 156–157*&fig*
opportunity to learn (OTL) 5, 8–9, 35–37, 40–41, 44–51, 79–80, 112, 114–115, 117, 120, 122–123*&tabs*, 124–125*tabs*, 126–128, 133*tab*–134, 136, 150–152, 155–156

P
participation levels 9, 106
political histories, differences 1, 3–4, 13–14, 33, 150
Potchefstroom Teacher Education College 28
poverty/inequality 53–54, 60
    Gini coefficient 54n3
Primary Education Improvement Project (PEIP), Botswana 17
principals/school leadership 33, 35, 47, 49, 51–52, 60–61, 150, 157
    administrative workload 68–69*&figs*, 70–71
    education levels 61, 71
    experience 61–63*&fig*, 71
    support/oversight of teachers 63–64*&n1*, 68–71
    use of time 68–70*&figs*, 71
production function methodology 2–4
Programme for International Student Assessment (PISA) 1, 8
pupil-teacher ratios 23, 29*&tab*–30, 55–56

R
racial classification 1n1
racial inequality 19
racial segregation 1, 18
    separate development 16
Ramotshere Moiloa 59–60*&tab*
reading skills 10*&tab*
Reeves, Cheryl 8–9, 45–46, 48–49
resources, classroom/school 2, 6, 8–10*tab*, 16, 18, 35, 38, 70–71, 150, 157
    potential efficiency gains 153–155, 158
    production possibilities frontier (PPF) 154*&fig*–156
Revised National Policy on Education (RNPE), Botswana 20

S
sample schools
    North West Province 56–57map, 58–59*&n9*, 60
    South East Botswana 56–58*&maps*, 60
school feeding programmes 64

school finances see resources, classroom/school
school organisational environment 4, 36
secondary education 23–25, 54
Seychelles 11*tab*
Singapore 1
socio-economic status (SES) of students 3, 6–8n1, 9, 11*&tab*, 12–13, 21, 33, 36, 47, 52, 80–81*&figs*, 82, 87, 89, 99–100*tab&fig*, 102, 104, 114, 122*&tab*–123, 126, 131, 134, 136–141*tab*, 143–144*tab*, 145, 147–148*tabs*, 149–150, 152–153*&n1*, 155
South African Native National Congress (SANNC) 15
South African Schools Act 20
South African War 14
southern Africa 9–10, 71, 74, 88, 158
state control over education 13–16, 22, 24
structural models used in study
    hierarchical linear model (HLM) 37–38
    ordinary least squares (OLS) 38, 143
student achievement research/surveys 8&n1, 9
    limitations of 8
    Southern African Consortium for Monitoring Education Quality (SACMEQ) 1–2, 9–11*&tabs*, 12, 33, 35, 137, 155
student tests/test scores 4–5, 7–9, 10*&tab*–11*&fig*, n3, 35, 37–39, 44–50*&tab*, 51, 73*&n1*, 74–75*&figs*, 76–77*&tab*, 78*fig*, 80–81*&figs*, 82*&tab*, 83–85*&figs*, 87–88, 96, 101–102*figs&tab*, 104, 115, 119, 123, 132, 134, 137
    classroom and teacher/peer effect 136, 139–141*&tab*, 142*&n1*–143, 147, 150, 153
    learner achievement gains 2–4, 6–8, 11, 35–38, 41, 45, 51–53, 73*&n1*, 75–79*fig*, 82, 84*&figs*, 86*&figs*–87, 112–114, 123*&n1*, 124–125*&tabs*, 126*&n3*–127, 131, 135–138*&tab*, 139, 142–143, 145–148*&tabs*, 149–155, 157*&fig*
    results by curriculum category 149
Swaziland 10–11*&tabs*

T
Taiwan 1
Tanzania 11*tab*
teacher characteristics 2–3, 5, 8–9, 14, 136, 143
    education 91–93*&tabs*, 97–98*figs*, 99–100, 103–104, 136
    experience 8, 25, 30, 37, 89–91*&figs*, 92, 99*&tab*, 128–130*&tab*, 132–133*&tab*, 134–136, 144*tab*
teacher identity 32
teacher pedagogical practice (TQ) 9, 19–20, 35–38, 40–41, 44, 109, 152 see also mathematical teaching quality
teacher recruitment 6–7, 22, 25–26, 32
teacher salaries/wages 26–27*&tabs*, 30, 32–33
teacher shortages 14, 22, 28–31
teacher supervision/evaluation 6, 14, 18, 20–23, 33
    Botswana Competency Teaching Instrument (BCTI) 22

Integrated Quality Management System (IQMS), South Africa 22
National Education and Evaluation Development Unit (NEEDU), South Africa 22
school inspections 15, 21–23, 33, 64, 132
Teaching Service Management (TSM) 22
teacher test scores 93–94&n2, 95figs–97, 98–99&figs, 112, 126–129, 131–133&tab, 134–135
  bias toward higher achieving students 89, 100–103figs&tab, 104, 128, 131, 153
teacher training/pre-service education 1, 1, 4–7, 9, 13, 15–16, 18, 20, 22–24&n2, 25–26, 31, 34, 36, 55, 152, 155–156
  bursaries for 28
  Initial Professional Education of Teachers (IPET) programmes 30–31
  National Teacher Education Audit 26
  see also education colleges/higher education sites; teacher characteristics: education
teacher unionism 3, 26, 32–33, 152
  National Association of Professional Teacher Organisations of South Africa (NAPTOSA) 32
  South African Democratic Teachers Union (SADTU) 32–33
  Suid-Afrikaanse Onderwyserunie (SAOU) 32
teachers, underqualified/unqualified 23, 28–29, 32, 155–156
Tiger Kloof 15–16, 18, 24
tripartite alliance 32

U
Uganda 11*tab*
unemployment 54
  unemployed educator database 30&n4
  youth 53–54

Unesco
  Institute of Statistics 52
  International Institute of Education Planning (IIEP) 10
Unified Teaching Service (UTS), Botswana 21
Union of South Africa 14–15
United Nations Development Programme (UNDP) 52
  Human Development Index (HDI) 54&*tab*, n4, 150
United States 6, 40, 44, 91
University of Bophuthatswana 16
University of Botswana 25, 92
University of North West 28, 92
urban/rural comparison 7, 11, 29–30, 60, 82&*tab*

V
violence, school 3, 9, 33–37, 45, 47, 64–67&figs, 136, 143–144*tab*, 148
  under-reporting of 67, 72

W
Western Cape Education Department (WCED)
  Joint Education Trust's WCED baseline study 74, 80
white supremacy, ideology of 16
World Bank 52–53

Z
Zambia 11*tab*
Zanzibar 11*tab*
Zeerust 46, 58–60